A Companion & Guide to the
Norman Conquest

William the Conqueror – modern statue at his birthplace at Falaise, Normandy.

A COMPANION & GUIDE TO THE
NORMAN
CONQUEST

PETER BRAMLEY

The
History
Press

To the Memory of my Father, Donald

Front cover photograph: *top*: The death of Harold as per the Tapestry. Most scholars now favour the king being cut down by Norman knights as on the right. *Bottom*: Norman 'might' at Portchester.
Back cover photograph: The glory of Durham Cathedral's Norman nave. (By permission of Durham Cathedral)

First published 2012

The History Press
The Mill, Brimscombe Port
Stroud, Gloucestershire, GL5 2QG
www.thehistorypress.co.uk

British Library Cataloguing in Publication Data.
A catalogue record for this book is available from the British Library.

ISBN 978 0 7524 6335 3

Typesetting and origination by The History Press
Manufacturing managed by Jellyfish Print Solutions Ltd
Printed in India.

CONTENTS

PREFACE

The concept of this guide derives from the belief that the understanding and enjoyment of history can be enhanced from visiting the actual sites of key historical events, as well as the monuments or memorials to the people involved. Television documentaries on historical topics now routinely follow this approach, using on-location shots of appropriate sites. This guide is different because it focuses on one particular historical period: the Norman Conquest.

I could not have completed the task of researching and writing this book without the help of my family. My daughter Lucy has produced the maps and helped me to cope with some of the finer points of digital photography and computers. My son Tom has made a number of important inputs on the history of the period, and my wife has encouraged me throughout. Many thanks are also due to Rachel, with whom it has been a pleasure to work as always.

PICTURE CREDITS

There are colour plates located between pp. 128 and 129.

All images are from my own collection unless otherwise credited. I am grateful to the following organisations for permission to reproduce images from their collections.

Ashmolean Museum
British Library
Corpus Christi College, Oxford
Dean and Chapter of Westminster
Dean of Durham Cathedral
Public Record Office
Reading Museum

All maps have been drawn by Lucy Bramley.

ONE

Introduction to the Guide

The Battle of Hastings stands out as the single most cataclysmic event in English history. 'Regime change' was in effect achieved in one long day and, what's more, endured for centuries. But just fifty years previously another battle had had very similar consequences – the Anglo-Saxon defeat at the Battle of Ashingdon in 1016 led, one month later, to the death of King Edmund Ironside and the usurpation of the throne by Cnut, King of Denmark. This regime lasted but twenty-six years however.

After nearly 1,000 years it is perhaps surprising that a considerable number of historic sites survive from these dark, turbulent times that can help to reconstruct the events and personalities of the period. These sites occur in the form of battlefields, castles, churches and cathedrals, monasteries, plaques, obelisks and church monuments. The objective of this guide is to introduce the reader to the best of these by providing for each site:

• A short description of what there is to see.
• A brief account of any events in the Norman or Danish Conquest that occurred there and/or biography of the person(s) commemorated, covering his/her role in the Conquests. Few battlefields and fewer churches contain any detailed information on this, either in a leaflet or with a display notice, but there are exceptions. This guide fills the gap.
• Summary directions on how to find the site and other entry details. These directions are designed to complement modern road atlases.
• A broad-brush 'star' rating.

The guide covers the historic sites in England, Wales and Normandy which I consider to be the most interesting and important. I have visited more than 500 of these sites throughout the three regions over the last five years, selecting those to visit by consulting recent historical literature (see Bibliography), including the Pevsner and Arthur Mee county guides. My criteria for including sites in the guide are:

• There must be something memorable to see to act as a focus of interest. So churches where someone is known to have been buried but where no memorial has survived have been excluded.
• The Normans were great builders and imposed themselves on both the urban

Construction of a motte and bailey castle at Hastings, October 1066.

Norman pillars at Norwich Cathedral.

and rural landscapes through the medium of stone, taking the form of churches (including cathedrals), abbeys and, above all, castles. Early castles were thrown up quickly as wooden motte and bailies but were usually fortified in stone before long. Sites have been selected which provide good examples of this Norman imposition – later to be known as the 'Norman Yoke'. These sites display the very distinctive early Norman style of Romanesque architecture.

• The Anglo-Saxons had also mastered the art of building in stone. A number of late Anglo-Saxon churches have therefore been included in the guide to emphasise that in many fields the Normans did not possess a superior culture.

• Last but not least, each site must be accessible to the public.

I have visited all the sites included in this guide at least once.

In order to provide the reader with background for their visit to the site, the guide includes a summary of the key dates of the period and the key effects of the Norman Conquest together with profiles of the main historical characters involved. The latter have been drawn from a number of sources, including the *Dictionary of National Biography*.

In order to cover the demise of Anglo-Saxon England fully, the guide covers the period from the accession of Aethelred the Unready (978) to the death of Henry I (1135) – by which time the Norman Conquest was secure. The disputed accession of Stephen I and the resulting civil war with Queen Matilda really belong to a different era of history.

Norman nave arches, Rochester Cathedral.

TWO

HISTORICAL
BACKGROUND

BEFORE THE NORMANS: ENGLAND IN 1066

- The total population was 2–2.5 million and called Anglo-Saxons, yet in the old 'Danelaw', north and east of Watling Street (the current A5), a significant minority was of Danish origin.
- The economy was predominantly rural with 90 per cent of the population employed in agriculture.
- A significant land area was held by monasteries.
- Society was highly stratified. The landed aristocracy was divided into thegns (gentry), ealdormen or earls, plus clerics. These earldoms represented semi-independent, regional powerbases.
- The government of the country was in the hands of the aristocracy.
- Slavery was widespread at the bottom of society.
- The country was prosperous, with a well-established government bureaucracy to collect Danegeld. However this tax had hit smallholders hard, which led to fewer freemen.
- The north and south were not fully united because of the large Danish minority in the north.
- An army could move at a maximum of 30 miles per day on foot, so the country was far-flung.

THE DEMISE OF ANGLO-SAXON ENGLAND AND THE DANISH CONQUEST: 975–1042

The First Phase of Viking Invasions

By the eighth century the Anglo-Saxons had established a prosperous, cultured and Christian country, but they had not yet achieved a lasting political union and the country remained a small number of separate kingdoms. The first Viking raids were recorded in 786 at Portland, Dorset, and grew steadily in number and frequency. By the late ninth century virtually the whole country had been overrun and the north-eastern kingdoms, in what was to become known as the Danelaw, were colonised widely by Danes. Only Wessex held out against Viking incursions.

The accession of a genius, King Alfred, to the throne of Wessex inspired an Anglo-Saxon fightback in the late ninth century. Starting in Wessex, Alfred undertook a systematic programme of fortification of the major towns as burghs (e.g. **Wallingford** and **Wareham**), together with the establishment of a fast-response naval force and an organised and rotating standing army from the peasantry (the fyrd). Alfred showed the Anglo-Saxons that they could defeat the Danes. Having first saved Wessex, Alfred, and later his son, Edward the Elder, and grandson, Athelstan, were able to re-conquer Mercia and eventually Northumbria (by 954) in a series of highly successful military campaigns throughout the Midlands and the north. This re-conquest included the areas heavily colonised by Danes in the previous century of turmoil, each kingdom was now prepared to accept the King of Wessex as overlord.

The High Watermark of the Anglo-Saxon Kingdom to 975

Superficially at least, England emerged strengthened from the first phase of Viking invasions. It was independent, united and had successfully absorbed a significant proportion of new settlers with different ethnic backgrounds in the Danelaw. Alfred and his talented descendants evolved a national monarchy which embraced the appointment of regional earls and bishops by the king, meetings of a nationally based council of magnates (although these usually took place in the south) and the authority to call out the militia throughout the country.

The sixteen-year reign of King Edgar the Peaceable represents the very apogee of the Anglo-Saxon kingdom. The impressive Edgar (he was only 16 years old when he came to the throne) presided over sixteen years of peace during which no significant Viking raids were experienced and no internal troubles developed. To quote Stenton: 'It is a sign of Edgar's competence as a ruler that his reign is singularly devoid of recorded incident.' The high spot of Edgar's reign itself came in 973, just after his delayed coronation, when six British kings rowed him on the river Dee to the church of **St John in Chester**. How was it that within only forty years the seemingly powerful Anglo-Saxon nation was conquered by the Danes, and within ninety-five years conquered a second time by the Normans?

The Second Wave of Viking Invasions to 1012

As far as the future of England was concerned however, Edgar made two fatal mistakes – he married badly and he died too young. Edgar's death at only 32 years old in 975 initiated the demise of Anglo-Saxon

England and the fall came quickly. He left behind him two young sons, both less than 15 years old and half brothers by two of Edgar's three wives (Archbishop Dunstan was unhappy with Edgar's unruly marital ways). The elder, Edward, succeeded, but his council was split into two camps. In 978 he was infamously murdered at **Corfe Castle**, Dorset, most probably on the orders of his stepmother Dowager Queen Aelfthryth. This brought to the throne her own son, aged about 10, and known to us all as Aethelred the Unready. No one was ever charged with the murder, and the atmosphere of suspicion damaged the prestige of the recently established national monarchy. A long minority followed, during which the council once again proved to be divided.

It can be no coincidence that within two years of Aethelred's accession the Vikings were back, ravaging Wessex and Cheshire. In twelve of the next twenty-two years they attacked in ever-increasing numbers (particularly in Wessex and East Anglia), and from fleets which remained away from home for years on end. In this 'Second Viking Age' the objective was to plunder and invade but not settle. By the mid-980s Aethelred had assumed the reins of power personally. The three cornerstones of his illustrious predecessors' successes in the 'First Viking Age' remained in place: fortified burghs, a royal fleet and a standing army. But perhaps never has the aphorism 'Cometh the hour, cometh the man' seemed so inappropriate. In a heroic age Aethelred presented himself as a non-fighting king – at least as far as the Danes were concerned. Alfred and the other successful kings in the ninth and tenth centuries had led armies into battle against invaders. This was not Aethelred's way, but neither could he organise someone else to provide adequate national defence against the Danes. Local resistance did occur but

only three full-scale battles were fought: Watchet, Somerset, in 984; **Maldon**, Essex, in 991; and Ringmere near Thetford in 1010. All ended in Anglo-Saxon defeats.

The only possible defence of Aethelred's approach is that at this time he was the sole survivor of the House of Cerdic. The Anglo-Saxon kingdom needed him to survive, though the situation did not prevail later in his reign. Aethelred's answer was to buy off the Vikings. The money paid was raised from a land tax (Danegeld) in England. The tactic didn't work – they just came back for more, as the table below shows. Later the tax was used to pay mercenary troops.

Payment of Danegeld or Heregeld (Army Tax)

AD991	£10,000
AD994	£16,000
AD1002	£24,000
AD1006	£36,000
AD1012	£48,000
AD1014	£21,000
AD1018	£82,000 (to King Cnut)

Heregeld continued to be levied until 1051 when Edward the Confessor stopped collecting it – whether temporarily or permanently is unclear.

By 1002 England was in crisis. That year Aethelred made two fateful decisions which sent Anglo-Saxon England into terminal decline. The first one had some semblance of logic to it. Aethelred's first wife, Aelfgifu (Elgiva) of Northumbria, had died, so he took as his second wife and queen, Emma, the daughter of Duke Richard I of Normandy and sister of the current duke, Richard II. This alliance offered the prospect of the Normans closing their ports to their kinsmen the Vikings. In practice this never really happened. Although no contract survives, subsequent events strongly suggest the quid pro quo was that Aethelred agreed that any offspring from this marriage would supplant the nine surviving children from his first marriage to Aelfgifu. Not surprisingly this helped to alienate Aethelred from his adult sons, particularly Athelstan and Edmund, and proved crucial as the crisis unfolded beyond 1011. This move was to prove equally disastrous in the long term after Cnut died in 1035 as we shall see later. Queen Emma proved to be one of the most formidable women in English history by marrying Cnut in 1016, shortly after Aethelred's death. A worm of Norman influence had been planted at the heart of the English court.

But the second decision Aethelred took in 1002 must rank as one of the most stupid in English history. He commanded that on Friday 13 November, St Brice's Day, all the Danish inhabitants in England should be put to death. Informed by his advisors that the Danes intended to kill him and his councillors, and perhaps emboldened by his recent alliance with Normandy, Aethelred had gone too far. In practice it was impossible to carry out the order in the Danelaw, where Danish settlers were often in the majority, but in some areas the order was carried out (e.g. Oxford) and the Danes were massacred. It is traditionally held that included in the list of victims were Gunhild, sister to King Sweyn of Denmark, and her husband, who were being held as hostages by the English. Sweyn Forkbeard had been involved in raiding in England since the mid-990s and was the most effective and feared Viking commander. Now he was honour-bound to add family revenge to his motives as he returned on a raid for the 1003 season. Not a clever move by Aethelred. From now on the pace of Danish raiding increased and became better organised and 'professional'. In 1003 Sweyn targeted Exeter, given by Aethelred to Queen Emma in dower on her

marriage. Almost unbelievably, her French reeve, Hugh, betrayed the city to the Danish raiders. A bad start for the Norman alliance. The Anglo-Saxon defences began to buckle under the increased pressure.

In 1006 Aethelred re-organised his council in a cabinet reshuffle eleventh-century style. Aelfhelm, Ealdorman of Northumbria was murdered on the king's orders by his new henchman, Eadric 'Streona' (the Greedy), and two of his sons were blinded and a third son exiled. Eadric and his numerous brothers now dominated the court. Eadric – probably a candidate for one of the least attractive personalities in English history – became Earl of Mercia and married one of Aethelred's daughters. Uhtred of Bamburgh became Earl of Northumbria around the same time. The new regime proved energetic and constructed at great cost a large fleet of ships specifically for defence against the Vikings. They were brought together at Sandwich. However the achievement seems to have gone to Eadric's head. One of his brothers, Beothric, accused Wulfnoth Cyld to the king. Wulfnoth was known to be an associate of Aethelstan, Aethelred's eldest son. Wulfnoth was not impressed by this move. He detached twenty ships from the grand fleet and ravaged the south coast. He was pursued by Beothric with eighty ships, but the latter's fleet was scattered and wrecked by gales in the Channel. Wulfnoth's superior sailing skills enabled him not only to survive the gales but also to set fire to Beothric's remaining ships. The grand fleet was now in tatters, destroyed by factional in-fighting so typical of England during Aethelred's reign. Wulfnoth was the father of Godwin, who came to dominate southern England in Cnut's reign.

The next few years really knocked the stuffing out of the English resistance to the Danish raids. In 1011 the Danes, led by Thorkell, sacked Canterbury following the treachery of an abbot named Aelfmaer, and captured the Archbishop of Canterbury, Aelfhaeh, who then refused to be ransomed. Thorkell lost control of his men and at an Easter feast in 1012 in **Greenwich** Aelfhaeh was pelted with animal bones by drunken Danes and then finished off with an axe. A truly low point in English history.

The Danish Conquest, 1013–16

By 1013 English resistance was in tatters. Sweyn's expedition of this year came not to raid but to conquer. He entered the Humber in August and sailed up the Trent to Gainsborough with his fleet. There he met with Anglo-Danish leaders from Northumbria, Lindsey and the Five Boroughs in the East Midlands. Highham even suggests that these leaders may have included Aethelred's eldest son, Athelstan, who through his mother, Aelfgifu of Northampton, was associated with leading Northumbrian families. These disillusioned men had given up on Aethelred and were prepared to support Sweyn, who was duly acclaimed king at Gainsborough. In a lightning campaign Sweyn then proceeded to invade Wessex: Winchester, Oxford and Bath all submitted without a fight, only London offered any resistance before finally submitting in late 1013. Before the year's end Aethelred followed his wife, Emma, and their two sons, Edward and Alfred, into exile in Normandy. That should have been the end of Anglo-Saxon England, but on 3 February 1014 King Sweyn died suddenly at Gainsborough – whither he had returned to his fleet. Foul play or perhaps a war wound? There had not been time for a coronation.

The Danish crews at Gainsborough immediately gave their allegiance to Cnut, the younger of Sweyn's sons who was still in his teens (Gainsborough's moment of 'glory' in English history had been short-lived indeed). Before Cnut could mobilise, the leading men in Wessex sent a deputation to Aethelred in Normandy. After agreeing a pact which specified that the king would mend his ways, Aethelred returned to England and reclaimed his throne. Cnut had been out-manoeuvred and decided to return home to Denmark with his army. Reprisals for supporting Cnut were ruthlessly carried out by Aethelred's agents in Lindsey. Early in 1015 a great council meeting was held at Oxford and once again the tendency to schism in England was to the fore. During the meeting, Eadric Streona organised the murder of Siferth and Morcar, the two leading thegns of the northern Danelaw. Siferth's widow was arrested but then abducted by Edmund, Aethelred's eldest surviving son (Athelstan had died in 1014), who married her against his father's wishes (her wishes are not recorded!). This act of rebellion against Aethelred was followed by another when Edmund took possession of both Siferth's and Morcar's estates in the Danelaw and was accepted as Lord of the Five Boroughs.

Meanwhile, at the end of the summer of 1015, Cnut appeared at Poole Harbour with a fresh army, probably accompanied by his elder brother Harold, who had inherited the throne of Denmark, and by Thorkell, who had once again changed sides. Eadric Streona quickly joined Cnut, who then over-ran Wessex. Mercia and Northumbria soon followed, leaving Aethelred and Edmund in control of only London and the south-east. Aethelred subsequently died in London on 23 April 1016, aged about 50. Edmund was quickly acclaimed king and crowned in St Paul's.

Fortunately, Edmund, known as Ironside, was a man of action (unlike his father) and he quickly regained Wessex from

Cnut – who then retaliated by blockading London. In a series of indecisive engagements across southern England, Edmund seemed to be getting the better of Cnut. He gained three victories against the Danes at Penselwood in Dorset, Sherston in Wiltshire and Otford in Kent (a sequence not achieved since the early tenth century, but none were decisive). However at **Ashingdon** in Essex, Eadric Streona, who had previously defected back to Edmund, infamously changed sides (again!) on the battlefield and helped Cnut's forces to an overwhelming victory with heavy casualties amongst the English leaders. Edmund escaped but may have been wounded in the battle. Dramatically, Edmund and Cnut met at **Deerhurst** on the Severn, north of Gloucester, and split the kingdom, Edmund taking only Wessex. Within a month Edmund was dead and Cnut became master of all of England before the end of 1016. Edmund most probably died of his battle wounds, but there was talk of other causes, including man-to-man combat with Cnut at Deerhurst or a very unpleasant murder on his toilet in London. With this heroic king died Anglo-Saxon England.

The Danish Occupation, 1016–42

Cnut proved to be a more ruthless politician and king than he had been military commander. His military record in England in 1015–6 was mixed and he was to lose the important naval battle at the Holy River in Sweden in 1026. In 1016, however, he moved decisively and married Aethelred's widow, Emma, in 1017 (even though he already had a family in the Danish manner by Aelfgifu of Northampton, who was not repudiated), as well as carrying out a cabinet reshuffle eleventh-century style in which he purged the English nobility. Eadric Streona finally got his comeuppance and was executed

without trial in 1017. Cnut also imposed a huge Danegeld at a much higher rate than anything paid previously (see earlier table).

Cnut ruled England as part of his Empire of the North, including Denmark and Norway (his elder brother was dead by 1019). He wanted England for its wealth but he did not engage in wholesale replacement of the indigenous ruling class, and there does not seem to have been further large-scale colonisation from Denmark. Cnut became a Christian and even went on pilgrimage to Rome – perhaps we see the influence of Queen Emma here. Not surprisingly, there were no problems with Viking raiders during his reign and Cnut ruled with a rod of iron for nearly twenty years. He is thought to have died after a short illness at Shaftesbury Abbey, which he patronised. He was still only about 40 years old.

The Danish Conquest of England ended more with a whimper than a bang. At the time of Cnut's death in late 1035, his son by Queen Emma, Harthacnut, was in Denmark and needed time to secure his position there. Harold Harefoot, a son of Cnut's first marriage with strong connections in Mercia and Northumbria, outmanoeuvred Dowager Queen Emma in the succession crisis in England and ruled until he died suddenly in 1040. Harthacnut was able to return from Denmark to claim his throne, but dropped dead shortly after 'at the bar'– at a wedding feast at the House of Osgod Clapa in Lambeth in 1042. He was all of 24 years old. Poison perhaps? Previously, the young Harthacnut had charitably invited his half-brother Edward back to England (following a long exile in Normandy). Edward may have been intended to act as a joint-king in England, thus allowing Harthacnut more time for Denmark. Once again I think we could be seeing the long arm of cunning Queen Emma here as,

Despite the dark times late Anglo-Saxon architecture also had style, see Deerhurst parish church.

whatever the truth of the matter, Edward was conveniently on hand to fill the vacancy on the occasion of Harthacnut's death. So the Danish occupation of the English throne came to a somewhat ignominious end. But what manner of cultural affinity did the new occupant possess?

The Norman Conquest and the Formation of Normandy

During the late ninth and early tenth centuries Viking raiders had menaced northern France as well as England. In around 911 the French king adopted an unusual solution to prevent further raids: he ceded lands around Rouen and Cherbourg to Rollo (Hrolr), the leader of one of the Viking armies. In time these lands expanded and became known as Normandy. Viking settlers took over the dominant positions in the new political unit and intermarried with the locals from early on. This Franco-Viking mix proved a heady brew, producing a people who were massively energetic, dynamic, ruthless and bellicose, but at the same time intelligent and methodical. Initially counts, but later dukes based in Rouen, the Norman leaders at least nominally paid homage to the King of France.

Alliance with England, 991–1002

By 990 the English and Norman courts were at loggerheads because of the Norman habit of offering anchorages and support to fellow Viking raiders intent on attacking England. English agitation with the Pope resulted in his intervention to secure a treaty with Duke Richard I of Normandy in 991, who promised not to support the Vikings. The treaty proved ineffective and was soon forgotten. However, by 1002, England had been badly mauled by succeeding Viking armies and King Aethelred was looking for new ways of countering the threat. That year he again tried to buy off the raiders with Danegeld but was unsuccessful. He also sent ambassadors to Normandy to negotiate a marriage alliance with the new Duke Richard II's sister, Emma.

Emma, twice Queen of England

The wedding duly took place in the spring of 1002 in the Old Minster, Winchester. Emma, aged only 16 years, was Aethelred's second wife (his first, Aelfgifu of Northumbria, is thought to have died earlier that year). It is highly probable that the terms of the marriage alliance required that any children of the new union would take precedence in terms of the succession to the English throne over the eight sons produced by Aelfgifu, the eldest, Athelstan, being already about 16 years old (just to confuse everybody, Emma was given the English name Aelfgifu as well). Emma lived until 1052, in England for all but a few years, marrying Aethelred's Danish enemy and successor, Cnut, along the way. Emma proved to be an intelligent and scheming queen. For fifty years the Normans had a redoubtable high-born 'mole' at the heart of the English court.

Emma's first child was probably born between 1003 and 1005, a boy, Edward, known to history as 'the Confessor', followed by Alfred and a daughter, Godifu. Godifu's second husband, Eustace of Boulogne, fought alongside the Normans at Hastings.

Development of the Norman Connection, 1013–37

In 1013 when Sweyn of Denmark seized the English throne and drove out Aethelred, Emma's second royal family was able to seek refuge at the Norman court. It is thought that Edward, despite only being about 12 years old, represented his father during the negotiations held with English clerics to secure the return of Aethelred in 1014–5, following Sweyn's sudden death. After Cnut, Sweyn's son won back the throne of England and Emma's children remained in Normandy even when she took on the rollercoaster option of being Cnut's wife, based in **Winchester**. Her children were well received in the duchy. Edward spent time in **Jumièges Abbey** and is referred to in Norman charters as 'King of the English'. In the early 1030s Duke Robert I even fitted out an expedition to invade England from Fécamp, but it was hit by Channel gales and blown off course to Jersey. The Norman court clearly believed Edward should be King of England.

In February 1037, during the succession crisis which followed Cnut's death, both Edward and Alfred crossed the Channel with retinues in support of their mother and her ally, Earl Godwin of Wessex. Edward arrived at Southampton, didn't like what he saw and returned to Normandy. Alfred landed in Kent, made his way to **Guildford** and met up with Godwin. Betraying the rules of overnight hospitality, Godwin took Alfred captive (who was subsequently blinded on the orders of King Harold Harefoot and died) and massacred his men. This incident was not forgotten by Edward.

King Edward the Confessor, king 1042–65

By 1040 Harthacnut had at last been accepted on the English throne. Aged only 20 and unmarried, Harthacnut invited his half-brother, Edward, to return from Normandy as joint-king and his heir. As mentioned previously, Harthacnut dropped dead two years later at a wedding feast in Lambeth 'whilst he stood at his drink'. So Edward, eldest son of Aethelred and Emma, now aged almost 40 years, became king. The royal line of Cerdic was restored – or was it? Edward had an Anglo-Saxon father but little else of Anglo-Saxon origin. Despite being only half Norman blood, his upbringing had been more Norman than English: he had spent time in the Norman church at Jumièges and been given active support to pursue the English throne by the Norman people. It is clear where his sympathies lay.

Fortunately a number of Cnut's old friends remained in power in England, and men such as Earl Godwin and Bishop Stigand were able to act as a counterbalance to the pro-Norman king. Like his father, Edward was not a fighting man and, fortunately, he had little need to be during his long reign. There was some serious skirmishing with the Godwins in 1051–2, but that subsided into an uneasy truce. A major factor during this time was the absence of Viking raids. Wessex farmers would have been very grateful to Edward for this continuation of the peace achieved in Cnut's twenty-year reign. Had Danish protection already been exchanged for de facto protection by the Normans?

With the benefit of hindsight we can see that Edward could hardly have done more during his reign to enhance the Norman interest in England, and in particular their designs on the throne.

Edward married Edith, Godwin's eldest daughter, in 1045, but they had no children (apparently because they didn't sleep together). Edward had no recorded illegitimate children or surviving full-brothers.

The son of King Edmund Ironside, Edward Aetheling (which meant 'throneworthy'), survived in exile in Hungary however, where he was sent to escape Cnut. In 1057 King Edward invited him to England. He accepted but died suddenly, shortly after his arrival and before seeing the king. A sign of dirty work, surely? The aetheling's young son Edgar had come with him and was adopted by the king and Edith as an aetheling himself. Pauline Stafford has pointed out, however, that based on around 300 years of Anglo-Saxon precedent a valid aetheling could only be the son of a king, not the grandson.

On King Edward's death in 1066 the crown of England was thus technically vacant. This opened the door for Harold Godwinson to become king through election by the Witan, but, more threateningly, it also allowed Duke William of Normandy to put forward a claim. This was based on the fact that King Edward is supposed to have promised the throne to the duke during the latter's visit to England in 1051. Queen Emma, married successively to Aethelred and then to Cnut, was William's great-aunt. William used this weak claim to underpin his case for papal support for his invasion of England (see next page). Harald Hardrada, King of Norway, also put forward a claim based on an old treaty from around 1039 between Harthacnut and Magnus, Harald's father, that if either should die without an heir his kingdom should pass to the survivor, which of course you could interpret from a Scandinavian viewpoint had happened to Harthacnut in 1042.

Although Edward signally failed to curb the power of the Godwins (they held earldoms throughout England by 1065), he did manage to split the family when Tostig was exiled in that year. Harold and Tostig were the eldest surviving and most powerful brothers but ended up fighting on opposite sides at Stamford Bridge where Tostig was killed.

From 1044 onwards, Edward invited a considerable number of Normans to take up aristocratic positions in English life, from Ralf, Edward's nephew who became Earl of Hereford, to Robert of Jumièges, who briefly became Archbishop of Canterbury. Not surprisingly this brought an immediate and ferocious response from the Godwins in 1051. Edward eventually reasserted his authority the following year. During his reign the first castles were built by the Normans in Herefordshire and Essex.

In 1064 Edward sent Harold Godwinson to the Norman court. He was shipwrecked en route and ended up swearing an oath over holy relics that he would assist Duke William to gain the crown of England. William wore these relics round his neck at the Battle of Hastings. This helped to damn Harold's reputation after his death.

Edward even succeeded in dying at the right time of the year, in early January, giving Duke William time to construct an invasion fleet in time for his late-summer adventure across the Channel, but not allowing King Harold much time to consolidate his hold on the throne.

Duke William of Normandy

Duke Robert the Magnificent died in 1035 while returning from pilgrimage to the Holy Land, leaving as his sole heir, his son, William the Bastard, aged about 7 years. William's mother, Herleve, was still alive but had been hastily married off to Herluin de Conteville.

Otherwise William had no immediate family, just two younger half-brothers named Odo and Robert. In the next few years William's upbringing belonged to the school of extremely hard knocks. His tutor was murdered and he himself narrowly escaped death on more than one occasion. Beset by rebels from western Normandy, a still young William had to prostrate himself in front of King Henry I of France in 1047 to solicit military support. The king and duke emerged successful from the confused Battle of **Val-ès-Dunes**, south of Caen, and saved Normandy for the duke. But the duchy remained as turbulent as ever, with further victories at Arques and Mortemer necessary to cement Duke William's hold on power. By the 1050s however, the King of France had sided with Geoffrey of Anjou against William. At the Battle of **Varaville** in 1057 William cunningly defeated their joint army, displaying a complete mastery of strategy and even managing to use the tide in his favour. The aggrieved king left Normandy well alone for the rest of his reign. This gave William some space to prepare for his expedition to England.

As a result of his successes William had acquired a formidable military reputation throughout northern France. This reputation was somewhat tainted, however, when he ordered the hands of the defeated townspeople of Alencon to be cut off simply because they had defied his siege. We shall see more of this side of his character in the conquest of England. This reputation was not confined to William himself. The Norman successes in southern Italy and Sicily in the 1050s and '60s ensured their prowess was known throughout Europe. Their military machine depended on three key strengths:

- They were amongst the most formidable cavalrymen in Europe and their horses (destriers) were the best.

The English Earldoms in 1065 (after E.A. Freeman)

- They made increasing use of crossbowmen and archers in battle. The Norman crossbow could penetrate chain mail at 100m at this time.
- They made widespread use of castles. Developed in northern France and the Rhineland in the early eleventh century, castles distinguish themselves by being small and high, acting as fortified barracks for the military elite. They were not designed to defend whole towns as were the burghs in England. When invading a new territory, castles had the huge advantage that they could be erected very quickly from earth and wood. Though it seems incredible, the Normans are thought to have brought two or three prefabricated castle 'kits' with them to England in the invasion fleet.

This unholy trinity was to prove ideally suited to the conquest of England. Amidst the military turbulence, Normandy itself was experiencing a period of rapid social mobility with a new and dynamic aristocracy coming to the fore. An intense revival of the Church also took place, epitomised in the new churches built in the Romanesque style (see Bernay and **Cerisy-la-Forêt**).

Military Alliances and Papal Support

In order to be in a position to launch an invasion of England, Duke William had two final strategic objectives to achieve. Firstly, he had to secure the borders of Normandy so they would be defensible during his prolonged absences abroad. His annexing of Maine in 1062 and his involvement in the affairs of Brittany in 1064 made this possible. The new King of France was still young so unlikely to be a threat, and the king's guardian and regent was Count Baldwin V of Flanders, conveniently William's own father-in-law.

Secondly, William had to gain access to military resources sufficient to ensure the invasion would be successful. In terms of population, in the mid-eleventh century Normandy was probably only half the size of England (1 million against 2). The duke was able to secure the military support of most of his neighbours in northern France through diplomatic and military means, and through marriage. Count Eustace of Boulogne was married to Edward the Confessor's sister, Godifu (though later Eustace saw himself as a potential King of England and caused trouble after the Conquest). Brittany sent the second-largest contingent under Count Alan the Red while Flanders was 'on-side' through William's marriage to Matilda, and many Flemish mercenaries joined William's invasion force. Nevertheless the Normans remained in the majority.

The final piece of the jigsaw was William's securing of papal support. In early 1066 Gilbert, the son of William Fitz Osbern and one of the duke's closest advisors, led a delegation to Rome to make the case for William's dubious claim to the English throne. Nevertheless, his support was probably achieved because Anglo-Saxon England was so out of favour with the Pope as a result of inappropriate appointments to bishoprics, simony and lapses in the payment of Peter's Pence. As a consequence the Pope deemed Duke William's invasion of England to be no more than a small war, ensuring that the penances required for any sins committed by participants during the invasion would be reduced by the Pope. This no doubt helped recruitment to William's expedition. William also received a papal banner that flew above the Norman army at Hastings. In return the Pope sought the re-instatement of England within the close-knit family of Rome, including proper payment of Peter's Pence.

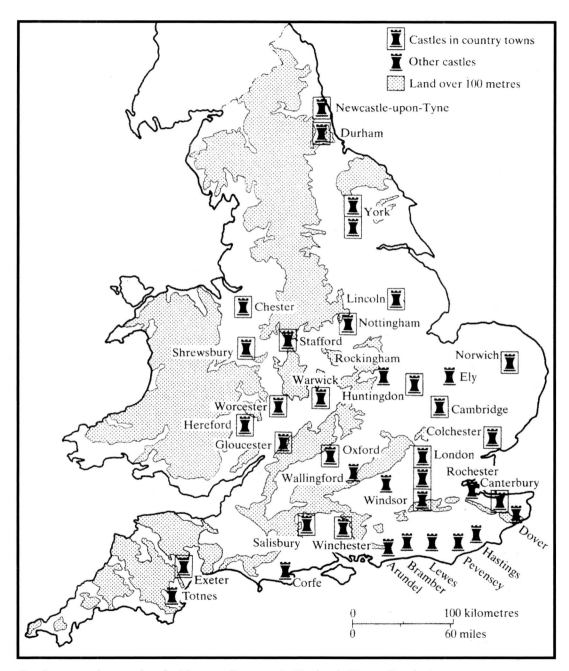

Castles erected soon after the Norman Conquest in England. (Trevor Rowley)

WHY THE NORMANS SUCCEEDED

1. Pure military might: the Battle of **Hastings** was fought at one of those rare moments in history when military technology was in the process of changing. Continental Europe had developed highly effective battlefield cavalry capabilities backed up by crossbowmen, whereas Britain and Scandinavia remained fully wedded to the foot soldier and the shield wall. One eminent historian has gone so far as to claim that the battle was 'a conflict between the military methods of the seventh century and those of the eleventh century.' The Normans were one of the leading exponents of the new technology, possessing high-quality horses termed 'destriers.' The Norman knights themselves made ideal fighting men because of their unique blend of Viking power and French sophistication.

2. In Duke William the Normans possessed a consummate general with a clear grip on strategy. His existing reputation enabled him to put together an unlikely military coalition involving the other provinces of northern France together with papal support. After arrival at Hastings in late September 1066, William had a plan: where he could re-supply his army, he made sure he stayed put. His early engagement with King Harold on the morning of 14 October probably ensured that, crucially, the English army was short of archers – most of whom would have been making their way to the battle on foot. In contrast, Harold can be seen as an experienced and perfectly competent general, but throughout 1066 he is 'on the back foot' responding to events.

3. In the run-up to the D-Day landings the Allies regularly used deception as an effective tool against the Germans. There is every reason to suspect that the Normans may have used this approach. He may not have been a Norman double agent, but the actions of Tostig, King Harold's brother, in the spring and summer of 1066 were immensely helpful to Duke William's cause. His raiding on the east coast brought out Harold's fyrd at too early a date, so they disbanded well before the Norman invasion. His alliance with Harald Hardrada not only ensured Harold's defending army was out of position in the north from mid-September, but also led to the elimination of Hardrada as a rival to the throne at Stamford Bridge. Tostig also lost his life (see Selby Abbey).

4. The English response to the crisis of 1066 lacked any overall coherence. Edward the Confessor had allowed the power of the Godwins to become so completely dominant in southern England that Hastings was, in effect, the Godwins versus Duke William. Two out of three of Harold's surviving brothers fought there and both died with Harold (the third, Wultnoth, was held hostage by Duke William). All the Godwin eggs had been in one basket and, more importantly, there was no back-up plan. The reign of Edward had ended with the other super-magnate houses of England in disarray. The House of Leofric was represented by two callow youths, Earl Edwin in Mercia and his younger brother, Earl Morcar in Northumbria. Waltheof, the son of Siward, had been

overlooked by Edward in 1055 for the earldom of Northumbria because he was a child, but even as a young man he was still not recognised. The only remaining member of the royal House of Cerdic was Edgar – another callow youth.

After Hastings these ineffectual youths were unable to organise any significant resistance to the Normans. London Bridge was defended by Edgar but, with no field army mobilised from the Midlands and the north, the south capitulated meekly. In reality, England was not truly united between the Anglo-Danish north and Anglo-Saxon south. The deep historical divisions had been exacerbated during the turbulent years since 990.

5. It is tempting to wonder whether there was in fact a pro-Norman faction at the English court, perhaps led by Dowager Queen Edith, who arranged for the early and bloodless surrender of Winchester. Edith had been Edward's queen, and Tostig was her favourite brother.

THE EFFECTS OF THE NORMAN CONQUEST

1. By the time of the Domesday Book of 1086, the Anglo-Saxon ruling elite had been all but wiped out. Deaths at the battles of Stamford Bridge and Hastings were compounded by exile (e.g. to Byzantium to join the Varangian guard), in addition to direct replacement by Norman knights at William the Conqueror's command. Only two Englishmen held lands of baronial size. King William carefully parcelled out the conquered lands amongst his Norman and other French supporters so that regional powerbases were generally avoided.

2. English foreign policy was re-orientated towards continental Western Europe (particularly France), away from Scandinavia, its focus for the previous 200 years.

3. The new Norman/French ruling elite in England ensured that the Anglo-Saxon language disappeared from use at the top level of society, in both written and oral forms. English only re-emerged over 300 years later after Henry IV spoke to parliament in the vernacular. In the meantime, driven underground, the language's grammar changed dramatically, losing the inflections of Anglo-Saxon.

4. It has been calculated that only 100,000 Normans and northern French came over with the Conquest in the eleventh and twelfth centuries (compared with a total population of 2 million in 1066). There was some attempt at Norman and Flemish colonisation and new towns were developed, but these were not always successful.

5. So England quickly ossified into a highly stratified class system: a small French-speaking aristocracy of nobles and gentry, a Norman/Anglo-Saxon/Danish middle class who may have spoken both languages, and an Anglo-Saxon/Danish working class.

6. Unlike earlier invasions of England, one thing the Norman Conquest did not affect was the base agricultural economy. The Normans were no agriculturalists – they were predominantly a military elite. There was little change to the daily grind lower down the social pile.

7. There was higher taxation however. The Normans were primarily interested in England for its revenue generating capacity, in order to finance their incessant wars with neighbours in northern France. King William and his successors were fortunate that the hapless Aethelred had laid the foundations of the Danegeld tax collection system.

8. More hidden economic penalties were imposed by the Normans. The livings of numerous churches in England were quickly granted to Norman monasteries and churches. Many new monasteries were founded in the eleventh and twelfth centuries, in part absorbing land previously farmed by the Anglo-Saxons. By the fifteenth century up to one-third of cultivated land in England was owned by monasteries and the church.

9. The most obvious short-term impact on the English countryside however, was the results of the huge building programme instigated by the Normans in the years after 1066. It has been said that this activity was without precedent until the nineteenth century. Motte and bailey castles, cathedrals, parish churches and monasteries were either built from scratch or rebuilt on Anglo-Saxon sites. In later centuries these very distinctive Romanesque buildings came to represent the 'Norman Yoke'.

10. The papal backing of the Conquest ensured that the English Church was brought more directly back into the fold of Rome. Peter's Pence payments were reinstated. Dioceses were re-organised and increased and new cathedrals were usually built within the major centres of the population, e.g. Chichester, Norwich. Archbishop Lanfranc provided the initial driving force.

KEY DATES

The Danish Conquest to 1042

975	**July**	Death of King Edgar. Accession of King Edward the Martyr.
978	**March**	Murder of Edward the Martyr at Corfe Castle, Dorset. Accession of King Aethelred II.
980		Viking raiders return to southern and midland England (Hampshire, Kent and Cheshire).
981		Viking raids in Devon and Cornwall.
982		Viking raids in Dorset.
984		King Aethelred comes of age at 18 years old.
991		Viking raids force imposition of land tax by Aethelred, later called Danegeld. £10,000 paid to Vikings.
		Treaty agreed between England and Normandy to co-operate against Viking raids.
	August	Battle of Maldon. Vikings defeat Anglo-Saxon force, latter led by Byrthtnoth Ealdorman of Essex who is killed.
992–1001		Viking raids of increasing force virtually every year, especially in southern England.
1002	**Spring**	Payment of further Danegeld – £24,000.
	April	Marriage of King Aethelred and Emma of Normandy (his second wife).
	November	Aethelred orders St Brice's Day massacre of 'all Danes in England'. Victims include Gunnhild, sister of King Sweyn of Denmark.
1003		Sweyn leads raiding army into England.
		French reeve of Queen Emma betrays Exeter to the raiders.
1004–5		Sweyn attacks East Anglia. Norwich is sacked. Ulfkell Snilling defeated at Thetford.
		Birth of Edward the Confessor.
1006		Vikings attack Kent and Isle of Wight, and raid inland to Reading and Wallingford. Wiltshire militia defeated near Avebury. £36,000 paid as Danegeld.
1007		Further Danegeld paid. Eadric Streona appointed Ealdorman of Mercia.
1009		Aethelred organises national fleet of warships to oppose Danes but fleet is wrecked by dispute between Eadric Streona's brother and Wulfnoth (Godwin's father).
	August	Danish fleet anchors unopposed off Sandwich with two formidable armies under Thorkell the Tall, Hemming (his brother) and Eilaf. They attack Canterbury, London and Oxford.

1010	**Spring**	Attack Ipswich. Battle of Ringmere Pit. Ravaged Norfolk, Lincolnshire. Swept through southern England and Wiltshire.
1011	**September**	Danes raid Kent. Sack Canterbury and capture Archbishop Aelfheah.
1012	**April**	Danegeld of £48,000 paid. Archbishop Aelfheah murdered at Greenwich by Thorkell's Danes. Thorkell defects to King Aethelred.
1013	**Autumn**	Sweyn acclaimed as King of England by leading men of the Danelaw at Gainsborough.
		Oxford, Bath and Winchester surrender. Initial attack on London failed but finally city submits. King Aethelred flees England with Thorkell to Normandy.
1014	**February**	Death of King Sweyn at Gainsborough.
	Before April	Aethelred returns as king on terms. Attacks Danes in Lincolnshire. Cnut returns to Denmark via Sandwich, where he mutilates hostages.
1015	**Summer**	Cnut returns with with Thorkell, Eric of Hathin and invasion fleet, and anchors in Poole Harbour. Cnut overruns Wessex. Edmund Ironside carries off the widow of Siferth – a leading thegn in the northern Danelaw – marries her and establishes himself as a leader in the Danelaw. Both Cnut and Edmund Ironside raise armies. Edmund ravages West Midlands whilst Cnut invades the Danelaw.
1016	**April**	Death of Aethelred. Edmund acclaimed king in London.
		Cnut probably acclaimed in Southampton.
	May	Edmund invades Wessex. Cnut besieges London.
	Summer	Cnut gives battle to Edmund Ironside at Penselwood (Dorset), Sherston (Wiltshire), on south bank of Thames, and at Otford (Kent). Eadric Streona comes over to Edmund's camp.
	October	Battle of Ashington.
	November	Treaty of Olney (Gloucestershire). Kingdom divided. Death of King Edmund. Cnut sole king.
	December	Edward the Confessor goes into exile in Normandy.
1016		Edward and Edmund, sons of King Edmund Ironside, go into exile, eventually in Hungary.
	Summer	Rising in favour of Eadwig Aetheling suppressed.
1017	**July**	Marriage of Cnut to Aethelred's widow, Queen Emma.
	December	Murder of Eadric Streona, Northman and others by Cnut.
1018	**Spring**	Cnut dismisses fleet. Massive Danegeld of £82,500 raised for Cnut.
		Godwin made an earl.
1018–9		Cnut's brother, Harold, dies and Cnut becomes King of Denmark. Thorkell the Tall regent in England.
1025–6		Ulf, husband of Cnut's sister Estrith, made regent in Denmark.

1026		Cnut defeated at battle of Holy River in Sweden by Ulf and Earl Eilaf, his brother soon afterwards. Ulf murdered on Cnut's orders.
1027		Cnut goes on pilgrimage to Rome.
1028		Cnut drives King Olaf from Norway and takes over the crown. Harthacnut made King of Denmark.
1029		Cnut's 'minor' wife, Aelfgifu of Northampton, and their son Sweyn become rulers in Norway. Cnut gives Estrith, his sister, in marriage to Robert Duke of Normandy but Robert repudiates her.
1035	**Autumn**	Aelfgifu and Sweyn are driven out of Norway.
	November	Death of Cnut at Shaftsbury.
1036	**Winter**	Council of Oxford divides England between Harold Harefoot as regent for Harthacnut and Dowager Queen Emma based in Winchester.
		Edward and Alfred Aetheling separately 'invade' England from Normandy. Alfred captured by Godwin at Guildford and murdered on King Harold's orders at Ely.
1037		Harold I recognised formally as king. Dowager Queen Emma exiled to Bruges in Flanders.
1039		Harthacnut joins his mother Emma in Bruges from Denmark.
1040	**March**	Death of Harold Harefoot.
	Summer	Harthacnut recognised as King of England.
1041		Edward Aetheling joins Harthacnut and Emma in England.
1042	**June**	Death of King Harthacnut. Edward recognised as king.

The Reign of Edward the Confessor

1043		Sweyn and Harold, sons of Godwin, appointed earls.
	November	Edward rides to Winchester with Earls Leofric, Godwin and Siward and confiscates their lands and property.
1045		Marriage of Edward and Edith, daughter of Godwin. Beorn Estrithson, brother of King of Denmark, made an earl in England.
1046		Earl Sweyn Godwinson invades Wales and abducts the Abbess of Leominster.
1047		Stigand made Bishop of Winchester. Earl Sweyn banished to Flanders.
	October	Harald Hardrada made King of Norway on death of Magnus. Ralf the Staller (a Breton and a son of King Edward's sister Godifu) made an earl.
1048		South-east raided by Vikings.
1049	**Autumn**	Returned exile of Earl Sweyn murders Earl Beorn (his cousin) off Dartmouth.

1051	**Spring**	The Norman Robert of Jumièges, made Archbishop of Canterbury.
	Summer	Marriage of Earl Tostig Godwinson to Judith of Flanders.
	September	Visit of Count Eustace of Boulogne, fracas in Dover and Godwin's failed rebellion.
	Autumn	Sweyn declared an outlaw. Godwin, his wife Gytha and his sons flee to Bruges, Flanders and Ireland.
		Duke William of Normandy probably visits England and is made King Edward's heir.
1052	**March**	Death of Dowager Queen Emma.
	September	Return of the Godwin family under arms. Stigand appointed Archbishop of Canterbury. Death of Sweyn on pilgrimage to the Holy Land.
1053	**April**	Death of Earl Godwin succeeded by his son Harold as Earl of Wessex.
1054	**Summer**	Bishop Ealdred of Worcester visits Germany to negotiate return of Edward Aetheling the Exile.
1055		Death of Siward. Earl of Northumbria succeeded by Tostig Godwinson.
	October	Earl Ralf the Staller defeated at Hereford by Aelfgar, son Earl Leofric and Gruffydd ap Llywelyn, ruler of Wales.
1056	**June**	Bishop Leofgar of Hereford defeated (and killed) by the Welsh.
	August	Death of Earl Odda.
1057		Edward Aetheling the Exile returns to England and dies.
	Autumn	Death of Earl Leofric of Mercia succeeded by Aelfgar. Aelfgar outlawed for treason.
1058		A Viking fleet led by Magnus, son of Harald Hardrada, menaces Wales.
1060	**December**	Ealdred promoted to Archbishop of York.
1061		Ealdred and Tostig visit Rome.
1063	**(probably)**	Earl Aelfgar dies succeeded by Edwin.
		Earls Harold and Tostig invade Wales.
1064		Peace treaty between Kings Sweyn of Denmark and Harald of Norway.
	Summer	Earl Harold visits Normandy.
1065	**Spring**	Earl Harold attacks south of Wales.
	October	Rebellion in Northumbria. Edward and Tostig hunt near Salisbury. Earl Harold negotiates with the rebels.
	November	Tostig exiled.
	December	Westminster Abbey dedicated.
1066	**January**	King Edward dies.
1161	**February**	Pope Alexander III canonises Edward.

Normandy to 1066

1028		Birth of William the Conqueror.
1035		Death of Duke Robert I of Normandy. Accession of Duke William.
1040		Count Gilbert of Brionne, tutor to the young duke and others, murdered in William's service.
1044		Lanfranc becomes Prior of Le Bec.
1046		King Henry of France supports Duke William in opposing revolt of Guy of Burgundy.
1047		Battle of Val-ès-Dunes. Victory for William and King Henry.
1049		Proposed marriage of Duke William to Matilda of Flanders prohibited by the Pope.
1051–2		William marries Matilda at Eu in Normandy.
1053	**Autumn**	William captures Argues and suppresses revolt of William, Count of Argues.
1054	**February**	Battle of Mortemor. William repulses invasion force led by the French king, Henry.
1057	**August**	Battle of Varaville. William defeats French force, led by King of France.
1063		Invasion and conquest of Maine by Duke William.
1064		Visit of Harold Godwinson to Normandy. Duke William invades Brittany.

The Norman Invasion of England

1066	**January**	Harold II crowned king. Harold marries Ealdgyth, widow of Gruffydd ap Llywelyn and sister of Earls Edwin and Morcar.
	Spring	Norman mission to Rome led by Gilbert. Bishop of Lisieux obtains papal support for the invasion.
	May	Tostig attacks Isle of Wight, Sussex, Sandwich and north Norfolk coast. Tostig ravages Lincolnshire but is defeated by Earl Edwin. Tostig sails to Scotland.
	Early summer	Harold calls out the militia (fyrd) to defend the English coasts.
	August	William's invasion fleet assembles at Dives-sur-Mer.
	End of August	Harold Hardrada, King of Norway, departs with invasion fleet.
	8 September	Harold stands down militia and fleet moves to London. Hardrada's fleet (including Tostig) arrives at mouth of the Tyne.
	12	William moves fleet from Dives to Valery-sur-Somme. Some ships wrecked by a storm.
	16–18	Hardrada and Tostig land at Riccall on the Ouse south of York.

18–21	Harold leaves London for York with mounted force.
20	Battle of Gate Fulford. Hardrada and Tostig defeat Earls Edwin and Morcar.
24 (evening)	York surrenders to Hardrada.
25	Battle of Stamford Bridge. Harold defeats and kills Hardrada and Tostig.
27 (evening)	Duke William's fleet sail from Valery-sur-Somme.
28	Fleet arrives at Pevensey. First castle built.
29	Move along coast to Hastings. First wooden motte and bailey castle built.
2 October	Harold hears of Norman landing and leaves York.
6	Arrives in London.
11	Leaves London for south coast.
13	Arrives at battle.
14	Battle of Hastings.

A page of the Domesday Book for Hampshire.

Late Anglo-Saxon sword recovered from the Thames at Wallingford.

THE COURSE OF THE NORMAN CONQUEST: 1066–92

Phase 1: Gaining the Crown of England, 1066

14 October	Battle of Hastings. King Harold killed. Power of Godwin family destroyed.
15 October	Rested army at Hastings camp for five days.
20 October	Army moves north-east to Romney to extract revenge for murder of crew of off-course Norman vessel.
Late October	Dover surrenders on demand. Eight days spent building castle. Norman reinforcements cross the Channel.
October/ November	Canterbury surrenders without a fight (but not Archbishop Stigand). Castle built. Duke William catches dysentery. Army rests near city at 'broken tower' for one month. Dowager Queen Edith arranges surrender of Winchester including Treasury. Edgar the Aetheling acclaimed king in London by remaining Anglo-Saxon nobility.
November	Duke moves up Watling Street (the current A2) to Southwark. Sally by Anglo-Saxon defenders of London Bridge under 'King' Edgar. Defeated but bridge not taken. Southwark set on fire. Duke moves through Surrey, northern Hampshire and Berkshire along south bank of the Thames. Scorched earth policy utilised (as shown by decline in Domesday manor values). Crosses Thames west to east at Wallingford. Camps on east bank in Oxfordshire. Archbishop Stigand submits to William.
Late November/ early December	Moves along Ickneild Way below the Chilterns to Berkhamsted, which commanded the main routes out of London to Mercia. Edgar, Earls Edwin and Morcar, plus Archbishop Ealdred of York, surrender to Duke William.
December	Moves 25 miles to City of London, adopting scorched earth policy. May have been some fighting within city walls.
25 December	Duke William crowned King of England in Edward the Confessor's newly built Westminster Abbey. First castle erected on site of the Tower.

Phase 2: Isolated Revolts, 1067–8

January 1067	King William is based at Barking. Edward and Morcar submit again. Normans sweep through East Anglia and parts of Mercia. Royal castles built at Norwich, Colchester and Hereford.

March 1067   King William confident enough to return to Normandy leaving his half-brother, Bishop Odo, and William Fitz Osbern as joint rulers of England. English hostages Stigand, Edwin, Morcar, Edgar accompany William.

Spring/ Summer   Revolts occur in Herefordshire (led by Edric the Wild, nephew of Eadric Streona) and in Kent, where rebels support the candidacy of Count Eustace of Boulogne as king. Both suppressed.

December 1067   King William returns to England. Archbishop Eadred of York declares his support.

Early 1068   Exeter, spurred on by Princess Gytha, Harold's mother, defies Norman demands. William mobilises army of both Normans and English and besieges city. Surrenders after eighteen days.

Castle built on highest part of city.

Devon and Cornwall and Bristol and Gloucester submit by Whitsun.

Later in year the three sons of King Harold attack Bristol and coast of Somerset, but pose no real threat.

Gytha retires to the island of Flatholme in Bristol Channel.

Whitsun 1068   King William's wife Matilda brought to England and crowned at Westminster.

Summer 1068   Edwin, Morcar, and Edgar leave William's court and raise a revolt in the north with Gospatrick of Northumbria.

William leads a force against them via Warwick and Nottingham. On his arrival resistance crumbles.

Edwin and Morcar pardoned and a castle established (later to be known as Clifford's Tower).

William negotiates a treaty with Malcolm Canmore, King of the Scots.

Castles established at Nottingham and Warwick, also at Lincoln, Huntingdon and Cambridge on William's return journey to London.

September 1068   Queen Matilda gives birth to the future King Henry I at Selby.

Phase 3: Crisis: The North on Fire, 1069–70

Late 1068   Robert de Commines sent by the King to Durham with an armed force to establish Norman rule.

Late January 1069   In the name of Edgar Aetheling, rebels surround the town, burn Robert in the bishop's house and wipe out his men.

York also attacked but castle holds out.

William undertakes rapid march to relieve city.

A second castle (Bailes) built on west bank of the Ouse and entrusted to William Fitz Osbern.

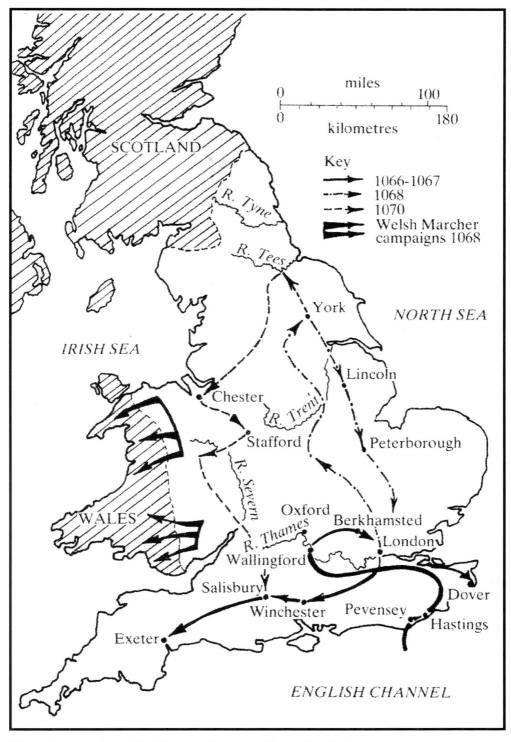

The main campaigns of the Norman Conquest. (Trevor Rowley)

Autumn 1069 Danish fleet arrive off the coast of Kent, consisting of 240 ships of both Danes and Norwegians and including three sons and a brother of the Danish king, Sweyn Estrithson, heir of Cnut's royal house. As fleet heads northwards landing parties are repulsed by local musters until it anchors in the Humber. A general rising by Edgar Aetheling, Gospatric and Waltheof (son of Siward, an earlier Earl of Northumbria), joins the Danes and attacks the two castles at York, destroying them and their garrisons. This defeat, the heaviest ever suffered in England by the Normans, is not followed up however. Danes withdraw to Isle of Axholme in north Lincolnshire. William's response is immediate: he moves directly on Axholme causing the Danes to cross back across the Humber/Ouse into Yorkshire.

Meanwhile, success at York inspires revolt in the south-west (Exeter and Montacute Castle) in West Mercia under Edric the Wild. William leaves his half-brother, Robert of Mortain, and Robert Count of Eu to watch the situation in north Lincolnshire while he leads an army across the Midlands to Stafford. Here the rebels are easily defeated. The revolt in the south-west is suppressed by Geoffrey, Bishop of Coutances but with more difficulty.

On his return from Stafford, William learns at Nottingham that the Danes are re-occupying York. He immediately turns north but is held up for three weeks at the Aire Gap as the rebels have destroyed the bridge and are holding the crossing (now celebrated as Pontefract or Pons Fractus). Despite this long delay the Danes withdraw as soon as William moves up to threaten York. As his army progresses, William redoubles his scorched earth efforts – the harrying of the north begins in earnest. William celebrates Christmas 1069 in York surrounded by urban and rural devastation. Small bands of Norman troops systematically continue to devastate Yorkshire. The terrible effects are still visible to the Domesday officials twenty years later.

Once in York William buys the Danes off, though allows them to over-winter in the Humber. Waltheof and Gospatric submit to William.

Easter 1070 William disbands the mercenary portion of his army at Old Sarum. The crisis passes.

Spring 1070 King Sweyn of Denmark joins fleet in the Humber and sails down to the Wash, joining English rebels under Hereward the Wake in the Isle of Ely.

In June a joint Anglo-Danish force burns and loots Peterborough Abbey. William buys off the Danes and they set sail for home laden with booty. This had been a Viking raid, not an invasion of England.

Spring 1071 Earls Edwin and Morcar leave William's court. Edwin murdered by his followers on the way to Scotland. Morcar joins the rebels in Ely. Willia advances to confront them and the rebels surrender. Morcar taken prisoner. Hereward passes out of history into legend.

Phase 4: The Final Touches

1075	Rebellion in East Anglia of Roger of Hereford (William Fitz Osbern's son). Earl Ralph Guader of Norfolk and Waltheof, Earl of Huntingdon quashed.
1076	Waltheof, son of Siward of Northumbria, executed at Winchester.
1092	Westmorland annexed from the Scots by William Rufus. Castle built at Carlisle.

The Normans in Wales

1067	William Fitz Osbern, Earl of Hereford, builds castles at Hereford and Clifford Ewyas on the border, and takes possession of the lordship of Netherwent in Gwent. He builds a castle at Striguil (now Chepstow).
1070	Hugh d'Arranches made Earl of Chester with forward defence against the Welsh at Rhuddlan near Rhyl.
1074	Roger de Montgomery made Earl of Shrewsbury. Forward defence against the Welsh established at Hen Domen (near Montgomery). Further expansion into Powys follows.
1081	King William undertakes expedition to St David's (Pembrokeshire) to assert his overlordship.
By 1086	In the south the Normans reach Caerleon and the line of the river Usk.
1093	Lordships of Brecon and Glamorgan established. Cardiff Castle built by Robert Fitz Haimon. Roger de Montgomery invades Ceredigion (Cardigan).
1135	By the end of Henry I's reign much of south and west Wales is under Norman control. Henry involves himself in detailed Welsh affairs, invading three times and establishing an effective hegemony.
1136	King Henry's death changes everything. The Welsh rise up in early 1136: in the Grynne Fawr Valley near Abergavenny, at a battle near Swansea and in Ceredigion. The Normans are repulsed and much of Wales remains independent for another 150 years before Edward I's invasion in the thirteenth century.

Scotland: Attack is the Best Form of Defence

1018	Lothian, largely populated by English, taken over by MacAlpin Kings of Scotland. The border established on the Tweed.
1061	King Malcolm III recovers control of Cumbria previously held by Earls of Northumbria.
1068	Malcolm marries Margaret, sister of Edgar Aetheling, the sole surviving member of the English House of Cerdic.
1070	Malcolm raids Teesdale. Edgar attempts invasion of England from Scotland.

1072	The Conqueror leads an expedition into Scotland, comprising of an army and fleet in the North Sea. The two kings meet at Abernethy on the Tay near Perth. Malcolm does homage and gives his eldest son as hostage. In return he is granted lands in England. Edgar forced to leave Scotland.
1079	Malcolm harries Northumbria. William sends his eldest son Robert northward; he reaches Falkirk. On his return Robert commences building a new castle on the Tyne.
1091	While William Rufus is absent in Normandy, Malcolm raids almost as far down as Durham. Later in the year both Rufus and Duke Robert march north.
1092	Rufus leads a large army and recovers Cumbria. A castle built at Carlisle. Malcolm visits Rufus in Gloucester but receives no special treatment.
1093	Malcolm crosses the Tweed. He is ambushed near Alnwick by Earl Robert de Mowbray. He and his son Edward are killed.
1102	King Henry marries Edith (renamed Matilda), daughter of King Malcolm of Scotland.
1113	David, brother of Edith, marries daughter of Earl Waltheof and niece of William the Conqueror, and is made Earl of Huntington.
1124	David succeeds his brother, Alexander, as King of Scotland.
1124–53	David initiates policy of inviting Norman lords to Scotland and granting them feudal lands, thus promoting cross-border holdings. Many are tenants of his Honour of Huntingdon.
1136	On King Henry's death David continues the policy of attack and seizes Carlisle and Newcastle. King Stephen regains them.
1138	King David launches three invasions of England. Ultimately regains control of Cumbria and Northumbria. Over 400 years of warfare follows but no conquest is made.

THREE

THE MAIN PROTAGONISTS

ANGLO-SAXONS

King Aethelred II (*c.* 966–1016, king 978–1016)

Here is a king who definitely lives 'down' to his reputation. Although known in modern times as the 'Unready' because of his disasters with Viking raiders, his nickname was actually 'Unrede', which formed a play on Aethelrede Unrede – good counsel, bad counsel, his regime was one of erratic policies and decisions. Aethelred was the second son of King Edgar by his second wife, Aelfthryth. On Edgar's death a disputed succession led initially to the accession of Aethelred's elder half-brother, Edward. In 978 however, Edward was murdered at **Corfe Castle** while being entertained by his step-mother. Aethelred's reign thus began under inauspicious circumstances. Aethelred was crowned at **Kingston-upon-Thames**, the last king to be crowned there. With a king aged only 12 years, Viking attacks soon recommenced, providing the dominant feature of his calamitous reign.

Unlike earlier members of the House of Cerdic (e.g. Alfred, Edward the Elder, Athelstan) Aethelred chose not to be a fighting king. He led from the rear and depended upon his ealdormen confronting the Viking raids (e.g. Byrhtnoth at **Maldon**). Instead his attempts to buy off the raiders with Danegeld proved fruitless and may even have encouraged further raiding. Danegeld was levied at very high rates across England and led to a sophisticated bureaucracy being developed for its collection, which was unique in Western Europe in its time. However this penal land tax led to a serious reduction in the livelihood and independence of the smaller landowners at the expense of the wealthier aristocracy. England became a more stratified society between rich and poor.

After a decade or so of this ineffectual approach to the Vikings, Aethelred changed tack. In 1002 he married Emma, daughter of Duke Richard I of Normandy, in an attempt to ally with Normandy against the Viking threat. The policy never really proved effective and may in fact have goaded King Sweyn of Denmark to increase his efforts. Furthermore Aethelred had previously been married to Aelfgifu (Elfreda) of Northumbria, daughter of an English ealdorman, by whom he had had thirteen children, the eldest being Prince Athelstan. It is thought Aelfgifu died in February 1002 and that the agreement relating to Aethelred's marriage to Emma included a clause giving precedence to any children of the new marriage in terms of succession to the English throne. The first nail had been inserted in the coffin of Anglo-Saxon England. Once Emma produced Edward (and later Alfred) by 1003–4 a great schism opened up between the two English royal families and within the English aristocracy. Furthermore, a secret Norman 'mole' had been introduced at the English court in the form of Queen Emma herself – a highly intelligent woman who was to become William the Conqueror's great aunt. Calamitous stuff indeed.

Aethelred followed up his new Norman alliance with one of his most celebrated mistakes. On 13 November 1002 (St Brice's Day) he ordered all the Danish men in England to be killed. The order was not carried out everywhere but clearly was in some places (e.g. Oxford). Included in the victims was Gunhild, sister of King Sweyn of Denmark, giving Sweyn the perfect motive for returning to England in revenge. The years that followed saw the rise to power of Eadric Streona, a thegn from West Mercia. Eadric effectively did Aethelred's dirty work for him, enabling the king to once again remain aloof from the action. The Danish raids continued, now more professionally organised, widespread and determined. Further payments of Danegeld were made but to no avail. By 1012, after the murder of Aelfheah, Archbishop of Canterbury, it was clear the Danes were now intent on conquest.

In February 1013 King Sweyn took up residence at Gainsborough on the river Trent. A considerable proportion of the English nobility submitted to him there, giving their support to his candidacy for the throne of England largely because of their dissatisfaction with the behaviour of Aethelred and Eadric Streona. By mid-summer these arrangements had been

Coin of King Aethelred II.

KINGS OF ENGLAND 975–1065

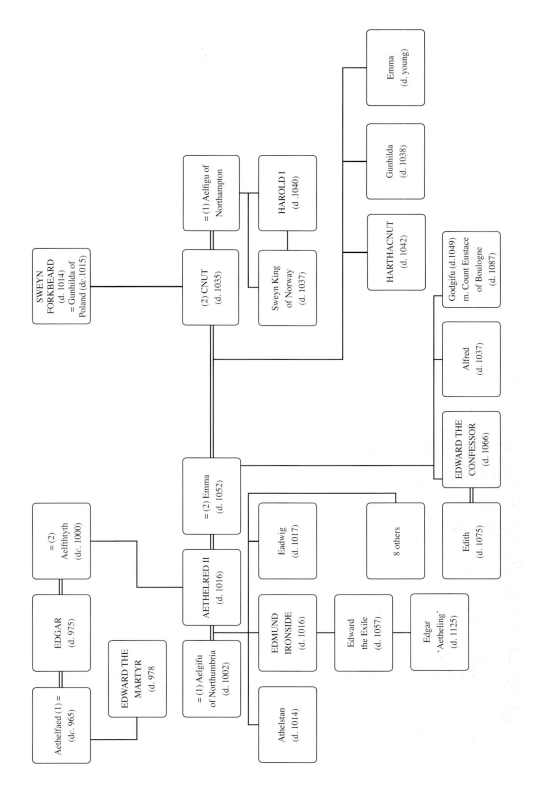

SWEYN FORKBEARD
(d. 1014)
= Gunhilda of
Poland (dc.1015)

= (1) Aelfigu of
Northampton

(2) CNUT
(d. 1035)

HAROLD I
(d. 1040)

Sweyn King
of Norway
(d. 1037)

HARTHACNUT
(d. 1042)

Gunhilda
(d. 1038)

Emma
(d. young)

Godgifu (d.1049)
m. Count Eustace
of Boulogne
(d. 1087)

Alfred
(d. 1037)

EDWARD THE
CONFESSOR
(d. 1066)

= (2) Emma
(d. 1052)

Eadwig
(d. 1017)

8 others

Edith
(d. 1075)

= (2)
Aelfthryth
(dc. 1000)

EDGAR
(d. 975)

EDWARD THE
MARTYR
(d. 978)

Aethelfaed (1) =
(dc. 965)

AETHELRED II
(d. 1016)

= (1) Aelgifu
of Northumbria
(d. 1002)

EDMUND
IRONSIDE
(d. 1016)

Athelstan
(d. 1014)

Edward
the Exile
(d. 1057)

Edgar
'Aetheling'
(d. 1125)

formalised in the Gainsborough Accord, and by the end of the year Aethelred and his second family had been driven into exile in Normandy. King Sweyn's unexpected death at Gainsborough in February 1014 gave Aethelred an unexpected second chance. He returned from exile but, despite promising otherwise, he and Eadric continued their brutal and arbitrary rule until Aethelred's death in April 1016 in London. He was to be succeeded by Edmund Ironside, a son from his first marriage, but the Anglo-Saxon kingdom was broken and at the mercy of the Danes. Aethelred was buried in Old St Paul's Cathedral, London, but his tomb was lost in the Great Fire of London.

Eadric Streona the Grasper (d. 1017)

This man is a candidate for being the most unsavoury person in this book, admittedly chosen from a very long list. History judges him as driving the final nail into the coffin of old Anglo-Saxon England in 1016. At the Battle of **Ashingdon** he had recently switched sides from Cnut to King Edmund Ironside, but halfway through the encounter he led his forces from the field – thus condemning the previously successful Edmund to defeat, and most probably to a fatal wounding. Eadric originated from the Welsh borders of Shropshire and was at King Aethelred's court from 1002. In a major coup in 1006 he helped Aethelred to eliminate Aelfhelm, Ealdorman of Northumbria, and to blind his two sons. He was appointed Ealdorman of Mercia by the king in 1007. A thoroughly ruthless and unprincipled operator, Eadric was Aethelred's principal counsellor for the next eight years and married the king's daughter, Edith. Along the way Eadric most probably arranged the disastrous St Brice's Day murders of Estrith, Sweyn's sister, and Pallig, her husband, which gave King Sweyn of Denmark the perfect excuse to invade

England. Eadric also organised the murders of Siferth and Morcar, two thegns from Lindsey who rebelled against Aethelred in 1014. It is even possible that he creamed off Danegeld to line his own pocket.

In the first of a number of changes of allegiance, Eadric submitted to Sweyn in 1013. In 1016, following the deaths of both Sweyn and Aethelred, he initially aligned with King Edmund Ironside but then defected to Cnut, who had invaded from Denmark. After the Battle of Otford he rejoined Edmund before his final betrayal at Ashingdon. Such ludicrous behaviour clearly did not impress Cnut, despite the benefit he gained from it. Eadric received his comeuppance from the young king as early as Christmas 1017, when the ruthless Cnut ordered his execution by Earl Erik of Hdathir in London and had his unburied body thrown into a ditch.

Edgar Aetheling: the King that Never Was (c. 1052–1125)

Edgar was the son of Edward Aetheling (d. 1057) and grandson of King Edmund Ironside. He was born in Hungary whither his father had fled in 1018 to escape Cnut, who was attempting to eliminate all descendants of the royal House of Cerdic. Edward married Agatha, a German princess, and also they had two daughters. In 1057 Edward was invited by Edward the Confessor to England as the only other surviving descendant of the line of Cerdic – the latter having no children of his own. But, suspiciously, Edward Aetheling died before he ever saw the king. Although not technically an aetheling (traditionally it had to be the son of a king), Edgar was brought up at Edward's court and declared an aetheling by the king. On the Confessor's death in January 1066, the northern Earls Edwin and Morcar initially supported Edgar's candidacy for the throne

THE MAIN PROTAGONISTS

but eventually swung behind Harold. After Hastings and Harold's death, Edgar was chosen as king by the Witan (including Edwin and Morcar) but was never crowned. Edgar meekly surrendered to Duke William with Edwin, Morcar and the rest of the magnates in early December at **Berkhamsted**.

Edgar's foreign upbringing meant that he held no land and had no natural support in England. After William became king he treated Edgar surprisingly well, giving him freedom and some land. But Edgar could not resist the temptation to rebel against the Norman regime. He took part in the great northern revolt of 1069–70 in which York was captured with Danish help. His sister Margaret married Malcolm, King of the Scots, so enabling Edgar to escape across the border when events got too hot. By 1074 Edgar had submitted to William again. Historical writers describe Edgar as simple and indolent, so it comes as no surprise to learn that he became close friends with Robert, Duke of Normandy and the Conqueror's eldest son – a man with a very similar character. Though initially expelled to Scotland by William Rufus in 1091, Edgar was later rehabilitated. He may have joined Duke Robert on crusade in 1098, and was certainly at his side at the Battle of Tinchebrai in 1106 when the duke was defeated and captured by his youngest brother, King Henry I of England.

Edgar was an altogether 'ineffectual claimant' to the throne of England, offering little or no leadership during his long but rather peripheral life. It reflects well on William the Conqueror's judgement of his opponents that he repeatedly felt able to spare Edgar's life, despite his much better claim to the throne. The man offered no effective threat to William's crown and, if executed, could have become a focus for English rebels.

Queen Edith (*c.* 1020–75, queen 1045–66)

Edith was the eldest child of Godwin, Earl of Wessex, and Gytha, and was educated at Wilton nunnery. In January 1045 she married King Edward the Confessor and became Queen of England. Edward was recognising the realpolitik of Godwin's dominating power in southern England. In all probability the marriage was never consummated – for religious reasons on Edward's part – and at any rate the couple had no children. In 1051–2, when the Godwins fell from grace and were exiled, Edith was dispatched by her husband to a nunnery, either Wherwell in Hampshire or Wilton, but returned to favour in September 1052. Edith's favourite brother is said to have been Tostig, who arranged to have Gospatric of Northumbria murdered in late 1064 and bizarrely organised the murder at court with the help of Edith. Edith is best remembered for commissioning the Latin tract '*Vita Aedwardi Regis*'; most of which survives and which in reality is a eulogy of the Godwins.

King Edmund Ironside (*c.* 990–1016, king 1016)

Edmund was the third son of King Ethelred II and Elgiva (Aelfgifu), daughter of Earl Thored of Northumbria, but on the death of his elder brother Athelstan in 1014 he became the eldest surviving son. During the chaos that reigned in England following Sweyn's invasion of 1013 Athelstan and Edmund became alienated from their father, who seems to have designated Edward and Alfred, his sons by his second wife Emma, as heirs to the throne. In 1015 the treacherous Eadric Streona arranged the murder of Siferth and Morcar, leading Danish thegns in the seven boroughs. Edmund abducted Siferth's widow, Ealdgyth, from Malmesbury, where she had been taken on Aethelred's orders;

thus effectively rebelling against his father, the king. Edmund now had a power base in the north, as well as in Wessex, with which to counter the Danish threat posed by Sweyn's son Cnut.

After Aethelred's death in April 1016, Edmund was acclaimed king in London. Unfortunately Cnut was also acclaimed in Southampton as he was sailing from Poole Harbour to London. In the battles that followed Edmund showed himself to be one of the very few fighting kings of late Anglo-Saxon England, inflicting defeats on Cnut at Sherston, Penselwood and Otford (Kent) during the campaign. Unfortunately at **Ashingdon** (Assandun) in Essex the Anglo-Saxon Chronicle tells us that he was betrayed on the battlefield by Eadric Streona and defeated. Although managing to flee, the initiative had passed to Cnut. The two kings famously met to divide the kingdom on an island in the Severn at **Deerhurst.** Edmund retained only Wessex. Unfortunately only weeks later Edmund died; possibly of injuries sustained at Assandun, although there are horrendous stories of his murder while seated on his toilet! With him died any real hope for the long-term future of Anglo-Saxon England. A warrior hero without any real blemish?

King Edward the Confessor (*c.* 1004–66, king 1042–66)

Edward was a complete enigma. Sanctified in 1163 through the efforts of Henry II, he remains the only King of all England to be thus honoured. He comes across as a highly religious and ascetic man who spurned sexual relations and possibly died a virgin. As king he was a clever, crafty non-confronter who was not a fighting man – rather like his father, Aethelred, in fact. Yet during his reign England was largely peaceful and exempt from serious Viking raids. His main military problems stemmed

from internal conflicts with the Godwins.

Edward was the elder son of Aethelred and his second wife, Emma of Normandy. Their marriage settlement probably insisted on precedence to the English throne being given to any aethelings produced by the couple over the sons already existing from the king's first marriage. Edward and his younger brother, **Alfred**, were brought up to be very pro-Norman, spending a lot of time there – especially after Aethelred lost the throne of England. The Danish conquest of 1013–6 meant that Edward missed out on his rightful inheritance as he made no attempt to invade England at this time.

After Cnut's death in 1035 Edward and Alfred made an abortive attempt to seize the throne from Harold I which ended in Alfred's capture at **Guildford** and subsequent murder at **Ely**. Once Harthacnut, his half-brother, had gained the throne in 1040 however, Edward's fortunes improved and he was invited to return to England. 'Fortune then favoured the weak' as Harthacnut dropped dead at a wedding feast in Lambeth in 1042 and Edward inherited the throne of England. Surely we see here the invisible hand of twice Dowager Queen Emma, mother to both kings? After Godwin's death in 1053 Edward was able to turn increasingly to the former's five sons as able lieutenants to run the country. In many ways a brief golden age of Anglo-Saxon England followed, only to be shattered by Hastings in 1066.

In many ways Edward's main contribution to our story is his total ineffectiveness when it came to the succession. He could not have done more to hand the throne to Duke William of Normandy even if he had tried (perhaps he had?). At his death in January 1066 the English throne was technically vacant. He and Queen Edith (Godwin's eldest daughter) had no children. He had no earlier wives and he had no known

Coin of King Edward the Confessor.

mistresses or illegitimate children (which is one of the reasons why he was seen as saintly). Furthermore there were no Anglo-Saxon aethelings (meaning those who were 'throneworthy') still alive. Anglo-Saxon precedent dictated that any son of a king was an aetheling, but a grandson was not. In 1056 Edward invited Edward, the sole remaining son of King Edmund Ironside, to return from exile in Hungary. He duly arrived in London but died shortly afterwards without even meeting the king. Edward the Exile had a son, Edgar, aged around 5 years at the time and the sole survivor of the English royal House of Cerdic. King Edward and Queen Edith declared the infant Edgar an aetheling and took him under their wing.

The major crises of Edward's reign were the two armed revolts led by Godwin in 1051–2. Edward weathered these storms and, during Godwin's exile in 1051–2, it is likely (though not certain) that he invited Duke William of Normandy to England and, during his visit, promised him the throne of England as Edward's successor. William of course could claim to be the 'great nephew' of Emma of Normandy, queen to both Aethelred and Cnut, but that constituted no credible claim to the throne of England. After Godwin's death in 1053 Edward built up the power of his sons. Tostig was his favourite. In 1055, on the death of Siward, Earl of Northumbria, Tostig was chosen to succeed him at the expense of the infant Waltheof, Siward's remaining son. In 1064 Tostig probably arranged the murder of Aelfgar, Earl of Mercia, leaving that powerful earldom in the hands of his son, Edwin, still a callow youth. In the autumn of 1065 Tostig was deposed as Earl of Northumbria by rebels. Brother Harold held talks with the rebels at Northampton but they utterly refused Edward's demand to reinstate Tostig. Harold chose not to settle the issue by force. Tostig went into exile and the power of the Godwins had been split. At the rebels' request the earldom of Northumbria was given to Edwin's brother, Morcar, an even more callow youth.

By early 1066 the fighting capability of England had become dangerously centred on the Godwinson brothers remaining in England. Harold, now king, Gyrth and Leowine, plus the two very inexperienced sons of Aelfgar, Earl of Mercia (Edwin and Morcar) – whose relations with the Godwins had been poor since 1064. Edward had also provided valuable English military experience by his appointment of Normans, including his sister's son Ralf of Mantes, to key positions in Herefordshire and Essex in the 1050s.

It is possible that the deposing of Tostig in the autumn of 1065 caused the old king to have a stroke or series of strokes (Edward was with Tostig at the royal hunting lodge of Britford near Salisbury when the rebels struck in York). His death took place conveniently for Duke William, who then had plenty of time to build and assemble his invasion fleet before the end of the 1066 campaigning season. England was ripe for the taking. Edward was buried in his own new abbey at **Westminster**.

King Edward the Martyr (*c*. 962–78, king 975–8)

King Edgar (king 959–75) 'the Peacable' was an effective king, little troubled by military strife. Unfortunately his marital affairs were less conventional. Before he became king he married Aethelflaed Eneda (the 'white duck'), daughter of Herefordshire landowner Ealdorman Ordmaer. She bore him a son, Edward, but was subsequently either divorced or died. Edgar then married Wulfthryth, later to become Abbess of Wilton near Salisbury, who produced a

daughter who was later known as St Edith. While Wulfthryth was still alive in 964–5, Edgar was married a third time to Aelfthryth, widow of Ealdorman Aethelwold. Aelfthryth was blessed by the church and anointed queen and produced two sons: Edmund (who died young) and Aethelred.

On Edgar's death, despite Aelfthryth's anointing as queen, it was first son Edward who succeeded to the throne, aged about 13 years. He was powerfully supported by Dunstan, Archbishop of Canterbury, and was crowned at **Kingston-upon-Thames**, the traditional location for the kings of Wessex. However, with both Edward and Aethelred being minors, the aristocracy was split between the rivals. Edward's short reign was disparaged by his successor, but he is best remembered by the manner of his murder at **Corfe Castle** in 978, most probably on the orders of his stepmother, Aelfthryth. The descent from the high point of Edgar's reign to the depths of Aethelred the Unready was to be a swift one. A groundswell of support developed for St Edward's canonisation, which Aethelred wisely encouraged.

Queen Emma (*c*. 985–1052, queen to Aethelred 1002–16, queen to Cnut 1018–35)

Surely one of the most extraordinary women in English history, Emma was the daughter of Richard I, Count of Rouen, and Gunnor from Denmark. She was sister to Richard II, Duke of Normandy (d. 1026). In other words, she was a senior member of the Norman ducal family and was to become William the Conqueror's great aunt. In 990 King Aethelred concluded a treaty with Richard I that aimed to prevent Viking ships from using harbours in Normandy as bases to raid England. In the spring of 1002 Emma was married to Aethelred with the same objective in mind. However, Aethelred was already married to Aelfgifu of Northumbria 'in the Danish style' and they had a large family, including sons now approaching adulthood. Emma took precedence in the eyes of the church, though she bizarrely adopted her predecessor's name, Aelfgifu, once in England.

Emma and Aethelred produced three children: Edward (later the Confessor), Alfred and a daughter, Godifu. Fairly soon rumours were circulating that Aethelred had little time for Emma, but in 1013 Aethelred and this second family escaped to Normandy when Sweyn and his Danes swept to power in England. In 1016, when Sweyn's son Cnut took the throne after the Battle of Ashingdon, Emma's children returned to Normandy (Aethelred had died). It is thought that Emma remained in England; she may even have been captured by Cnut in London. At any rate, in 1017 – in an extraordinary twist – Emma was married to Cnut, the son of the man who had driven her first husband from the throne of England! He was about 22 years old and she about 32. It is said that her firstborn, Edward, never really forgave her for abandoning her first family in this manner.

With Cnut, Emma had two surviving children, Harthacnut and Gunhilda (a girl, Emma, died young – see Bosham), but this king also retained a first wife, Aelfgifu of Northampton, in the 'Danish manner'. They had had two sons, Sweyn and Harold, but once again Emma insisted that only Cnut's son by her should have the right to the English throne. As Cnut's queen, Emma was a great patron of the church, involving herself with Bury St Edmunds, Ely, Christchurch, St Augustine's Canterbury and particularly **Winchester**. Emma had acquired the manor of **Godbegot** in that city in 1012, which became her powerbase. She was able to assist Cnut in projecting 'an image of royal piety'.

After Cnut's death in 1035 Emma featured in two notorious events as Queen Dowager. In 1036 a power struggle developed between Emma, as regent for Harthacnut (who was detained in Denmark), and Harold Harefoot, Cnut's son by Aelfgifu. Harold was gaining the upper hand so Emma wrote to her sons by Aethelred, Edward and Alfred, in Normandy, urging them to come to her rescue. Alfred landed in Dover and was travelling overland to Winchester when he was tricked and captured by Godwin in Guildford and handed over to Harold. Alfred Aetheling was subsequently blinded and died. This infamous event became a cause célèbre between Edward (as king) and Godwin, and between Edward and his mother.

On Harold I's accession in 1036 Emma was exiled to Flanders (not to her native Normandy). Here she worked hard towards ensuring that Harthacnut inherited his father's throne, which he achieved in 1040 on Harold's death. Emma returned to England at this time and was no doubt instrumental in persuading Harthacnut to invite his half-brother Edward to return to England from Normandy. One of the first acts carried out by Edward on becoming king in 1042 was to ride down to Winchester, accompanied by Earls Godwin, Leofric and Siward, and drive his mother out of Godbegot and the city, confiscating all of her property – apparently because of her role in these unsavoury events.

This queen to two very different kings, and mother to two more, played a key role behind the scenes during the turbulent years in the first half of the eleventh century. She died in 1052 and was buried next to Cnut in **Winchester**.

Godwin, Earl of Wessex (d. 1053)

Most famous for being the father of King Harold II, Godwin was himself a major

Queen Emma receives her Encomium watched by her two sons, Edward and Harthacnut.

figure in Anglo-Saxon politics from 1018. His own father is thought to have been Wulfnoth Cild, an important Sussex thegn, who rebelled against Aethelred in 1009, was exiled and then disappears from record. It is likely that Godwin was amongst Cnut's early supporters in England; in 1018 he was appointed to the key post of Earl of Eastern Wessex as Cnut divided the country by region. The western shires followed in 1020 and by 1023 he was the undisputed 'top' earl. In 1019 he was given the hand of **Princess Gytha**, daughter of Danish magnate Thorgils Sprakaleg and Cnut's sister-in-law (her brother Ulf had married Cnut's sister Estrith).

Below the king, Godwin remained the most powerful man in the country throughout Cnut's reign. Cnut is quoted as describing him as 'the most cautious in counsel, the most active in war'. But political life became more of a struggle when Cnut died. Initially supporting Harthacnut and Dowager Queen Emma in the 1036 succession crisis, Godwin switched sides to support Harold Harefoot and was blamed for the lamentable massacre at Guildford and the subsequent blinding and death of Alfred, Emma's second son and brother to Edward the Confessor. When Harthacnut (Alfred's half-brother) returned to claim the throne in 1040, the relationship was not easy and Godwin had to buy forgiveness for his part in Alfred's murder by presenting the king with a mighty warship.

This uneasy relationship continued after the accession of Edward the Confessor. Godwin became the leader of the resistance to Edward's pro-Norman policy. Godwin and Gytha had at least three daughters and six sons – five of which were given Scandinavian names, so the family's allegiance is clear. By the 1050s five of the sons had acquired earldoms and soon found themselves dominating the country. In 1051 however, Edward felt strong enough to move against the family, provoking Godwin over his failure to punish the townspeople of Dover after an affray with Count Eustace of Boulogne, Edward's brother-in-law. South of Gloucestershire, an armed confrontation looked on the cards, but Edward was saved by the timely support of Earls Leofric, Siward and Ralph. The Godwins were exiled to Bruges in Flanders under the protection of Count Baldwin, and to Ireland. Nevertheless, the very next year Godwin gathered a large fleet, menaced London and forced Edward to reinstate the family.

In April 1053, barely six months after his return from exile, Godwin collapsed while dining with the king and surrounded by his family. He was carried from the chamber unconscious and later died – another untimely and suspicious death. After Hastings, Gytha upheld family honour by opposing the Conqueror in the south-west (see Exeter).

King Harold II (*c.* 1021–66, king 1066)
Harold was the second son of Godwin, Earl of Wessex. His elder brother Sweyn, one of the wildest individuals you will come across in this book, died while on pilgrimage to Jerusalem in 1052. Harold steadily gained power in England in a more conventional manner under the guidance of Godwin. In 1044 he was made Earl of East Anglia followed by Earl of Wessex on his father's death in 1053. He was then the most powerful man in England beneath the king. Harold acquired considerable military experience and reputation while subduing Gruffydd ap Llywelyn in Wales, especially in the 1063 campaign when he co-operated with his brother Tostig. Gruffydd's severed head was presented to King Edward as proof of success.

THE HOUSE OF GODWIN

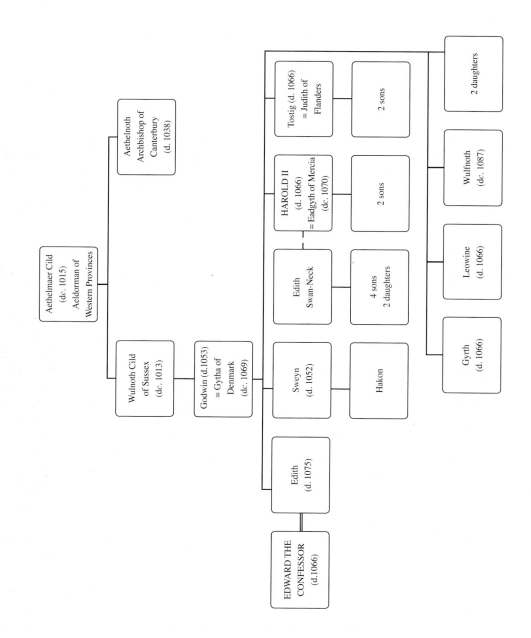

Aethelmaer Cild
(d*c*. 1015)
Aeldorman of
Western Provinces

Aethelnoth
Archbishop of
Canterbury
(d. 1038)

Wulnoth Cild
of Sussex
(d*c*. 1013)

Godwin (d.1053)
= Gytha of
Denmark
(d*c*. 1069)

Edith
(d. 1075)

EDWARD THE
CONFESSOR
(d.1066)

Sweyn
(d. 1052)

Hakon

Edith
Swan-Neck

4 sons
2 daughters

HAROLD II
(d. 1066)
= Eadgyth of Mercia
(d*c*. 1070)

2 sons

Tostig (d. 1066)
= Judith of
Flanders

2 sons

Gyrth
(d. 1066)

Leowine
(d. 1066)

Wulfnoth
(d*c*. 1087)

2 daughters

In 1064 Harold made a somewhat mysterious visit to northern France. He was shipwrecked in Pontieu (perhaps blown off course), captured by the count and handed over to Duke William of Normandy. During his stay both men saw a lot of one another; Harold also got to see the Norman military machine on campaign in Brittany. Crucially, Harold is said to have sworn on holy relics to support Duke William as King of England. William made much use of this event in his propaganda ahead of and after the Conquest.

In the autumn of 1065 Harold failed to back his brother, Tostig, who had been supplanted as Earl of Northumbria by Morcar. Tostig was exiled by the dying King Edward. No reconciliation appears to have been attempted once Harold became king, so Tostig became an important player in the events of 1066 alongside Hardrada of Norway.

Harold developed this re-alignment with the House of Leofric further by marrying Morcar's sister, Ealdgyth (widow of the same Gruffydd on page 53). After Hastings she was dispatched (heavily pregnant) to Chester, where she gave birth to a boy, Harold, in December 1066. He died in exile sometime after 1098. Harold, of course, had had a long-standing relationship with Edith Swan-Neck, by whom he had four sons and two daughters. The sons were to invade the West Country from Ireland in 1068 with no success.

On Edward the Confessor's death the throne of England was technically vacant since, strictly speaking, no aethelings of the House of Cerdic now survived. Even though Edgar Aetheling, a grandson of King Edmund Ironside, was alive, Edward nominated Harold as his successor on his deathbed in the English tradition. The Witan gave its support and Harold was crowned the same day. He had no other claim to the throne.

It is impossible to judge Harold as a peacetime king. From early spring he was engaged with pretenders to his throne: his brother Tostig, Harald Hardrada and finally Duke William. He is said to have been brave and resolute and an inspiring leader, but also cautious. His victory at the Battle of **Stamford Bridge** over Hardrada and Tostig was one of the outstanding Anglo-Saxon victories over the Vikings. In many ways Harold could have made a fine Anglo-Saxon king, had he not the misfortune to be opposed by the might of the Norman military machine, led as it was by a strategic genius. But why did Harold head north to Yorkshire in mid-September 1066, when he knew Duke William was the main threat? He and his two younger brothers were killed at the Battle of **Hastings**.

Earl Leofric and Countess Godifu (Godiva) of Mercia and the House of Leofric

Yes, she was very much a real person – only the details of her ride through **Coventry** are the stuff of legend. **Godifu** (d*c*. 1067) probably came from a substantial East Midlands family, holding sixty hides of land in her own right in the East and West Midlands. Roger of Wendover claimed she had both beauty and piety. She and husband Leofric were certainly great benefactors of the church. They supported churches and priories at Much Wenlock, Leominster, Chester, **Stow** near Lincoln, Burton and Evesham. They also founded **St John's Abbey** at **Coventry**.

Leofric (d. 1057) was the son of Leowine, created ealdorman by Aethelred in 994. The family originated from the Worcester/Gloucester region. Despite Northman, Leofric's elder brother, being executed by Cnut for rebelling in 1017, the family seem to have made their peace with Cnut – such that Leofric was able to inherit the earldom of Mercia in about 1023. Leofric provided a haven of continuity through the turbulent reigns of four kings until his death in 1057. On Cnut's death in 1035 he acted as kingmaker for Cnut's son Harold I, and later provided the main counterbalance to the Godwins during the reign of Edward the Confessor. He died at King's Bromley in Staffordshire and was buried at Coventry. Godifu outlived him, dying in around 1070.

After Leofric's death the fortunes of his family waned. His son **Aelfgar** was twice outlawed by King Edward and then disappeared from history in 1063 – probably murdered by Tostig. Aelfgar's eldest son, **Edwin** (c. 1048–71) assumed the earldom but was still in his teens. On Tostig's exile in 1065 Aelfgar's second son, **Morcar** (c.1050–87), received the earldom of Northumbria. Though things sounded good for the family, both sons were young and inexperienced and in attempting to combat William the Conqueror after 1066 they were to prove a disaster for their families and for England.

In the spring of 1066 King Harold II, who had backed Morcar against his own brother, Tostig, in the autumn 1065 crisis, married Edwin and Morcar's sister Eadgyth (Edith). She was the widow of Prince Gruffyd ap Llywelyn of North Wales, whose severed head Harold had personally delivered to Edward the Confessor in 1063–4! This obviously political alliance was an attempt by Harold to bind the brothers to the House of Godwin. Initially it worked; the brothers drove Tostig out of Lindsey in mid-1066 and then bravely engaged with the mighty Hardrada, King of Norway, at the Battle of Gate Fulford near York. This allowed Harold to surprise Hardrada and Tostig a few days later at Stamford Bridge and kill them. Thereafter the brothers fade from view however, making a largely supine and ineffective contribution to the campaign against William the Conqueror. They may

have become disaffected because Harold replaced Morcar with Maerleswein as Earl of Northumbria after Stamford Bridge.

After the complete demise of the Godwins at Hastings, the defence of England rested crucially on the two brothers as the only nationally powerful military force in the country. They flirted with supporting Edgar Aetheling, but in the end meekly joined the other English leaders in surrendering to Duke William at **Berkhamsted.** Their sister, by now heavily pregnant, was dispatched to Chester where she gave birth to a boy, Harold in the December. He died sometime after 1098 in exile. In March 1067 both brothers were taken as members of the hostage party to Normandy by the newly crowned King William. An accommodation seems to have been reached with the new regime and there was even talk of Edwin marrying one of William's daughters.

However in the summer of 1068 they left court in London and headed north. An insurgency based on York was attempted but snuffed out without a battle by the Conqueror's rapid counter march to York, where he built a castle. The brothers appear to have taken no part in the more effective revolts of 1069–70, but left court again in 1071. Edwin was quickly killed by his own men, while Morcar took refuge with rebels in the Isle of **Ely**. He was captured here and imprisoned in the custody of Roger of Beaumont, one of the Conqueror's close confidants.

Earl Odda (d. 1056)

A splendid pamphlet by Anne Williams (available in St Mary's church, Deerhurst) tells us that Odda was a distant kinsman (in-law) of Edward the Confessor – possibly through Aelfgifu, wife of King Edgar. Odda was born in the 990s and was a major landowner in the West Country, holding

THE HOUSE OF LEOFRIC

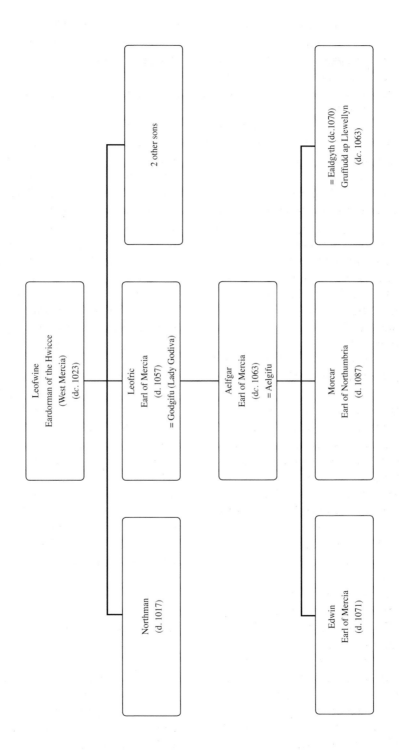

Leofwine
Eardorman of the Hwicce
(West Mercia)
(dc. 1023)

2 other sons

Northman
(d. 1017)

Leofric
Earl of Mercia
(d. 1057)
= Godgifu (Lady Godiva)

Aelfgar
Earl of Mercia
(dc. 1063)
= Aelgifu

Edwin
Earl of Mercia
(d. 1071)

Morcar
Earl of Northumbria
(d. 1087)

= Ealdgyth (dc.1070)
Gruffudd ap Llewellyn
(dc. 1063)

manors in four counties (Gloucestershire, Herefordshire, Worcestershire and Devon).

Odda's place in history was cemented at the fall of Godwin, Earl of Wessex in 1051. King Edward made Odda Earl of the Western Shires (Cornwall, Devon, Dorset and Somerset) and the next year appointed him to command the royal fleet at Sandwich together with Ralph, Earl of Herefordshire and the East Midlands. Their task was to prevent Godwin returning to England from Flanders where he had been exiled. Sure enough, in mid-1052, Godwin made a sortie to Dungeness and Pevensey, eluding the earls, but was forced to return to Bruges by bad weather. The earls were stood down by Edward and the fleet relocated to London under new leaders.

Later that year Godwin made a successful return to London, forcing Edward to re-instate him and his family to their positions of power. Odda was not disgraced however. He was given a new earldom in the West Midlands in Worcester and possibly Gloucestershire. He died childless in 1056 and was buried at Pershore Abbey. His lands passed to Edward, who gave the **Deerhurst** estate to St Denis Abbey in Paris.

Archbishop Stigand (d*c*. 1072)

Stigand was the last Anglo-Saxon Archbishop of Canterbury. The state of the Anglo-Saxon church in 1066 and the behaviour of its primary archbishop in particular were *casus belli* for both William the Conqueror and the Pope. The career of Stigand demonstrates the problem. Born an Anglo-Scandinavian in or near to Norwich, Stigand comes to view when he was appointed a royal priest at Cnut's new minster at Assandun (**Ashingdon**), built to commemorate his victory there. He attested charters during Cnut's reign, indicating a position of some influence.

His rapid rise to power started soon after Edward the Confessor came to the throne. In 1043 he was made Bishop of Elmham in Norfolk, but was soon deposed on the fall of his mentor, Dowager Queen Emma. Stigand was even accused of being Emma's lover! He was restored in 1044 and quickly promoted to Winchester in 1047. He was prominent at court from 1047–52 and acted as mediator between the king and Godwin during the crises of 1051–2. In 1052 he was appointed Archbishop of Canterbury when the previous incumbent, Robert Champart, fled the country with Edward's other Frenchmen. Stigand continued to hold his Winchester see in plurality with Canterbury and the deposed Robert travelled to Rome to present his case to the Pope. Stigand's appointment was deemed uncanonical (he had received his pallium from anti-Pope Benedict X) and he became *persona non grata* with the Pope.

At home he was an effective administrator, but more interested in furthering his own financial interests. With possession of the two wealthiest sees in England he held land in eighteen counties, including one-third of Norfolk. He built up large private holdings here and in Gloucestershire. He probably crowned Harold in early 1066. After the disaster at Hastings, Stigand appeared to back Edgar Aetheling, but at **Wallingford** in early December he set the precedent and submitted to William. This early act probably prolonged his tenure until 1070 when he was taken into comfortable custody in Winchester. He did not, however, crown William or Matilda. Stigand was buried at **Winchester**.

Tostig Godwinson (*c*. 1025–66)

Third son of Godwin and Gytha, history tried to assign Tostig a lesser role than his illustrious brother, King Harold II, but

Stigand, Archbishop of Canterbury, crowns King Harold II (Bayeux Tapestry).

he would have none of it. In 1051 he was exiled by Edward the Confessor after the fall of the Godwins, and chose to go to Flanders with his father. There he married Judith, half-sister to Count Baldwin V of Flanders, whose daughter Matilda married Duke William of Normandy at about the same time – dangerous relations for an Englishman. A man with plenty of charisma, Tostig was said to be a favourite of King Edward's and Queen Edith's favourite brother. In 1055 Edward, on the death of Siward, Earl of Northumbria, overlooked the infant Waltheof, Siward's son, and appointed Tostig to be Earl of Northumbria. It was a truly amazing move and the first time a southerner had ruled this traditionally independent and racially diverse part of England. Despite spending considerable time in the south, often in the king's company, Tostig initially did well and even appointed another southerner to be Bishop of Durham.

In 1063–4, however, Tostig had three Northumbrian nobles murdered – including Gospatric, in whose death at court he bizarrely involved his sister Edith. In summer 1065 the Northumbrians finally revolted in Tostig's absence, murdering his household troops and inviting Morcar, brother of Edwin of Mercia, to be their earl. In the subsequent negotiations brother Harold refused to back Tostig and sided with Edwin and Morcar. King Edward had no alternative but to exile Tostig in what was surely the most disastrous fraternal argument in English history. England needed its most important political family to be united at this crucial time but it was split firmly down the middle.

Tostig left court at Christmas in 1065, as King Edward was dying. There is no evidence of any attempt at reconciliation between the Godwinson brothers after Harold became king. By May 1066 Tostig was raiding the south coast of England with a fleet provided by Count Baldwin of Flanders, before turning his attention to the east coast. Although repulsed from Lindsey by Edwin and Morcar, these actions had the major effect of causing King Harold to call out the militia at the beginning of the 1066 campaigning season. Consequently Harold had to stand the force down in early September, when Duke William had not even left his Normandy ports. But worse was to come for Harold when Tostig joined up with King Harald Hardrada of Norway in early September. It was the appearance of their joint fleet in Yorkshire in mid-September which prompted King Harold's wild plan to dash up north rather than wait for Duke William to cross the Channel. Tostig was killed at **Stamford Bridge** fighting his own brother.

As Hardrada also fell at Stamford Bridge, the only beneficiary of this fraternal conflict was Duke William, who landed unopposed at Pevensey on 28 September, three days after Stamford Bridge. Tostig could not have been more helpful to William's cause if he had tried. The Normans obviously thought so as Tostig was buried in York Minster, though sadly nothing survives today.

Waltheof, Earl of Northumbria (*c*. 1050–76)

Of particular importance as the only Englishman to be executed by the Conqueror himself, Waltheof was predictably considered a martyr by Englishmen, especially at Crowland and Romsey abbeys. The Normans usually preferred to blind and castrate nobles in need of punishment. Waltheof was the second and much younger son of Siward, Earl of Northumbria, by Aelfflaed of Bamburgh. His elder brother Osbearn died in 1054, so when Siward died the next year the infant Waltheof was overlooked by Edward the Confessor, who controversially appointed southerner Tostig

Godwinson. Even ten years later, on Tostig's downfall, Waltheof was passed over for Morcar of Mercia. It is probable that he was made Earl of Huntingdon and Northampton, which had also been ruled by his father, at this time however. By 1066 he had acquired land in eight counties and much influence in the East Midlands. Waltheof submitted to Duke William in 1066 and was one of the hostages taken by the new king to Normandy in 1067. On returning to England in 1068 he later left court and joined the rebellion in York in 1069. On William's arrival late in 1069 Waltheof and his cousin, Gospatric, now Earl of Northumbria, fled from York and submitted to the king on the banks of the Tees. Both were pardoned and surprisingly Waltheof was married to Judith, the king's niece (she was the daughter of his sister, Adelaide). He continued to acquire lands in the south of England but remained outside the top level of magnate landowners.

William expelled Gospatric in 1072 and made Waltheof Earl of Northumbria – his true inheritance. Unfortunately he was lured into a plot against the king with Ralph, Earl of East Anglia, and Roger, Earl of Hereford (the son of William Fitz Osbern), both Normans. Although he had misgivings before any action actually took place and threw himself on the mercy of Archbishop Lanfranc, the king was not impressed, probably because Waltheof had already had to be pardoned for the 1069 rebellion. He was arrested, tried in a much drawn-out process and, after further delay in prison, executed on 31 May 1076 on St Giles' Hill, Winchester. His body was thrown into a ditch and left unburied until retrieved by the Abbot of Crowland at the request of his widow, Judith (despite this, there were rumours that she was one of those insisting he be executed). Waltheof was buried in the chapter House of **Crowland Abbey**. On a happier note, the couple had two daughters who went on to found three important noble families, including the family of King David of Scotland.

DANES

King Cnut (*c.* 996–1035; King of England 1016–35)

One of the giants of our story, Cnut was born the second son of Sweyn, King of Denmark and England, and his wife Gunhilda of Poland. But his strengths were more those of a ruthless gangster than a battlefield general. Cnut accompanied his father to England in 1013 during the latter's successful expedition to wrest the throne from Aethelred the Unready, but, on his father's sudden death in February 1014, Cnut surprisingly returned home to regroup and conveniently obtained the allegiance of Thorkell (the experienced Viking commander who had previously fought for Aethelred). He had the hands, ears and noses of Sandwich hostages cut off in 1014 as he returned to Denmark. Cnut returned in force to England in the autumn of 1015, now opposed by Aethelred's son Edmund Ironside, an altogether more formidable opponent on the battlefield. In a vigorous campaign covering much of southern and south-eastern England, Edmund got the better of Cnut and his Danes in six battles but never achieved an outright defeat. At the final Battle of **Ashingdon** in Essex in 1016 it was Cnut who pulled off the decisive victory, largely due to the battlefield defection of the notorious Eadric Streona.

Cnut's ruthless streak is also shown by the number of executions without trial he carried out in England in 1017–8 during his usurpation of the throne: Uhtred of Northumbria, the hapless Eadric Streona and probably Eadwig Aetheling, son of Aethelred. Later he arranged for the murder of his sister's husband Ulf, whom he had appointed as Regent of Denmark in 1023–4 but who had fought against him at the Holy River. In 1027 Cnut suffered this decisive naval defeat in Sweden at the hands of a coalition of the kings of Norway and Sweden. Nevertheless this did not prevent Cnut from returning to Scandinavia in 1028, where he added the throne of Norway to those of England and Denmark (Cnut's elder brother Harold had died in 1021) by overawing the incumbent (who probably fled) with naval force. Cnut was now at the height of his power, ruling a maritime empire of the north unparalleled before or since. He managed to keep it together until his early death in 1035, but the empire then disintegrated. Cnut ruled absolutely as a conqueror.

Cnut's interest in England appears to have been largely financial: he wanted the wealth of this relatively prosperous and sophisticated country as a war chest to shore up his regime in Denmark and to finance his imperial ambitions. In 1018 he imposed a massive Danegeld on England of £18,000. From so far back it is impossible to estimate an accurate present day equivalent of this but it has been claimed that this could represent the highest level of taxation England has ever been subjected to! Given this gangster style to government, there are two surprising twists to Cnut's life. In July 1017, less than a year after Ashington, Cnut married Emma, Aethelred's dowager queen and ten years his senior. This somewhat primeval move was probably designed to square off the Norman threat to his new kingdom – Emma was the daughter of Duke Richard I of Normandy.

Cnut's grandfather, Harold Bluetooth, is said to have brought Christianity to Denmark, but religion didn't seem to feature in the life of Sweyn, his father, to a great degree. Cnut, contrastingly, paid a lot of attention to religious matters even going on pilgrimage to Rome in 1027. In 1023 he transported the body of St Aelfheah, who had been murdered by Danes in **Greenwich** in 1012 and whose coinage bore Christian symbolism to Canterbury. By such acts he acquired a reputation for piety and munificence. It is quite possible that these actions were really the work of his bishops – they are certainly in sharp contrast to his political style, as touched on earlier. Emma, a great patron of the Church, would also have been a great help. The famous story of Cnut and the waves fits in with the religious approach. It was designed to show a humble monarch displaying to his flatterers his weakness compared with the power of God. Tradition suggests three locations on the south coast of England: Southampton Water, Dover or Bosham (Cnut had a royal palace here).

In one crucial sense Cnut did not pursue a Christian path: that of marriage. In 1015, soon after his return to England, Cnut married Aelfgifu of Northampton, daughter of a former Earl of Northumbria. This political connection proved important to Cnut's drive for the throne in 1015–6. Cnut and Aelfgifu had two sons, Sweyn (King of Norway, died 1036–7) and Harold. When Cnut married Emma in 1017 – despite all the Christian ceremony – Aelfgifu was not repudiated. Trouble was stored up for the moment of Cnut's death. There is even a tradition that the love of Cnut's life was actually Gytha, a Danish princess, whom Cnut gave in marriage to his right-hand man, Godwin (see Bosham).

I see Cnut as a highly intelligent and ruthless king, but like kings before and since he was not able to arrange his kingdom sufficiently well to guarantee the succession of his line. Danish rule in England collapsed with the sudden death of Harthacnut in 1042, only to be replaced by Edward the Confessor, son of Aethelred and Queen Emma. Cnut died after a short illness at Shaftesbury Abbey in 1035 and was buried in **Winchester Cathedral**. Chaos soon descended on the English polity.

King Harold I (Harefoot) (c. 1015–40, king 1035–40)

The most obscure king of the eleventh and twelfth centuries, Harold was the son of Cnut by his first wife (probably not consecrated by the church), Aelfgifu of Northampton. Cnut had married her as part of the Gainsborough Accord of 1013–4, put together as Cnut's father Sweyn seized power in England. This dynastic union gave Cnut a strong powerbase in the north of England; Aelfgifu was the only daughter of Aelfhelm, Earl of Northumbria.

On Cnut's early death in November 1035, Harthacnut, son of 'official' wife Emma of Normandy and most likely to have been Cnut's chosen heir in England, was detained in Denmark by the need to secure the throne against Magnus of Norway. Magnus had just evicted Sweyn, Cnut's eldest son, from that kingdom, as well as his mother, Aelfgifu. A conference was held at Oxford to determine the best way forward in England. Two opposing parties developed: Harold Harefoot strongly supported by Earl Leofric of Mercia, the Midland thegns and the shipmen on the one hand, and Dowager Queen Emma supported by Godwin, Earl of Wessex, on the other. Armed confrontation is thought to have developed, but eventually a compromise was agreed in which Emma was to act as regent for Harthacnut in Wessex, backed by Godwin and by Cnut's house earls, leaving Harold as full king north of the Thames, supported by Leofric. Within twelve months Harold had sent a force to Winchester to claim his father's treasure. Emma's supporters tried to spread doubt about Harold's parentage and, in further desperation, she attempted to arrange military backing from her two sons by Aelthered, who were refugees in Normandy, and Alfred. Neither of their separate invasions were successful – indeed, Alfred was murdered on the orders of Harold in early 1037 – so before the end of 1037 Queen Emma was driven out of England and into exile in Bruges, under the protection of Count Baldwin V. King Harold was left to rule the whole country but little is known of his reign as no charters survive. He died in March 1040, aged perhaps 24 years, possibly at Oxford, but no details are known. He was buried at Westminster; the first king of England to be buried there.

In the same year Harthacnut at last secured peace in Denmark with Magnus of Norway and, at the same time as Harold's death, just happened to be leading a fleet of sixty-two ships from Bruges (his mother's haven) to England. Down the ages many political figures, reputations have suffered at the hands of their immediate successors. Harold Harefoot received the ultimate desecration: his body was dug up on the new king's orders and flung into a ditch! He was eventually re-buried.

It is impossible to form a coherent view of his competence as a king but we should give him much credit for out-manoeuvring that wily old fox Dowager Queen Emma at the beginning of his reign. It is in fact possible that his mother Aelfgifu had returned from supporting her eldest son as King of Norway and was the real force behind Harold's coup – redoubtable lady indeed.

King Harald Sigurdsson/Hardrada the Ruthless (1016–66, King of Norway 1046–66)

Harold was one of the great European warriors of the eleventh century. He succeeded to the throne of Norway on the death of his nephew Magnus, also inheriting the latter's claim to the throne of England through a deal made in 1039 between Magnus and Harthacnut. Harald had fled Norway after being wounded during the Battle of Stiklestad in 1030. He became a soldier of fortune in Russia, Byzantium and other parts of the Middle East, acquiring much booty and a fearsome reputation over the years.

Harald was seduced by the silver-tongued Tostig Godwinson in early 1066 to pursue his claim to the English crown. Harald and Tostig's fleet penetrated up the river Ouse in September 1066. At the Battle of **Gate Fulford** on 20 September they defeated the forces of Earls Edwin and Morcar, but five days later were annihilated and killed at **Stamford Bridge** by Kind Harold II's army.

King Harthacnut (c. 1018–42, king 1040–2)

Harthacnut (meaning 'tough knot') was the son of Cnut and Queen Emma, and his full sister, Gunhild, was to become Empress of Germany. From 1029 Cnut appointed Harthacnut King of Denmark. As the only son of Cnut's 'legitimate' marriage it was expected that he would inherit the English throne as well on his father's death. However, by 1035, Magnus Olafson had taken the Norwegian throne from Cnut and was threatening Denmark. When Cnut died that same year Harthacnut did not therefore hasten to England to claim his second throne. This allowed his half-brother Harold Harefoot, son of Cnut and Aelfgifu, to usurp the English throne from 1037. In 1039 Harthacnut finally joined his exiled mother in Bruges, Flanders, with ten ships. After Harold's death in 1040 envoys were sent to Flanders from England inviting him to take the throne.

Given the short duration of his reign and the paucity of sources, it is difficult to form a coherent picture of his character and achievements. What we *do* know is not flattering. He seems to have behaved like an extreme example of his father, but because his reign was never established only the negative survives. He began by exhuming the body of his predecessor, Harold Harefoot, and throwing it into a ditch. The Danish community in London later retrieved the body and re-buried it. Like his father he imposed very high taxation, thus causing a revolt in Worcestershire during which two housecarls were killed. The revolt was put down with great severity – Worcester burned for five days.

Harthacnut had no wife or children. In 1041 Edward the Confessor, his half-brother, was surprisingly invited to return to England from exile in Normandy. He may even have been declared heir to Harthacnut (do we detect the hand of Emma here?). On 8 June 1042 Harthacnut dropped dead while enjoying a drink at the wedding feast of Gytha, daughter of Osgod Clapa, to Tovi the Proud in Lambeth. Was it poison? Possibly, though commentators have suggested Harthacnut may have actually suffered from frequent illness. So ended the Danish annexation of England as Edward took over the throne. Harthacnut was buried in **Winchester Cathedral**.

King Sweyn (Forkbeard) (d. 1014, King of Denmark, King of England 1013–4)

The son of King Harold Bluetooth of Denmark, Sweyn raided England between 994 and 1013 and may even have been present at the Battle of Maldon in 991. But in 1013, goaded by Thorkell's defection to the English, Sweyn decided upon conquest of all England. Landing at Gainsborough on the Trent in the autumn, he was soon acclaimed king by large numbers of thegns from northern England. Laying waste to the countryside as he went, Sweyn swept

through in an arc from Oxford to Winchester and on to London, which he finally took at the second attempt. Sweyn is credited with bringing a more organised, 'professional' approach to Viking raiding in the late tenth to early eleventh centuries when compared with the raiding and Viking colonisation of the late ninth century. Stenton sees him as the pre-eminent military commander: 'The rapidity and precision of his movements place him as a general above every other Viking leader of his time.' All seemed set for Sweyn to establish a powerful empire based around Denmark and England when he died apparently without warning in February 1014 at Gainsborough, leaving the task of establishing his empire to his son Cnut. There are not many towns outside London where kings have been both acclaimed and have died. Not surprisingly nothing survives of Sweyn in Gainsborough.

Thorkell Havi the Tall, Earl of East Anglia

Of Danish descent, Thorkell burst upon England in the summer of 1009 with a very large raiding fleet that landed in Kent. For three years Thorkell plundered the south and east of the country, including Canterbury where they seized Archbishop Aelfheah, until 1012, when Aethelred paid Danegeld of £48,000 to buy Thorkell off. By then, he had lost control of his men anyway – at Easter in 1012 they had murdered Aelfheah at **Greenwich**. So Thorkell stayed in England but allied himself to Aethelred with forty-five ships. He fought for Aethelred in 1013 against Sweyn Forkbeard, probably attempting to defend London, and helped Aethelred escape to Normandy when Sweyn was acclaimed king.

After Sweyn's death, Thorkell sailed back to Denmark but this time joined Cnut. He fought for Cnut with distinction at the Battle of Sherston in the summer of 1016, and again at the Battle of **Ashingdon** (where he killed the much-vaunted Ulfcytel Snilling who had killed his brother Heming). Thorkell is said to have married Ulfcytel's widow, Wulthild, a daughter of Aethelred. Between 1017 and 1021 Thorkell was the most powerful magnate in England, probably helping to arrange the marriage of Cnut to Emma, Aethelred's widow. He was regent in 1019–20 when Cnut returned to Denmark, then outlawed and exiled in 1021, before being reconciled to Cnut once more and made regent in Denmark by 1023. Thereafter he is lost to history.

NORMANS

Alan the Red (Rufus), Count of Brittany (d. 1093)

Alan Rufus was the second son of Count Eudo, who acted as Regent of Brittany from 1040–7 after the reign of his brother, Duke Alan III. Their mother, Hawise, was the great aunt of Duke William of Normandy. Because of this family involvement, Brittany joined the English invasion in 1066 and Alan and his brother, Brien, most probably led the Breton contingent on the left wing at Hastings. In return, Alan was granted the Honour of Richmond, which included vast lands throughout Yorkshire, Lincolnshire, Northamptonshire and London. Alan settled in England and was personally close and very loyal to King William. His principal residence was **Richmond Castle** in North Yorkshire, and he became one of the wealthiest men in England (in fact a recent comparative study using modern-day land values places him as the wealthiest man ever to have lived in Britain). Many of his tenants were Breton immigrants. Alan founded St Mary's Priory in York and was a benefactor of St Edmundsbury Abbey, where he was buried.

Count Eustace of Boulogne (d. 1087)

Eustace was a vassal of the Counts Baldwin of Flanders. In 1066 he dropped his recent opposition to Duke William and became a major player in the Conquest. In 1036 he had married Godifu (or Goda), daughter of Aethelred Unrede and Emma, and sister to Edward the Confessor. It was his visit to Edward in England with the murderous affray in Dover in 1051 which brought about the confrontation between Godwin and Edward. Godifu died in 1047 and Eustace was remarried two years later to Ida of Lorraine. His main claim to fame is that the Bayeux Tapestry depicts him at the early crisis in the Battle of Hastings, urging Duke William to take off his helmet to show the Norman troops that he is still alive at a time when the cry was up that he had been killed. The Tapestry shows him '*aux Gernons*', his trademark moustaches.

After the Conquest, Eustace was given lands worth £770 in Essex that were based around his caput at **Chipping Ongar**, which made him the wealthiest man in Essex. Despite this, in September 1067, Eustace answered the call of Kentish rebels who saw him as a more acceptable king of England than the Conqueror. He crossed the Channel with a substantial force of knights but failed to take the new castle of Dover where his force was cut to pieces by the defending force. He slunk away back home but retained his English lands.

King Henry I (1068–1135, king 1100–35)

Henry was born in England, allegedly at **Selby** in Yorkshire, and was the third surviving son of William the Conqueror, the only one to be born both after William had become King of England ('born in the purple'). Henry was more than fifteen years younger than his eldest brother, Duke Robert, and is the brother in whom we can most easily discern the full character of the Conqueror. Henry was highly intelligent, energetic, ordered, careful in his planning, but utterly ruthless in implementation (i.e. a classic Norman). He could also be brutal and had a ferocious temper: he personally pushed the rebel leader Conan off a tower of Rouen Castle to his death in 1090 and later, in 1124, insisted on carrying out the blinding of his grandchildren as a result of his illegitimate daughter's murder of a hostage. Poole's words seem very apt for Henry: 'The Norman rulers of England were disagreeable men, masterful, stern and cruel.'

Unlike his father or brothers Henry was not necessarily a natural warrior, but he did always 'step up to the plate' and lead his armies in the field. His victories at Tinchebrai over his brother Robert, and Bremule (1119) over the King of France demonstrated his skill as a general, but usually he preferred to avoid fighting. Henry's main achievement in England was one of consolidation of the Conquest. He secured the borders and achieved a lasting peace. A testament to this success is the fact that after his death the country was thrown into prolonged civil war (the Anarchy) and at no time did the resulting chaos lead to rebellion by the Anglo-Saxons – the Normans (or rather the French) were here to stay.

There was another side to Henry; perhaps a surprising one. He was something of an accountant-king in the mould of the later Henry VII. He was very interested in monetary matters and is accredited with the establishment of the very first 'exchequer' or accounting office for national government in Western Europe, along with the pipe rolls (records). Henry was also a great builder and is remembered at many sites in this book.

His main achievement was the re-uniting of Normandy and England. At William

the Conqueror's death his two elder sons shared the principalities, while Henry, aged 18 years, inherited no land but was given a large pile of silver. William knew his youngest son well. Henry used the money to buy territory in the Cotentin in Western Normandy from his impoverished brother, Duke Robert, in 1090, and steadily built up a following in the dukedom. Henry's triumph over Robert at the Battle of Tinchebrai in 1106 led to the latter's imprisonment and Henry's accession to the dukedom. Awesome is the word that comes readily to mind with Henry; very much a case of 'like father like, son'. Henry was present in the New Forest when his middle brother William Rufus was killed, and within four days had secured the throne of England. After Tinchebrai he imprisoned Robert in successive castles in England and Wales for twenty-eight years before the latter's death. No hint of an escape attempt was noted, so could Robert have been blinded? Henry certainly used this punishment with other nobles.

However there was a field in which Henry differed completely from his father: sex. William the Conqueror was almost unique in the early medieval period. His marriage to Matilda of Flanders seems to have been genuinely happy and at no time is there a hint of other women in his life. Henry, by contrast, although conventionally married to Edith/Matilda (Maud) of Scotland, fathered and recognised twenty-five royal bastards – a record for an English king. Henry obviously enjoyed the company of women and no doubt possessed a deal of charm himself, but like everything else in his life Henry had a purpose here. With one brother dead and one in prison, Henry's immediate family was small. He used the illegitimate sons as support (e.g. Robert, Earl of Gloucester) and the daughters for marriage alliances.

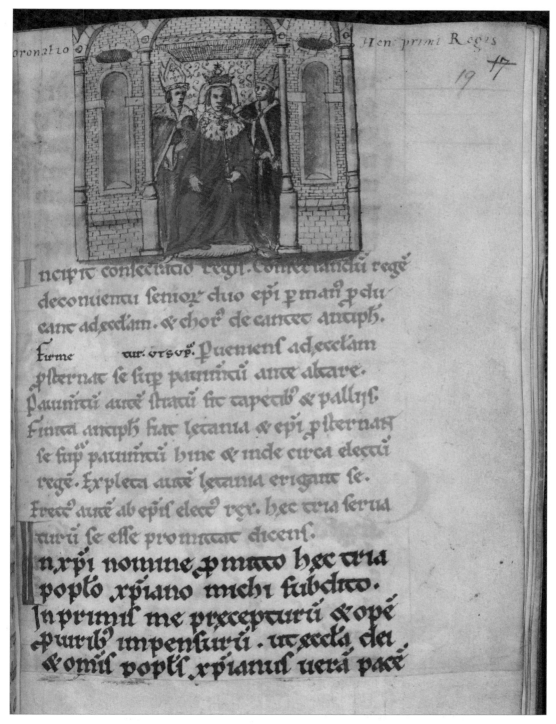

Coronation of King Henry I in 1100, just three days after the death of his brother.

While Henry's overall legacy was strong, it is in the area of succession where even he could not control matters to provide a secure future for his realm after his death. His wife, **Queen Edith or Matilda**, had the singular advantage of being of the Anglo-Saxon House of Cerdic. She and Henry had four children, with one daughter dying young. The eldest, **William**, was born in 1103 and styled 'Aetheling' in the English tradition. In 1120 he was made Duke of Normandy but then disaster struck in late 1120 when William was drowned off **Barfleur** in Normandy in the *White Ship* disaster. Henry I was travelling in a sister ship and had just turned down the opportunity to sail in the brand new *White Ship* himself. Henry was distraught (Edith had died in 1118) but managed to rally himself sufficiently to marriage within two months to Adeliza of Louvain. She was described as 'nubile', i.e. around 18 years. Henry was 52. Adeliza did not conceive with Henry although she managed seven children with her second husband, William d'Alibini.

Henry had no choice but to acknowledge his daughter Matilda as heir. Her first husband, Henry V, Emperor of Germany, died in 1125 so Matilda was then married to Geoffrey Plantagenet, Count of Anjou, in 1128. A somewhat tempestuous relationship produced three sons, including Henry, later to become Henry II, King of England. On Henry's death however, Stephen of Blois, Matilda's cousin and son of the Conqueror's sister, Adela, seized the throne of England, which led to civil war with Matilda. Stephen eventually triumphed, but a compromise saw his sons debarred from the succession and Henry Plantaganet took the throne after Stephen's death in 1154. England had not been ready for a queen regent, although Matilda had not helped her cause by being high-handed and arrogant.

Henry was buried in **Reading Abbey**, his own foundation made after the *White Ship* disaster.

Hugh d'Avranches, Earl of Chester (d. 1101)

Hugh d'Avranches was the son of Richard Goz, Viscomte d'Avranches, in the Cotentin. He came to England with the Conqueror in 1067–8 and was initially given command of Tutbury Castle in Staffordshire. In 1070 he was transferred to Chester and given a huge landed estate, the Honour of Chester and an earldom. His lands were mainly in the north but with elements scattered through the Midlands and south. Hugh was a larger-than-life character. To quote the *Dictionary of National Biography*: 'he indulged himself to excess; hunting, womanising and eating.' He became fat and fathered many bastards. But he also fought hard, attacking the Welsh and gaining the nickname Hugh Lupus ('the Wolf'). He partnered Robert of Rhuddlan in commencing the conquest of North Wales and attacked Anglesey and re-conquered North Wales in 1098 with Hugh de Montgomery. He founded St Werburgh's Abbey in Chester in 1092, where he was buried. At the Dissolution of the Monasteries Henry VIII gave this abbey cathedral status.

Odo Bishop of Bayeux and Earl of Kent (*c.* 1032–97)

William the Conqueror's elder half-brother, Odo, has a special place in our story as the sponsor of the magnificent Bayeux Tapestry. His life was as colourful as his tapestry. William the Conqueror's mother, Herleva, was married off to Herluin de Conteville (d*c.* 1066) and their union produced two sons, Odo and Robert of Motain. Odo was made up to bishop at the incredibly young age of 20. He was much involved in the planning for the invasion of England and

THE FAMILY OF WILLIAM THE CONQUEROR

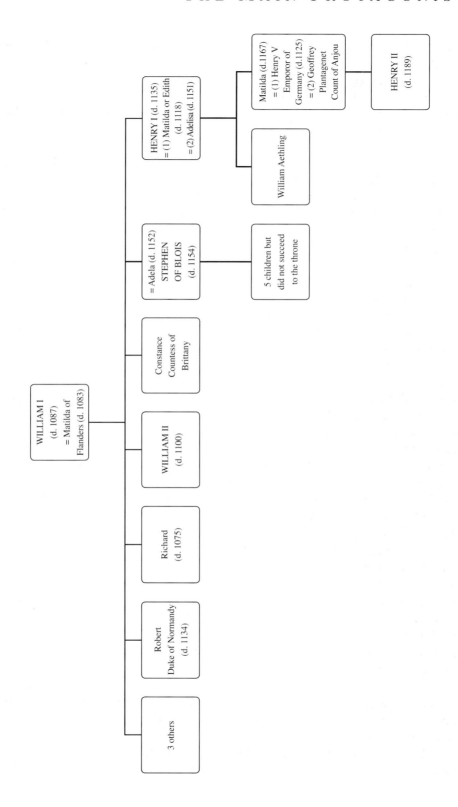

WILLIAM I
(d. 1087)
= Matilda of
Flanders (d. 1083)

3 others

Robert
Duke of Normandy
(d. 1134)

Richard
(d. 1075)

WILLIAM II
(d. 1100)

Constance
Countess of
Brittany

= Adela (d. 1152)
STEPHEN
OF BLOIS
(d. 1154)

5 children but
did not succeed
to the throne

HENRY I (d. 1135)
= (1) Matilda or Edith
(d. 1118)
= (2) Adelisa (d. 1151)

William Aethling

Matilda (d.1167)
= (1) Henry V
Emporor of
Germany (d.1125)
= (2) Geoffrey
Plantagenet
Count of Anjou

HENRY II
(d. 1189)

supplied 100 ships to the expedition. He is shown on the Tapestry as being involved in the battle planning for Hastings but it is unclear whether he actually fought. He may have used a mace, the traditional weapon for clergy because it supposedly did not draw blood.

When William the Conqueror returned to Normandy in the spring of 1067, Odo acted as his deputy in England along with William Fitz Osbern. There was much to do to consolidate the victory at Hastings and he continued to be active militarily – leading Norman armies into Northumbria and East Anglia to suppress revolts. Odo became the wealthiest landowner in England with vast lands in the south, Midlands and Norfolk, but became known for being rather grasping and tyrannical. He achieved almost the same status as William the Conqueror in England.

His apogee was perhaps the consecration of a new cathedral in **Bayeux** in 1077. Unfortunately this building was fired by the future Henry I in 1105 and only a small part of that structure remains. In 1082–3 Odo was imprisoned by William the Conqueror after trial, where he was discovered to be scheming to become the next pope. On William the Conqueror's death Odo was somewhat reluctantly released by William Rufus, who returned to England. In spring 1088 Odo led a rebellion against King Rufus in favour of Duke Robert of Normandy, Rufus' elder brother. This was decisively defeated by Rufus, and Odo exiled from England. He returned to Normandy and sided with Duke Robert, even imprisoning Henry, Robert's youngest brother, during the interminable in-fighting between the three brothers in Normandy in the 1090s. Odo joined Robert on the First Crusade but died and was buried in Palermo, Sicily, leaving one acknowledged son, John de Bayeux,

who became one of Henry I's chaplains. Clearly a forceful and colourful character, Odo was a 'prince-bishop on a grand scale'.

Ranulf Flambard (c. 1060–1128, Bishop of Durham 1099–1128)

Ranulf came from humble origins, the son of a parish priest in the diocese of Bayeux. He was sponsored first by Bishop Odo and then by Maurice, Bishop of London, and made his name as an administrator/justicular under William Rufus. He became chaplain and Rufus' right-hand man ('Mr First'), perpetrating much of Rufus' abuse of the church through the exploitations of vacant sees. In 1099 Ranulf was made Bishop of Durham.

Not surprisingly Henry I decided to make an example of Ranulf on his accession. Ranulf was imprisoned in the Tower in 1100 – the first prisoner ever to be sent there. With typical ingenuity and flair Ranulf escaped by the use of blankets, etc. and joined Robert Curthose in Normandy. Ranulf helped Robert to achieve a surprise landing at Southampton with a significant force, but the invasion soon lost momentum. By the Treaty of Alton Ranulf secured his pardon from Henry and was reinstated to Durham. Ranulf was a colourful rogue, having a mistress and several children. The former was conveniently married off when Ranulf was made up to bishop (although he still managed to visit her in her new home). As Bishop of Durham however, he does have a special place in this book. He was responsible for the majority of the building work at **Durham Cathedral**, which was completed in 1133, not long after his death. He also proved to be 'a bastion of Norman influence' in Durham and the border regions, holding Durham Castle and building the first castle at Norham on the Tweed border.

DUKES OF NORMANDY 995–1105

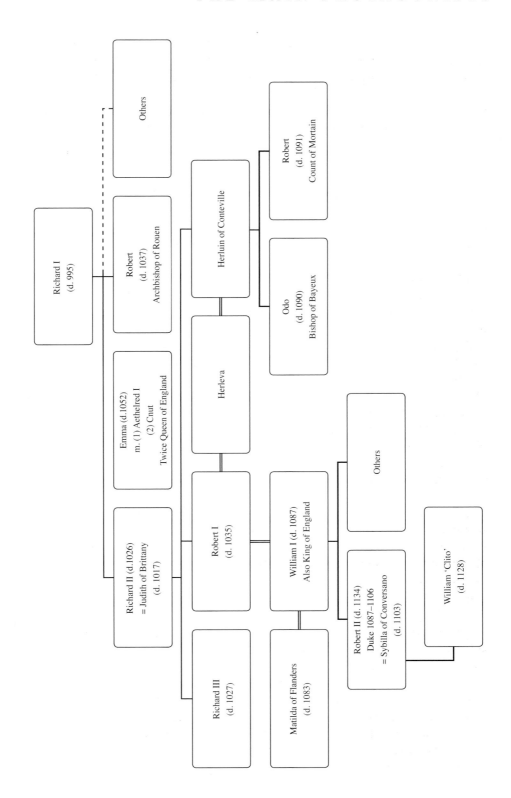

Richard Fitz Gilbert (1030–c. 89) and the House of Clare

Richard was one of the super-magnates, with vast lands in both England and Normandy. His major bases were **Tonbridge** and **Clare** (Suffolk) in England and Orbec in Normandy. He married Rohese Giffard and his successors took the name 'de Clare'. Richard was descended from illegitimate son Guy, of Duke Richard I of Normandy. His father, Gilbert of Brionne in Normandy, was tutor to the young Duke William for a few months in 1040, before being murdered during the turmoil which ensued during the first few years of his reign. Richard was present at Hastings and was quite naturally one of the Conqueror's inner circle, helping to suppress the rebellion of Roger Bigod et al. in East Anglia in 1085.

In 1088 Richard retired to a monastery and handed over his English lands to his son **Gilbert Fitz Richard** (d. 1117), with Roger the eldest son inheriting in Normandy. Gilbert of Tonbridge and Clare comes across as a more rumbustious and awkward character. He immediately joined Bishop Odo's revolt against William Rufus in the spring of 1088; he fortified **Tonbridge Castle** and was attacked by the king. But within two days the castle had surrendered and Gilbert had been wounded, though he was pardoned after the revolt faded out at Pevensey. He became embroiled in the unsuccessful plot against Rufus, which was, however, led by Robert of Mowbray in 1095. This time, along with another conspirator, Gilbert 'shopped' his fellow conspirators and probably saved his own life – but this didn't get him back into favour with Rufus. Gilbert's sister Adelaide was married to Walter Tyrel, castellan of the Pontoise in the French Vexin. Gilbert and Roger of the House of Clare were present at the New Forest hunting party when Rufus was killed by an arrow fired by Walter.

Early in Henry I's reign Gilbert attended court with large unruly followings that are said to have bullied Henry and his courtiers. Despite this behaviour Henry granted the whole of Ceredigion to Gilbert in 1110, who proceeded to invade and take over the area. Henry also made grants of land in England to Gilbert's younger sons. Belated recognition of Gilbert's acquiescence in 1100 or an astute move to head off trouble from an awkward and wealthy subject?

Gilbert married Alice of Clermont. Their eldest son, **Richard Fitz Gilbert** (d. 1136), inherited and continued the consolidation of the Welsh lands. Richard is most famous for the much-celebrated manner of his murder a few weeks later on 15 April 1136 (see Abergavenny).

Robert of Caen, Earl of Gloucester (c. 1095–1147)

Robert was the eldest of Henry's twenty-five acknowledged bastards and, from 1120 at least, certainly his favourite. After the death of Henry's legitimate son in the *White Ship* disaster, Robert was made up to earl and received many lands from Henry. He married the daughter of Robert Fitz Haimon, thus inheriting further lands around Gloucester and elsewhere. He became a member of Henry's inner circle and one of three super-magnates of the reign. He helped put down a rebellion in Normandy in 1123 and then received the marcher lordship of Glamorgan. A rivalry with Stephen, Count of Blois, the king's cousin and another of the English super-magnates, developed. Henry even considered making Robert his heir but dropped the idea because current ideals now demanded legitimacy.

Robert supported his legitimate half-sister Queen Matilda and spearheaded her cause during the Anarchy from 1139, following Stephen's usurpation of the throne after

Henry's death. It is said Robert was well educated and a patron of letters, supporting the historians William of Malmesbury and Geoffrey of Monmouth.

Robert, Count of Mortain (d. 1095)

Robert was half-brother to William the Conqueror, the second son of Herleva (previously concubine to Duke Robert of Normandy) and Herluin de Conteville (created Vicomte). His elder full-brother was Bishop Odo of Bayeux. He was brought up with the Conqueror and given lands close to the border of Normandy with Brittany and Maine and in the Cotentin. Before 1066 he married Matilda, daughter of Roger de Montgomery. Loyal to Duke William throughout the chaos in Normandy in the 1040s, he provided the largest contingent to the Conqueror's invasion fleet; 120 ships. He was given control of the Rape of Pevensey after the Conquest (a key part of William's strategy to secure movement between England and Normandy) and re-fortified the castle within the Roman fort at **Pevensey**.

In 1069 he beat the Danish forces threatening Lindsey. He was present at the Conqueror's deathbed in Rouen in 1087. Perhaps surprisingly, in 1088 he joined Odo in revolt against William Rufus and Pevensey was besieged and surrendered. Unlike Odo, Robert was pardoned by Rufus and fought for him against younger brother Henry in Brittany in 1091. Seen by chroniclers as a stupid and dull man, he had re-married in 1088 to Almodis, daughter of the Count of Toulouse. In England however he was second only in wealth to Roger de Montgomery, with lands in twenty shires – particularly in the West Country, which he administered from Montacute and Launceston. He was a generous patron of the church, founding an abbey at Grestain near Conteville where he was buried.

Robert Curthose, Duke of Normandy (c. 1051–1134)

The eldest son of William the Conqueror and his queen, Matilda, and said to be the latter's favourite, he was everything the Conqueror wasn't: talkative, clubbable and approachable but at the same time weak and indolent. His father nicknamed him 'short legs'. As early as 1063 he was recognised as heir in Normandy. In 1078, however, he revolted against his father at L'Aigle in eastern Normandy and at the subsequent siege of Gerberoi Castle personally unhorsed his father, probably wounding him.

His involvement in English politics was small. William judged correctly that he should not be made king here and on William's death the crown went to his younger brother, William Rufus. Curthose even failed to support a revolt in his own name in England by Bishop Odo in 1088. However he did lead a successful expedition against Malcolm Canmore, King of the Scots, in 1080 on behalf of Rufus, during which he stood godfather to Edith/Matilda, Malcolm's daughter who subsequently married youngest brother Henry. He also built a 'Newcastle' on the Tyne. In 1101 he invaded England via Portsmouth after Henry's usurpation of the English throne, but the brothers were reconciled at Alton through the treaty of that name.

Curthose was in fact a fine and brave soldier but less of a general, crucially lacking political judgement. In 1095 he joined the First Crusade (and was financed by brother William) and distinguished himself at the capture of Antioch, the Battle of Ascalon and the capture of Jerusalum. He returned to Europe something of a hero in September 1100, immediately after Rufus' death. Both of his younger brothers separately invaded Normandy during his dukedom. Robert struggled to prevent his polity from descending into chaos or financial insolvency – or both. Rufus came in 1091, forcing Robert to cede Aumale, Eu and Cherbourg. His struggle against Henry lasted until 1106 when Henry invaded Normandy and defeated Robert's forces at the Battle of Tinchebrai. Robert was captured and then incarcerated in various castles in England, including Devizes and Bristol, ending his days in the custody of Robert, Earl of Gloucester (Henry's eldest natural son), in **Cardiff**. He languished for an incredible twenty-eight years until his death, aged 80 years or more (you will not find a longer-lived person in this book). There was talk that Henry had Robert blinded and castrated, a traditional Norman punishment. Altogether a most unfortunate end for such a chivalric and likeable man in an age that hardly brimmed over with others of his ilk. However, in one of history's little ironies, it is Curthose, not his illustrious father or brothers, who is commemorated by the finest funeral monument. His colourful thirteenth-century effigy can be seen in **Gloucester Cathedral**.

On his way home from the Crusades Robert had married the beautiful Sybil, daughter of Count Geoffrey of Connersano in Italy. Their son William 'Clito' was to become a thorn in Henry's side until his death in 1128. Sybil died in 1103, possibly poisoned by a rival for Curthose's affections.

Robert Fitz Haimon (d. 1107)

Robert was the son of Haimo, steward to both William I and II and Sheriff of Kent, who had come over with the Conquest with Bishop Odo, the Conqueror's half-brother. Robert in his turn was a loyal supporter of both William Rufus and Henry I, who witnessed many charters and may possibly have been Rufus' lover. In 1088 Robert wisely sided with Rufus when his father's patron, Odo, rebelled. Robert held lands in Kent/Buckinghamshire and the south-west and landed a top-class marriage to Sybil, daughter of Roger de Montgomery, one of the most powerful Norman magnates. The couple had four daughters, the eldest of whom married Robert of Gloucester, Henry I's eldest bastard.

Robert led the conquest of Glamorgan in around 1093 and gave a considerable portion of the conquered lands to Gloucester and Tewkesbury abbeys. He was present at the hunting party in the New Forest on 2 August 1100 but not at the stand where Rufus was killed – he would have a very interesting tale to tell were he alive today. He immediately went over to Henry I and acted as intermediary at Alton, where Henry met the invading Robert Curthose in 1101.

In 1105, Fitz Haimon, fighting for Henry against Curthose, was surprised by the latter's forces at Falaise. He took refuge in the tower of the church at Secqueville-en-Bessin but was captured and imprisoned. Henry hotfooted to Bayeux, rescued Robert and torched the city. Later that year Robert was struck on the head with a lance at the siege of Falaise and lost his senses. He lived on for another two years 'almost in a state of idiocy' and died in 1107. He was founder of the new Norman abbey at **Tewkesbury** where he is commemorated by a magnificent thirteenth-century chantry chapel. His son-in-law, Robert of Gloucester, inherited his estates.

Roger de Montgomery and the House of Montgomery

This family was a member of the new aristocracy in eleventh-century Normandy, who had initially gained land in central Normandy at the expense of the monasteries but later became leading patrons of the Norman church. **Roger de Montgomery II, Earl of Shrewsbury** (d. 1094) was a close confidant of Duke William who, in 1066, remained behind in Normandy with Roger de Beaumont to assist Duchess Matilda in governing the Duchy while the Duke invaded England. Although not actually present at Hastings, Roger contributed sixty ships to the invasion force. He came over to England in December 1067 with the Conqueror and was granted substantial landholdings around Arundel and Chichester in West Sussex. In 1070–1 he received further lands in Shropshire, and in 1074 was made Earl of Shrewsbury.

In 1050 he had married a major heiress, **Mabel Talvas** of Belleme, a border region of southern Normandy. Mabel competes with Eadric Streona for the prize as the most unpleasant character in this guide – see **Mount Bures** for more detail. Perhaps as a distraction, Roger was a great builder; he founded **Shrewsbury** and Much Wenlock Abbeys together with **Hen Domen** Castle on the Welsh border. Montgomeryshire in Wales was named after him. Roger was a key element in the Norman incursions into Mid-Wales from 1074. Four days before his death he became a monk in Shrewsbury Abbey (this was a common practice at the time) and was buried there. His effigy survives.

After Roger II's death this hugely wealthy family did not prosper as it should have. His eldest son **Robert of Bellême** (d*c*. 1133) had inherited his mother's lands in Normandy after her murder in 1079–80. Unfortunately he seems to also have inherited her loathsome character; he was seen as arrogant and overbearing but was an expert in castle-building (see **Gisors**). He sided with Duke Robert of Normandy firstly against William Rufus and then Henry I. He fought for Duke Robert at the Battle of Tinchebrai, after which he was imprisoned by Henry until his death. Roger II's third son, **Hugh** (d. 1098), was much involved in the acquisition of

lands in Wales but was killed on Anglesey opposing Magnus Barelegs, King of Norway, in July 1098. He was buried with his father in Shrewsbury Abbey.

Roger of Salisbury (d. 1139, Bishop of Salisbury 1101–39)

Roger had humble origins in Normandy. In the 1090s he came to the attention of Henry, the youngest of the Conqueror's sons, allegedly because of the rapidity with which Roger delivered Mass in a church near Caen. Roger became Henry's chaplain, then steward. His administrative and financial skills clearly impressed Henry for, once the latter became king, Roger was appointed chancellor. His power and authority increased steadily and, in effect, he became Henry's chief minister, acting as regent during the king's absence in Normandy from 1123–6. After the Battle of Tinchebrai in 1106 Roger was given custody of Henry's captive brother, Robert Curthose, who was imprisoned in Roger's Castle in Devizes. He is credited with a number of important government innovations, including the Exchequer in the Treasury in Winchester and pipe rolls.

Roger was notoriously acquisitive and became very wealthy. He was a great builder, rebuilding the cathedral and castle at **Old Sarum** and building castles at **Sherborne**, Malmesbury and Devizes. He also kept a mistress, Matilda of Ramsbury, with whom he acknowledged a son, Roger, and energetically promoted the interests of his family (two nephews became bishops). Despite these weaknesses Roger was a conscientious and effective cleric. In 1126 however, the return of the Empress Matilda to England saw some diminution of his power – probably because he was unsure whether Matilda should succeed King Henry. Custody of Robert Curthose was transferred to Robert, Earl of Gloucester, Matilda's half-brother. On Stephen's accession in 1136 Roger rapidly switched allegiance, despite his previous oath to Matilda. However his allegiance was seen as suspect and, in 1139, Roger and his family were arrested by Stephen. Roger died before the end of the year and was buried in his cathedral at Old Sarum. In 1226 his remains were moved to the new cathedral in nearby **Salisbury**; his grave slab memorial survives.

King William I/William the Bastard/Conqueror (*c*. 1029–87, Duke of Normandy 1035–87; King of England 1066–87)

William was the illegitimate son of Robert the Magnificent, Duke of Normandy, and his concubine, Herleve of Falaise, daughter of a tanner or undertaker. Herleve was quickly married off to Herluin Conteville and produced two more sons, Odo and Robert. In 1034 Duke Robert announced that he was going on pilgrimage to Jerusalem. Robert had never married so before leaving he insisted his nobles swear allegiance to the young William and his heir.

William's accession as duke was disputed by the legitimate descendants of Duke Richard II, Robert's father. But thanks to the support of Duke Robert's core followers, most notably Archbishop Robert of Rouen, William's great uncle, William's initial position was secured. The archbishop died in 1037 and Normandy descended into a chaos of private wars. William's was the 'school of hard knocks' and his life was in serious danger on more than one occasion. In 1047 William, now 19 years old, had, in effect, to be rescued by King Henry of France when a revolt by Guy of Burgundy flared up. At the Battle of **Val-ès-Dunes** south of Caen, William and the king decisively defeated the rebels and William displayed

his own fighting prowess. Further feuding continued and in 1052 the King of France deserted William and sided with Geoffrey, Count of Anjou, with whom William had been disputing the border lands of Bellême. During this campaign William displayed his barbarity by cutting off the hands and feet of the townspeople of Alencon in retaliation for their mocking of his mother's origins. The King of France now supported Norman rebels against William and invaded the Duchy of Arques, Mortemer and Varaville between 1053 and 1057, establishing a first-rank military reputation for Duke William. His victory at Varaville illustrates his strength in careful strategic planning.

By 1060, however, both King Henry (who left a minor) and Count Geoffrey had died. Duke William had survived twenty-five years of almost continuous warfare, latterly against the French king himself. He was a battle-hardened military commander and had established an enviable reputation as a leader of men, as well as one for barbarity to his opponents. He was something of an expert in siege warfare and was then able to go on the offensive, invading Maine to the south and Brittany to the west. By 1065, therefore, William had established a position of pre-eminence in northern France. With his marriage in 1051–2 to Matilda of Flanders, William had the support of Matilda's father Count Baldwin V – who just happened to be guardian of the young French king.

It is William's strength in careful strategic planning that comes to the fore in the invasion of England. Examples include the construction of the alliance of northern France, the achievement of papal support, the provisioning of the invasion force through the summer of 1066 at Dives-sur-Mer, and the inclusion of pre-fabricated motte and bailey castles in the invasion fleet. To these we may add some kind of co-ordinated action with the exiled Tostig, King Harold's brother, who was married to the step-sister of Matilda, William's wife. William's approach comes across as well organised, methodical – almost 'modern' – in sharp contrast to the actions of King Harold, appearing to come from a heroic age.

After the Battle of Hastings William's military reputation 'went before him' as he swept through the south of the country. Canterbury and Winchester surrendered on demand and even in the north rebels were very often unwilling to confront the Norman army when he was in command. His military exploits in England during the 1067–70 conquest were of the highest rank, always conducted with speed and decision and, on occasion, in the depths of winter. But his harrying of the north in 1069–70 further increased his reputation for cruelty. Although he displayed battlefield prowess as a young knight, William's strength was not necessarily as a field commander. He was unhorsed and defeated by his eldest son, Robert, at Gerberoi, in 1079. After 1073 William was in fact relatively unsuccessful on the battlefield. Perhaps the death of his old friend William Fitz Osbern in 1071 may have removed a key cog in the wheel?

Fitz Osbern is a good example of another of William's strengths: his choice of subordinates. From the early days William had been supported by a tight-knit group of young men – Fitz Osbern, Roger of Montgomery, Walter Gifford, William de Warenne – all of whom were to play major parts in the conquest of England. His choice of Lanfranc as Archbishop of Canterbury was inspired; perhaps only in his faith in his half-brother Bishop Odo did he go wrong. His 'privatisation' of the conquest of Wales was an interesting experiment in delegation. It may well not have been any more successful if he had taken charge directly.

William made some very considerable achievements as King of England. He radically revised the system of land tenure, abolished outright slavery, reformed the church and relocated cathedrals – not forgetting the achievement of the Domesday Book. To begin with, William seemed determined to work with the Anglo-Saxons. He made an attempt to learn English and not all the members of the old elite were replaced by Normans. However, he appears to have taken against the country; perhaps after the continued rebellion from 1068–70 or perhaps because of the weather, or perhaps both. After 1072 the king spent 80 per cent of his time in Normandy, waging interminable wars including against his eldest son, Robert. At the end of the day William conquered England in order to harvest the huge wealth generated by the English agricultural economy and to use these funds to secure and expand his position at home in Normandy. In that sense he was not particularly successful given the resources at his disposal.

Nevertheless, the personality, strategic insight and drive of William the Bastard dominate this book. William's remains in his abbey in **Caen** indicate he was perhaps 5ft 9in (quite tall for the age), but well built and immensely strong. His voice was said to be harsh and rough – not a man to cross.

It is in the area of marriage that William's career is perhaps most puzzling. In 1049 the Pope forbade the proposed marriage between Duke William and **Matilda of Flanders,** daughter of Count Baldwin V. The exact reasons for this were never made public but speculation focused on consanguinity. Nevertheless the marriage went ahead in 1051–2 at Eu in eastern Normandy with Baldwin's support and involvement. Fairly soon afterwards Matilda was delivered of her first child, Robert. The Pope's blessing to the marriage was finally achieved in 1059, but only on the condition that William and Matilda founded separate abbeys in which they were to be separately buried. This is exactly what happened – the abbeys were built in **Caen** and form a monument unique in Europe.

William and Matilda, who was a lively 4ft 2in, were to have a total of nine children and seemed happy as a couple. Yet William had shown little interest in sexual activity as a young man and acknowledged no bastards. There were rumours of impotency. Matilda got herself into trouble with William by siding with their eldest son, Robert, in his disputes with his father. Later she acted as a mediator between the two, but after her death in 1083 Robert was again in revolt. William did not re-marry after her death.

He died in September 1087 at Rouen, of wounds received during the sack of Mantes in a campaign to regain full Norman control of the Vexin. The city had been torched and the tradition is that William's horse reared up in front of the flames, incapacitating him. On his death the Anglo-Norman kingdom was split between his three sons. Robert, the eldest, inherited the Duchy of Normandy, William Rufus the kingdom of England, while Henry, the youngest, inherited only silver – but plenty of it. The scene was set for nearly twenty years of family in-fighting.

King William II 'Rufus' (c. 1058–1100, king 1087–1100)

William was the second surviving son of William the Conqueror; on the death of his father, he inherited the throne of England. His elder brother Robert inherited only the dukedom of Normandy, where primogeniture was said to be more firmly established. Rufus (based on the colour of his hair) was short and thickset but brave and chivalrous. He was in essence a soldiers' king, with no graces or dignity. His primary strengths were energy and dynamism. He never suffered serious defeat on the battlefield and in so doing he restored peace in Normandy during Robert's absence on crusade, took Scotland under his lordship, and extended Norman territory in Wales and in Cumbria.

Rufus was probably homosexual and left no children, legitimate or illegitimate. He was generous to monasteries but did not get a good press from contemporary historians because of his prolonged dispute with Archbishop Anselm and his habit of keeping lucrative sees open and pocketing their income. He ensured the continuity of his father's rule in England and provided the same degree of ruthless direction. The rule of his elder brother was thus avoided here and the Norman Conquest and dynasty made safe. It is, however, the manner of his death in the New Forest (see **Cadnam**) for which history best remembers Rufus. He was buried in **Winchester Cathedral**.

William Fitz Osbern, Earl of Hereford (d. 1071)

William was roughly the same age as Duke William and had family connections to the ducal house. He was brought up with the duke and became his oldest and most loyal friend. William inherited vast estates around Ivry on the eastern borders of Normandy from his mother. He married Adelize de Tosny, who owned lands around Breteuil, where he built a castle in 1054. William is credited with persuading the smaller nobles to back Duke William's invasion of England. Fitz Osbern himself brought sixty ships and fought at Hastings. After the Conquest, William acted as steward to the new king for Wessex, based in Winchester with the rank of earl. When the Conqueror returned to Normandy in March 1067 he left Fitz Osbern and his own half-brother Bishop Odo as regents in England, which was no easy task so soon after Hastings.

Fitz Osbern became associated with the western border of Wessex, building one of the early castles at **Chepstow** as the Normans pushed into Gwent, and completing a chain of fortifications at Wigmore, Clifford, **Ewyas Harold** and Monmouth, along the South Wales border. William was prominent in the suppression of the northern rebels in 1068–9 and was given command of the second castle in **York** (**Bailles**). William was killed at the Battle of Cassel in Flanders in February 1071 during a succession crisis after the death of Count Baldwin VI, Duke William's brother-in-law. He was succeeded in Normandy by his son William de Breteuil, in England by his second son Roger, and was much mourned as a brave and strong character who gave sound advice. After his death it is noticeable that William the Conqueror's military success was limited.

William de Warenne, Earl of Surrey (d. 1088)

William was the younger son of a modest landowner named after the river Varenne near Rouen. He serves as a good example both of how William the Conqueror's invasion force contained a high proportion of recently promoted aristocracy and how loyalty to a successful duke or king could pay huge dividends. After the great revolt in Normandy against Duke William in 1052–4, Warenne was singled out for special reward with the grant of the castle of Mortemer and lands around Bellencombre, which became Warenne's caput in Normandy.

It was the invasion of England, however, that catapulted Warenne to the top echelon of aristocratic wealth. He fought at Hastings and gained lands in thirteen counties, including the Rape of Lewes in East Sussex, Conisborough in South Yorkshire, and Reigate. When the Conqueror created a fifth rape in Sussex based around Bramber Castle in 1073, Warenne was compensated for this loss with extensive estates in north-west Norfolk. In 1075 he was made Chief Justicar for the second time and fought for the Conqueror in Maine in 1083–5.

When the Conqueror's half-brothers, Bishop Odo and Robert Count of Mortain, rebelled against William Rufus in 1088 Warenne supported Rufus and was given the Earldom of Surrey at Easter. At the siege of **Pevensey Castle** in May he was mortally wounded and died in **Lewes**, where he was buried beside his first wife. He had married Gunrada, sister of Gerbod, Earl of Chester, and together they had founded the first Cluniac priory in England there in 1077. Gunrada died in 1085 during childbirth at **Castle Acre**, where William and his son William II founded a second Cluniac priory.

King William, famous for the manner of his death.

FOUR

THE GUIDE BY REGION

VISITING THE SITES

- It is better to go in summer as houses, castles and even churchs are often closed to the public in winter. Motte and bailey castles are the exception however; they are often tree-lined.
- Afternoons are best, until 4.30 p.m.
- Access to churches can be difficult, even in summer, because of problems of theft and vandalism. Parish churches in urban or semi-urban environments are often likely to be locked. churches in very isolated rural environments may also be locked. Cathedrals and large town churches are usually open with supervision. A phone call or letter before your visit is the best idea. Alternatively, a phone number is usually given on the board in the churchyard or in the church porch, or a key is sometimes available locally.
- Phoning clergy and parish offices in the morning is better.
- Most cathedrals ask for visitors' donations.
- All of the sites in this guide are open to the public.
- Directions are given to each site, and are designed for use with modern motoring atlases. Where there is more than one church in a town (tower) or (spire) is indicated.

RATING SYSTEM FOR SITES

*	Standard monument. Person involved in battle or a royal official.
**	More detail known of involvement or some architectural interest.
***	A significant participant in the period.
****	Outstanding historical interest.
*****	Truly national importance.

RATING SYSTEM FOR BATTLEFIELDS

+	Site known but little survives.
++	Site known and some interesting survivals.

+++   Plenty to see or key battle with some survivals.
++++   Key battle with much to see.
+++++   Decisive battles with plenty to see.

POUND SYMBOL

£   Entrance fee charged.
££   Higher entrance fee charged.

ABBREVIATIONS

NT   National Trust property.
EH   English Heritage property.
Cadw   Welsh Historic Monuments
KAL   Key to church available locally (check porch/board).
PO   Parish office phone number.

UNDERLINING

Underlining is used to highlight the person(s) involved in the period who is being celebrated at a particular site.

BOLD TYPE

Bold type is used in site descriptions in three ways:
1. To highlight locations in a building, e.g. **chancel**.
2. To indicate a secondary site, e.g. **Alnwick**.
3. To highlight a memorial at a site to a person who features in Chapter 3, 'Main Protagonists', where biographical information is given, e.g. **William Fitz Osbern**.

SITE CATEGORIES

Sites are split into primary sites (205) and secondary sites (6). Secondary sites are conveniently close to primary sites but do not necessarily warrant a long-distance visit on their own merit. They are 'while you are in the area do also visit' sites. Full directions are not necessarily given for secondary sites.

MOST REWARDING PLACES TO VISIT

Top-rated sites

*****	Bayeaux
	Caen
	Durham
	Hastings
	Pevensey
	The Tower of London
	Westminster Abbey
	Winchester
****	Abergavenny
	Cadnam
	Corfe Castle
	Deerhurst
	Fécamp
	Gloucester
	Reading
	Selby
	Shrewsbury
	Waltham Abbey

Top-rated battlefields

| +++++ | Hastings |
| +++ | Stamford Bridge |

LONDON AND THE SOUTH-EAST

BOSHAM ***

Church and quay form an attractive group at the heart of the old village. At high tide follow signs to car park and then walk west for ¼ mile to church. IF YOU PARK ON THE WATERFRONT AT LOW TIDE TAKE CARE TO CHECK WHEN THE TIDE WILL RETURN. Even Cnut couldn't control it!

Bosham is immortalised for the historian through its inclusion in the Bayeux Tapestry. The manor house, the church and the port all feature because it was from here that Harold Godwinson set sail in 1064 for his fateful encounter with Duke William in Normandy. The Godwin family held the manor (probably as their chief seat) and may have originated here. They had made Bosham their main

seaport. The delight of Bosham is that the quay still feels very much like a medieval port, the church retains much of its Anglo-Saxon architecture and the surroundings are beautiful. In many ways it is better to visit in winter unless you adore modern yachts and dinghies.

Holy Trinity Church

The tower (built 980–1000) and chancel arch are Saxon, along with parts of the chancel walls (1040–50). **Godwin, Earl of Wessex** may have sponsored the building of the latter. To the right of the chancel arch is a modern gravestone to Emma, alleged daughter of King Cnut, who died in 1035 aged 8 years. By local tradition she drowned in the nearby millstream. Her coffin was unearthed in 1865 following excavations conducted in response to another tradition, which long

THE·REGIONS·OF·
ENGLAND·&·WALES·

THE NORTH
Northumberland
Durham
Lancashire
Cheshire
Cumbria

YORKSHIRE

EAST MIDLANDS
Derbyshire
Nottinghamshire
Lincolnshire
Leicestershire
Northampton-
shire

WEST
MIDLANDS
Shropshire
Staffordshire
Warwickshire
Worcestershire
Herefordshire

EAST OF
ENGLAND
Norfolk
Suffolk
Essex
Cambridgeshire
Bedfordshire
Hertfordshire

WALES

THE
SOUTH
Oxfordshire
Buckingham-
shire
Berkshire
Hampshire

THE WEST COUNTRY
Gloucestershire, Wiltshire
Dorset, Devon, Cornwall,
Somerset

THE SOUTH-EAST
London, Surrey
Sussex, Kent

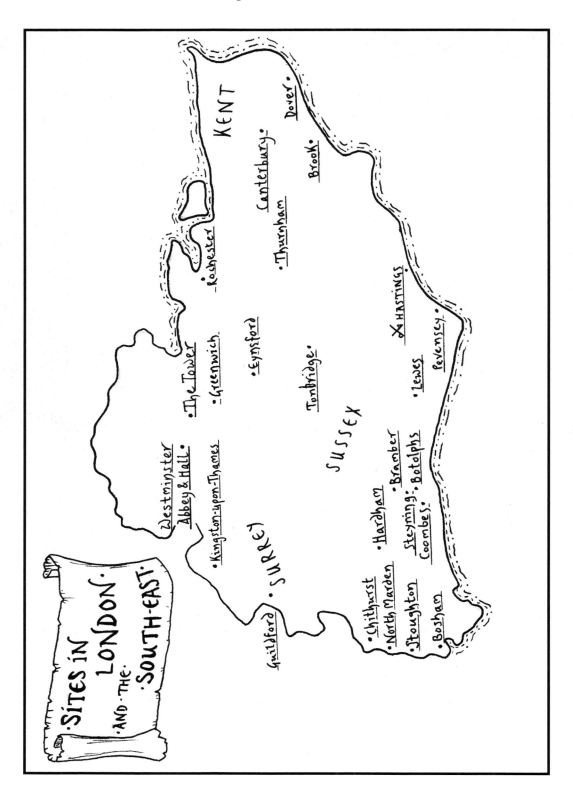

Sites in London and the South-East

KENT

Dover

Canterbury

Brook

Thurnham

Rochester

Eynsford

Greenwich

The Tower

HASTINGS

Tonbridge

Pevensey

Lewes

SUSSEX

Westminster Abbey & Hall

Kingston-upon-Thames

Bramber

Hardham

Botolphs

Steyning

Coombes

Guilford

SURREY

Chithurst

North Marden

Stoughton

Bosham

The church at Bosham, the main residence of the mighty Godwins, as depicted on the Bayeux Tapestry.

held that a daughter of Cnut was buried in Bosham. We assume, given the date and her name, that her mother was Queen Emma.

There was said to be a royal palace in Bosham at this time, just north of the church. There were rumours that Gytha, Godwin's wife, was the love of Cnut's life. The first three of Godwin and Gytha's children all had Danish names and Sweyn, the eldest, did boast that Cnut was his father – but Sweyn was a bit of a wild man (see Leominster). So was Bosham Cnut's secret love nest? Indeed it would be surprising if he did not have mistresses.

It has been claimed that the remains of a headless body found in the chancel in the 1950s are those of King Harold, but a firm identification has not been possible (see Waltham Abbey and Hastings). The **church tower** may have been used as a watchtower because the entrance to Chichester Harbour, 3½ miles away, is just about visible from it.

Other Political Events and Legends
Because of the presence of the Godwins and the royal palace, Bosham is steeped in eleventh-century political activity and legend:

• It is one of the candidates for being the location of Cnut's famous attempt to either hold back the waves or tide or to ridicule his flattering advisors, depending on your viewpoint (Southampton and Dover are other candidates).

- Godwin is said to have acquired Bosham Manor from the Archbishop of Canterbury by a trick. One day, on meeting the archbishop, Godwin apparently requested to have the kiss of peace from him in Latin, '*Da mihi basium*'. The archbishop complied but then Godwin deceitfully insisted that the archbishop had actually said '*Da mihi Boseam*' ('give me Bosham') and called his followers to witness the gift. Was Godwin a gifted Latin scholar?

- It is known however, that in 1049 Sweyn tricked his cousin Beorn, bundled him onto a ship at Bosham and headed west down the Channel. Beorn was later murdered on board off Dartmouth, probably in revenge for failing to support Sweyn in his struggle against Edward the Confessor.

- In October 1051 Godwin and a large part of his family (his wife Gytha, Sweyn, Tostig, a younger son and his wife Judith) set sail from Bosham into exile in Flanders with Count Baldwin, after having been faced down by King Edward. Sweyn was never to return but the others went home in 1052.

- After the Conquest Bosham was held by Osbern, brother of William Fitz Osbern, Earl of Hereford. Osbern had served in the household of King Edward and was related to him. In 1071 the Conqueror made him Bishop of Exeter. Osbern may have constructed the lovely chancel arch.

BOTOLPHS Church *

1 mile south of Bramber Castle on minor road to Lancing on west bank of river Adur. From roundabout at south end of Steyning bypass take Maudlin Lane exit. Go left at T-junction through Annington. Church on left.

A tiny hamlet close to the Adur with a great view of a cement works! Look the other way though and all is rural splendour. It owes its existence to the nearby footbridge across the river that, in Roman times, carried the tin road from Cornwall to Pevensey, the port used by the Romans to transport materials to France. The church was originally known as 'St Peter de Vetere Ponte', but in the thirteenth century was re-dedicated to the holy Saxon abbot, Botolph. The nave (south wall) and chancel arch are described by Pevsner as 'Late Saxon'. Close to Coombes and Bamber Castle.

BRAMBER Castle and St Nicholas Church **

At southern end of Steyning bypass (A283 Pulborough–Shoreham road). Exit directly to castle off roundabout.

William de Broase took command of this site immediately after the Conquest and was able to create a **motte** and **bailey** castle based on an existing pre-Conquest motte, which in turn sits on a natural and much larger mound. In 1073 the Conqueror created a fifth rape in Sussex, based on Bramber, which was carved out of the Lewes Rape commanded by William de Warenne (who was compensated by lands in Norfolk). The new rape was given to de Broase, who perhaps at this time constructed the magnificent **tower keep** (said to be eleventh century), part of which survives. De Broase developed Bramber as a port on the river Adur as a rival to nearby Steyning, but on the opposite bank because of a dispute with the monks of Fécamp who owned Steyning church.

St Nicholas church was constructed as a chapel for the castle in 1073 and given to the Abbey of St Florent at Saumur in 1075. The chapel suffered badly in the English Civil War (it was used as a gun emplacement during a siege of the castle) and the chancel and transepts have gone. The tower crossing now serves as the chancel. In 1080 the monks moved to Sele Priory across the river in Upper Beeding. Very close to Botolophs.

BROOK, St Mary's Church *

4 miles north-east of Ashford, 3 miles from J10 of M20 on minor road north-east through Hinxhill.

A complete early Norman church with a splendidly large west **tower**. The tower is in fact a 'westwerk', continental in style with a priest's room in the middle of the three storeys. The church has a fine Norman **chancel arch** and thirteenth-century wall paintings. Post-Conquest the parish living was owned by Christchurch Monastery in Canterbury.

CANTERBURY **

St Augustine's Abbey £

½ mile east of city centre – signposted outside city walls.

The other major religious site in Canterbury was established outside the walls in 613 to house the body of St Augustine. In typical fashion the first Norman abbot, called <u>Scotland</u>, demolished the existing Saxon churches and commenced building a massive new church, the remains of which are still visible. Its nave had eleven bays. The structure was finished in around 1120 and the clearly Romanesque original **west end** and **crypt** can still be seen today. Also visible is the base of the crypt of <u>Abbot Wulfric</u>'s **rotunda**, consisting of eight huge piers. Wulfric was abbot from 1047–59. Built around 1050, this was one of the buildings destroyed by the Normans. Note also at the south-east corner of the site the seventh-century remains of the church of St Pancras.

Castle

South-west corner of the city wall and ring road by exit for A28 Ashford.

The massive Norman tower of Brook church.

After the Battle of Hastings, the Conqueror headed to Dover rather than risk a direct march to London through the Weald. Having secured this burgh without a fight the Normans made for Canterbury. Their stay there was to be unexpectedly long because William was laid low for a month with dysentery. His time recuperating was spent near the city at a place called 'broken tower'. Canterbury had also surrendered without a fight. It is thought that the Normans constructed one of their wooden motte and bailey castles on 'Dane John' almost immediately – an ancient **mound** which can still be seen today, just inside the city walls, 400yds east of the castle. In the eighteenth century the area was remodelled as a pleasure garden.

In the reign of William Rufus this first castle was moved ¼ mile further west. The remains of its **stone keep** can be visited. It was probably completed in around 1120 during the reign of Henry I.

CHITHURST, St Mary's Church **

Turn off A272W Midhurst–Petersfield road ¼ mile before Trotton Bridge down Chithurst Lane. Church lies ¾ mile on left-hand side of narrow lane just after river bridge.

You will not find another entry in this guide closer in atmosphere and spirit to the mid-eleventh century than this one. Go in summer; the location oozes rural tranquillity and the surrounding country and buildings feel ancient. The church is mentioned in Domesday Book as an ecclesiola and is early Norman in style. In Domesday Book it was held by Morin from Roger de Montgomery, Earl of Arundel, and is believed to have been built on a pagan burial mound. Only the windows have subsequently been altered and enlarged (c. 1300). Otherwise this is a complete Norman period piece.

Enjoy a 2-mile round walk along the banks of the river Rother eastwards to Iping in beautiful rural surroundings, but watch out – as recently as 1757 the Reverend John Denham, priest-in-charge at Chithurst, was murdered in these fields as he returned home from Iping. Truly Norman country still.

COOMBES Church *

2 miles south of Bramber Castle on west side of river Adur on minor road. By farm in middle of hamlet. Access from Steyning bypass roundabout next to Bramber Castle.

Fortunately you approach this delightfully situated spot with your back to the cement works which dominates the lower Adur Valley. Early Norman nave and chancel arch plus wonderful **wall paintings** dated no later than 1100. Paintings of this date are rare in England (see Copford). Very close to Botolphs.

DOVER CASTLE, Church of St Mary-in-Castro ** £

High above east side of town within the castle grounds. Signposted to castle. (EH)

It is believed that pre-Conquest Dover town was situated inside the hilltop fortifications of what is now the castle, as a burgh (even though it is not included in the Burghal Hideage). It was on this hilltop, therefore, that Count Eustace of Boulogne's forces famously clashed with the townsfolk in 1051 in the leadup to the banishment of the Godwins by Edward the Confessor. Sometime in the twelfth century the townspeople were 'persuaded' to abandon their hilltop site and move down to the harbour – thus enabling Henry II to build his magnificent castle after 1168. The Saxon **Church of St Mary-in-Castro** is the only surviving structure from the earlier era. Built around 1000, it is an outstanding late-Saxon example despite heavy nineteenth-century restoration by Gilbert Scott.

After the Battle of Hastings the Conqueror made a beeline for Dover, taking a revengeful side-swipe at Romney on the way as revenge for having murdered some members of William's invasion force who had lost their way across the Channel. This act of terror no doubt helped to achieve the peaceful surrenders of Dover and Canterbury. Possession of Dover Castle had in fact been part of the Bonneville Accord of 1065 between William and Harold Godwinson. William's invasion army spent eight days in Dover and may have received reinforcements there. It is almost certain that he ordered the immediate construction of a wooden motte and bailey castle on this site but nothing survives today. It was this castle that Eustace of Boulogne failed to take during his short-lived and ill-fated attempt on the throne of England in 1087 after the death of William the Conqueror. William Rufus, showing his father's dynamism, counter-attacked the besiegers and cut them to pieces.

EYNSFORD, Castle *
Just north of village centre and church. Across river Darent from A225 Dartford–Sevenoaks road.

A very early and interesting example of a Norman stone keep, erected before 1100 by William de Eynsford, a tenant of the Archbishop of Canterbury. It sits on a low, oblong motte. The castle guards the crossing of the river Darent by the North Downs.

GUILDFORD ***

Castle
Town centre, ¼ mile south of High Street, above the river.

Before the Conquest, Guildford was a Saxon burgh guarding the Wey Gap in the North Downs. Such a strategic position on the main London–Winchester road demanded the early construction of a motte and bailey royal castle by the Conqueror. The original and impressive 63ft-high motte remains but was later overlaid by a splendid **tower keep**. The first documentary evidence for this keep dates from 1173 but recent thinking suggests it was actually constructed by **King Henry I** in the 1120s or '30s.

Site of 1036 Guildown Massacre
From the town clock in the High Street proceed west down the hill. Cross A286 Horsham road and river Wey. In front of you looms the Mount. Ascend this steep climb for ¾ mile beyond row of houses on right and onto the North Downs. In the eleventh century this road was part of the M3 from London to Winchester. 150yds beyond the last house brings you to the location of one of the most notorious events in English history. Note that you can drive and park fairly close to this spot but it is much more evocative to climb as the victims had to do.

There is no memorial to grab your attention but it doesn't really matter because the story associated with this site is so vivid. In 1929 in the back garden of the house over the left-hand fence, the remains of an Anglo-Saxon cemetery were discovered. Archaeological digs revealed two distinct cemeteries. In the first were thirty-six skeletons buried at a normal depth with proper spacing and alignment and thought to be sixth-century pagan, but in the second were 222 skeletons often buried less than 18in below the surface and thrown haphazardly into the grave in multiple burials. Many of these skeletons showed signs of brutal murder by beheading, scalping or spearing while fettered. These burials are seen as late Saxon and are accepted as evidence of the massacre of the forces of **Alfred Aetheling** (Edward the Confessor's younger brother) in 1036, well known from Anglo-Saxon sources. Since this appalling event became something of a cause célèbre between Godwin, Earl of Wessex, and both Harthacnut and Edward the Confessor in the 1040s and '50s it is worth exploring the background in a bit more detail.

Political Background
Cnut died in 1035 at Shaftesbury, probably without too much warning. The political situation thus became complex and fraught. It is likely that his 18-year-old son Harthacnut by Queen Emma, his 'official' wife, had

been designated heir – he had already been king in Denmark since 1025. Harthacnut however was unable to sail immediately for England because he had to deal with an invasion by Magnus, now King of Norway. This left an opening in England for Harold Harefoot, Cnut's second son by his first marriage to Aelfgifu of Northampton, who was backed by Earl Leofric of Mercia.

A meeting of the royal council was held soon after Cnut's death at Oxford. It resulted in a confrontation between Leofric and Godwin, backed by Dowager Queen Emma to represent Harthacnut's interests. A compromise was again reached in which Emma, assisted by Godwin, was to act as regent for Harthacnut in Wessex, while Harold was recognised as full king north of the Thames, i.e. joint kingship. Emma held Winchester where both the treasury and Cnut's housecarls lay. Yet within the year King Harold had sent a force down to Winchester to claim his share of Cnut's treasure.

During 1036 Emma appears to have despaired of Harthacnut's return and developed a plan to bring over to England one or both of her sons by her first husband, Aethelred Unrede. Aethelings Edward and Alfred had both been in exile in Normandy since 1016. She may have wished for one to be crowned king in Wessex to counterbalance Harold Harefoot in Mercia. Letters have survived inviting the two sons to come to England, which Emma later claimed were forged by Harefoot. Edward, by now aged around 30, is said to have sailed with a fleet to Southampton, taken one look at the situation there and sailed home again. Alfred, aged 23, chose a different route via Boulogne to Sandwich and then via the North Downs towards Winchester; one story is that Alfred was on his way to King Harold in London.

The Guildown Massacre

At some point Earl Godwin and retainers joined Alfred on the march and escorted the aetheling's Norman force along the way. They halted overnight in Guildford where the combined force feasted together before being billeted in the town. During the night, however, Alfred's men were attacked, overpowered and, in some cases, murdered. At dawn the remainder of the force, perhaps as many as 600, were butchered. Alfred himself was captured and sent to Harold. Subsequently Alfred was sent to Ely where he was blinded in the Norman tradition. However the deed was carried out, in so ferocious or inexpert a fashion, Alfred probably died in early February 1037 in the care of the monks of Ely.

This dreadful event broke all the rules of hospitality even at the time. It is not clear whether the victims were murdered in the town or along the grave site; probably a bit of both. This is why it is better to walk to this site up the Mount. You can follow in the footsteps of some of these poor souls who would likely have suspected they were climbing to their deaths.

Aftermath

Following this disaster Emma was driven out of Wessex and into exile in 1037. Harold became King of all England. But by 1040 he was dead and Harthacnut was finally able to claim his inheritance. The political importance of the Guildown Massacre really lies in the role of Godwin, Earl of Wessex. Why had he suddenly changed sides from Queen Emma to Harold Harefoot? Perhaps Emma had not consulted him before inviting her sons to come to England. After all, Godwin was no lover of Aethelred the Unready, who had exiled his father Wulfnoth in 1009.

The massacre at Guildford in 1036 occurred here on the North Downs.

Godwin later claimed that he was simply acting on the orders of King Harold. Harold may in fact have had his own troops hidden in Guildford who carried out the massacre. The accession of King Harthacnut in 1040 turned the whole incident into a cause célèbre. As half-brother to Alfred, Harthacnut was bound by family duty to extract revenge. Godwin was forced to make a gift in atonement to the king of a warship with a crew of eighty. After the accession of Edward the Confessor in 1042 this position only hardened with Edward being Alfred's full-brother. In 1051 Edward threw down Alfred's gauntlet and Godwin was forced into exile rather than stand trial for Alfred's murder. Although Godwin soon recovered power in 1052, the whole issue was a useful way for Edward to curb the power

and influence of England's most powerful subject. It is quite likely King Edward had the final word. Godwin dropped dead while dining with the king in 1053 (poisoned?).

HARDHAM, St Botolph's Church **
Hamlet centre 1½ miles south-west of Pulborough, just south of and bypassed by A29 to Bognor Regis.

A virtually complete and unaltered mid-eleventh-century, pre-Conquest church, which is unusual in that only a limited number of small windows have been opened up in the nave and chancel. This period feel is enhanced by the real delight of this church: the early twelfth-century **wall paintings**. These were produced by the so-called 'Lewes Group' of travelling artists belonging to the Anglo-Norman style represented in churches on both sides of the Channel (see also Coombes).

Hardham's special importance is that so much of the painting survives one can begin to visualise what a twelfth-century church interior really looked like – if much darker. The remains of the thirteenth-century priory can be visited ½ mile south-west.

HASTINGS, Castle ** £

High up above the town on a cliff top. Access via Old Town or A210 Hastings to Silverhill loop. Keep climbing!

After making landfall at Pevensey, Duke William quickly moved his invasion force to Hastings, which in 1066 still had a decent harbour (it was destroyed in a storm in the thirteenth century). On this promontory he erected one of the pre-fabricated wooden forts he had brought with him across the Channel. The **motte** for this fort still survives at the present entrance to the stone castle. It represents the very first motte and bailey castle in England built by Duke William (Pevensey didn't need a motte), which as a group played such a vital part in William's conquest of the country. This formed William's base as he waited the two weeks for King Harold to arrive.

The other side of the motte is visible within the stone castle, together with the ruins of the collegiate **church** of St Mary, built in 1070 on the site of a pre-Conquest church. The castle was rebuilt in stone very soon after the Conquest by Robert, Count of Eu, who had been granted the Rape of Hastings by William. Later it was much modified and extended by Henry II. Robert had been present at the battle.

BATTLE OF HASTINGS (14 October 1066) +++++

Strategic Background

With the death of Edward the Confessor in early January 1066, Duke William of Normandy initiated the process of pressing his claim to the throne of England. This included cementing his alliances with neighbours in northern France either to secure peace at home in Normandy (e.g. Flanders) or more directly to enlist support for his invasion force (e.g. Brittany), achieving papal support for the project and building an invasion fleet at Dives-sur-Mer near Caen. William held meetings with his magnates at Lillebonne, Bonneville-sur-Toques and Caen during the summer of 1066, involving them in his planning for the invasion.

By early August the transport and warships were ready. It is estimated that around 700 ships were involved in a venture that required the shipment of large numbers of Norman war horses, and even three or four fabricated wooden castles. Tradition has it that William suffered adverse northerly winds throughout August, which prevented the fleet from putting to sea – more likely he was waiting for the right moment (but the former is still entirely possible given the English climate).

The Ship List

Number of ships with soldiers offered by Duke William's magnates for the invasion of England (n.b. the size of the ships was not constant).

Robert of Mortain (half-brother)	120
Bishop Odo of Bayeux (half-brother)	100
Bishop William of Evreux	80
William Fitz Osbern	60

Roger de Montgomery	60
Roger de Beaumont	60
Hugh d'Avranches	60
Hugh de Montfort	50
Fulk the Lame	40
Gerald the Seneschal	40
Walter Giffard	30
Bishop Vougrin of Le Mans	30
Abbot Nicholas of St Ovens'Rouen (kinsman)	20

On 8 September King Harold is said to have stood down the militia (fyrd) which had been brought out of the raiding of the exiled Tostig (Harold's brother) and his small Flemish force from May onwards. Harold may have run out of provisions for the militia as he also moved the Isle of Wight-based fleet to London at the same time. The coast of southern England was now completely open to invasion, although the king and his housecarls were only one day's ride/two day's march away. Presumably learning of this from his spies in England, on 12 September Duke William moved the invasion fleet along the coast of Normandy to Valery-sur-Somme over the border in Ponthieu, which was tied into William's alliance.

Despite this move, on 21 September at the latest, King Harold left London with his housecarls and rode north to Yorkshire – a moment of true decision in English history. Harold turned his strategic direction on its head, having learnt of the arrival of Harald Hardrada, King of Norway, at Tynemouth in Northumbria, on around 19 September. Hardrada, a much-feared warrior, had been joined by Tostig, but while Hardrada *was* a threat to Harold, he was still a long way from London. Duke William, on the other hand, was renowned throughout northern Europe and Harold had spent time personally with him. The Norman invasion force was in being and likely to land much closer to London. Yet in the sources there are hints of something else. On 12 September it is known that part of William's fleet suffered storm damage in transit from Dives to Valery. Casualties were suffered, which not surprisingly William had to cover up to maintain morale. At the same time the English fleet moving from the Isle of Wight to London was also hit by 'storms'. We cannot be certain, but either a naval engagement ensued in the Channel or both fleets were hit by the same storm on 11–12 September – or a bit of both.

In London, did Harold overestimate the extent of the damage to the Norman fleet or had there been some deception employed? Whatever the reason this would credibly explain why Harold changed his plan. With the benefit of hindsight we can say that the decision to go north removed the only realistic chance Harold had of defeating Duke William, i.e. by catching him within a day or two of his landing on the south coast, before the Norman army could be fully offloaded from the invasion fleet and readied for battle.

On 25 September King Harold crushed Hardrada's Norwegian invasion at the Battle of Stamford Bridge. However, on the evening of 27 September, Duke William's fleet left Valery-sur-Somme (blessed at last with a fair southerly breeze) for an overnight Channel crossing and arrived at Pevensey at noon the next day completely unopposed: in 1066 this was located on a large inlet of the sea (now called Pevensey Levels and probably somewhat similar to present-day Chichester Harbour). The Norman force immediately began fortifying the old Roman fort here and moved their men by land and sea to the bigger port of Hastings on the 29th. One of the prefabricated wooden castles was assembled there on the cliff top.

Meanwhile it is probable that Harold heard of this calamity in York around 2 October, while still recovering from the exertions of Stamford Bridge. The very next day he rode out of York with his remaining housecarls and other mounted troops, and headed back to London to confront the Norman threat. Speed was now of the essence. Another army had to be assembled and moved down to East Sussex before the Normans ran riot through southern England. Harold stayed in London for only five days and left again on 11 October, arriving in the vicinity of where the battle would take place in the evening of 13 October – this after a two-day march of 58 miles through the Weald, having employed his favourite tactic of marching at maximum speed to catch his opponent unprepared.

Interestingly, despite their strength in mounted troops, the Normans had not ventured far from their base in Hastings in their two weeks on shore. They had harried and burnt some of the surrounding villages, all of course part of Harold's earldom of Wessex, but had not attempted to break out of their Sussex bridgehead. Duke William preferred to remain close to his marine supply lines from Normandy and must have liked what he saw of potential battle sites north of Hastings. Then, when the Anglo-Saxon forces arrived hotfoot from London during the evening of 13 October, the Normans were far from unprepared, being well dug-in in Hastings and ready for the inevitable confrontation.

Version D of the Anglo-Saxon Chronicle tells us that King Harold 'assembled a large army and came against him [Duke William] at the hoary apple tree'. The hoary apple tree is usually interpreted as Harold's pre-arranged meeting point where his principal army coming down from London would meet up with additional levies and troops assembled from the south coast. This tree is generally believed to have stood on or near the present-day windmill on Calbec Hill, a

mile north-west of Battle Abbey. In 1066 this point was the junction of three local hundreds and probably well known. There are some suggestions that Harold's lightning march was intended as a prelude to a night raid on William's camp down in Hastings. This was never attempted; probably because William had carefully stationed scouts in the region of Calbec Hill and perhaps because Harold's troops were exhausted after the march.

In addition to the rapid deployment of his army to Hastings, Harold had also ordered a fleet of seventy ships to station themselves off Hastings. Superficially, at least, it looked as if Harold had trapped the Normans in the Hastings 'peninsula' and they might be at his mercy.

The Battle

> **Note of caution:** The amount of detail known about this battle far exceeds that of any other in the medieval period in England thanks largely to the fabulous Bayeux Tapestry and other early medieval chronicles – and yet important questions remain (e.g. the death of King Harold). We should never forget that this is military history written only by the winners and in their own glorification.

In many ways the defining moment of the battle is the beginning. The Normans, confident, well prepared and rested, left their camp in Hastings just after daybreak and marched the 6 miles to Telham Hill, arriving at about 8 a.m. According to the Anglo-Saxon Chronicle, their arrival in the vicinity of Calbec Hill came before all the locally recruited Anglo-Saxon troops had joined up with Harold's army, catching

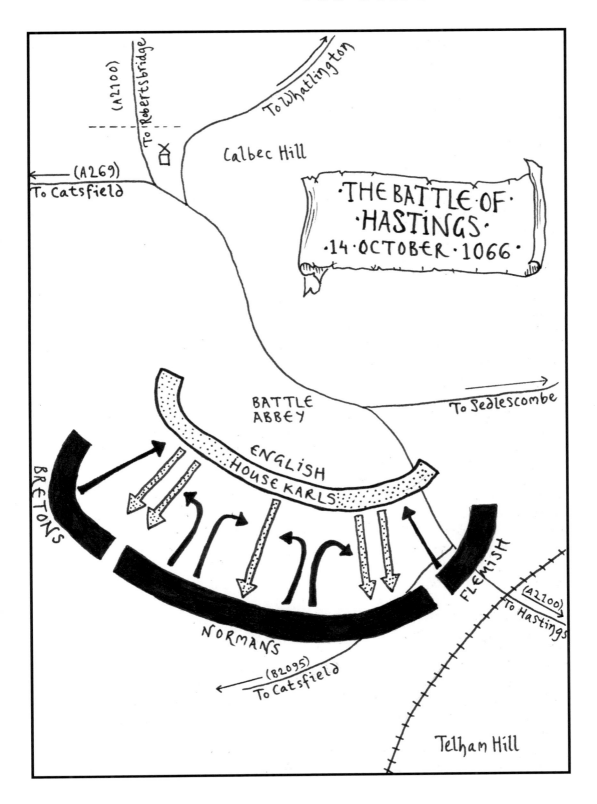

The iconic gatehouse of Battle Abbey.

the Anglo-Saxon army by surprise. These would probably have been foot soldiers and archers, generally recruited from the lower classes. Harold was forced to deploy his forces in a hurry. The conventional view is that they spread out along the plateau of Battle Hill to prevent the Normans gaining the ridge. Some sources indicate that there was not actually enough room on the ridge for the whole of Harold's army. The strategic tables had been overturned and the would-be surpriser had been surprised.

Important Aspects of the Battle

Hastings is a rare example of a major battle fought with significantly different battlefield technologies on each side. Anglo-Saxons fought on foot with swords, axes and spears formed into a shield wall, plus archers – largely as they had done for centuries. The king's housecarls, highly skilled professionals, provided the backbone of the

shield wall. Normans fought in the continental manner developed in the tenth century, with foot soldiers supported by heavy cavalry, crossbowmen and archers. Crossbows could penetrate chain mail at 100m.

At first sight the slopes of Senlac Ridge look truly awesome. How could the Normans contemplate trying to storm a shield wall in that position? While it must be noted that the height of the ridge is believed to have risen through accumulation over the centuries – and certainly the slope is less steep to the side of the abbey – the task would still have been daunting.

Considered the other way round however, the Anglo-Saxons were in fact quite stuck. Devoid of significantly large numbers of archers themselves (to provide cover for an advance), they were unable to move forward without being struck down by cavalry or crossbow archers. In other words, how could the Anglo-Saxons win? The contrasting

The Normans attacked up this slope to Battle Abbey.

technologies provide a classic example of the crucial importance of weapon range. Indeed, without sufficient archers, a defensive formation on the ridge was vulnerable to sustained archery fire as well. Archers were also key to the Anglo-Saxons as their best defence against the famed Norman cavalry, who were vulnerable to sustained fire from the ridge.

Archery at that time was still developing and most bows could kill at 100yds (by the fourteenth century the long bow was deadly at 250yds). The crossbow range was shorter but the bolt could more easily penetrate through chain mail. Here may lie one of the keys to understanding the outcome of the battle. From the moment he left London for York on 18/19 September, Harold had been in a constant hurry. He used mounted troops to and from the south, with probably only a restricted number of mounted archers. So it is quite likely that Harold arrived at Calbec Hill on 13 October with limited numbers of archers in his own contingent. He was very probably expecting local reinforcements to arrive at the meeting point the next morning. Certainly the Bayeux Tapestry depicts large numbers of Norman archers and crossbowmen but only a small number of Anglo-Saxon ones. Could this be the real meaning of the arrow in Harold's eye: an allegory? The importance of archery to a military victory was often devalued in medieval times simply because it was not what the aristocracy did – they were knights on horseback or part of a shield wall.

Hastings: King Harold's Strategic Position at 9 a.m. on 14 October 1066

1. Harold has had the exact battle site chosen for him in his own country – Duke William has surprised him.
2. Since mid-September Harold had been 'on the back foot' and in a great hurry. As a result, not all of his forces have arrived by the start of the battle. In particular there is no mention of the involvement of the northern earls, Edwin of Mercia and Morcar of Northumbria, in the battle. It is effectively the Godwins v. Duke William.
3. The English army is probably very short of archers – vital to the defence of the shield wall.
4. Both of Harold's younger but fully adult brothers, Gyrth and Leofwine, have front-line roles in the battle. In the event of Harold's death there is no fallback. The king has insisted on this situation.
5. The strength of the shield wall depended crucially on the housecarls. Their numbers had been depleted at Stamford Bridge and they may have been exhausted from the long journey to Yorkshire and back.
6. The steep downward slope from the Senlac Ridge would ensure that any isolated forays by the English would struggle to regain the ridge – they would be very vulnerable to Norman cavalry. High levels of troop discipline would be needed to prevent such occurrences.
7. English military technology had not kept up with the European developments over the last century. The English fought only on foot.

A visit to the battlefield run by English Heritage will provide you with all you need to know about the main events of the battle. Some of the highlights include the following:

The Anglo-Saxon shield wall, particularly the housecarls, proved formidable – Duke William was said to have been much impressed by their effectiveness. French archers proved ineffective against it early on, as did charges by infantry and cavalry. The Bretons on the French left were initially driven back. Shouts went up that Duke William had fallen and, encouraged by Count Eustace of Boulogne, William had to show himself to his troops.

A large part of the battle was attritional, with French archers, crossbowmen and cavalry gradually picking off the English shield wall. It was not until early evening that a breakthrough was achieved. Overall, however, Anglo-Saxon casualties were high; Norman and other French casualties were low.

The Normans used feigned retreats to lure the English down the slope and then isolate and destroy them. Given the high level of Anglo-Saxon attrition on the ridge it is very likely that discipline broke down, causing unplanned Anglo-Saxon advances as well. Harold's brothers, Gyrth and Leofwine, were killed early on, perhaps in these circumstances.

As the shield wall thinned, the Norman and other French archers increased their trajectory to swell casualties. It is perhaps at this time that King Harold was hit in the eye. Modern scholarship tends to favour the view that he was cut down by four Norman knights specially selected by Duke William (they are depicted on the Bayeux Tapestry immediately *after* the famous arrow scene), usually listed as Walter Giffard, Hugh de Montefort, Eustace of Boulogne and Hugh of Ponthieu.

After Harold's death the housecarls may have fought on but eventually the shield wall disintegrated and the English fled northwards.

The pursuing French were led into a trap at the Malfosse Incident (Evil Ditch) about 1 mile north of Battle Hill. Count Eustace was badly wounded and several French killed. Much has been made of this incident over the centuries in an attempt to claim some glory for the defeated English. Actually the battle had already been decided.

Aftermath

The remaining Anglo-Saxon forces slunk away under the cover of the Weald and then darkness. The south of England and the way to London now lay open to him. William rested his army at Hastings for five days and then, rather than take the direct route to London through the Weald, commenced a circuitous route through the south-east first, picking off the major towns. His first stop was Romney to exact revenge for the destruction of some wayward ships from the invasion force by the local people. His reputation now went before him and Dover, Canterbury, Winchester and Wallingford all submitted without a fight. Only London put up any resistance. Edgar Aetheling, grandson of King Edmund Ironside, who had been ignored as king when Harold emerged in January 1066, was now acclaimed as king by Earls Edwin and Morcar and the other remaining Anglo-Saxon leaders. He was never crowned and submitted to William at Berkhamsted in December. William was crowned king of England on Christmas Day 1066.

King Harold's badly mutilated body was by tradition identified by his handfast wife Edith Swan-Neck and handed to William Malet (see York) for burial. Tradition suggests that with typical medieval humour Harold was buried on the shore near Hastings so that he could forever keep watch over it (which of course he had signally failed to do). Sometime later his body was moved to his foundation at Waltham Abbey.

Participants and Casualties

The Norman Army

William, Duke of Normandy
Odo (half-brother), Bishop of Bayeux
Robert (half-brother), Count of Mortain
Eustace, Count of Boulogne
Geoffrey, Bishop of Coutances
Alan the Red of Brittany
Robert, Count of Eu
William Fitz Osbern
Aimeri, Vicomte of Thouars
Turstin, son of Rollo, standardbearer
Hugh (Ivo) of Ponthieu
Walter Giffard I
Walter Giffard II
Roger of Beaumont
William, son of Count of Evreux
Geoffrey, son of Count of Mortagne
Humphry of Tilleul
Ralf of Tosny
Hugh of Montfort
Hugh of Grandmesnil
William of Warenne
William Malet
Gulbert of Auffay
Robert of Vitot (k)
Engenulf of Laigle (k)
Rodulf (Ralf) de Tancarville
Gerelmus of Panileuse
Robert Fitz Erneis (k)
Roger, son of Turold (k)
Taillefer (k)
Erchembald
Vital
Wadard
Pons
Hugh of Ivry
Richard Fitz Gilbert

The English Army

Harold, King of England (k)
Gyrth (brother), Earl of East Anglia (k)
Leofwine (brother), Earl of Kent (k)
Hakon (nephew), son of Sweyn (k)
Aelfwig (uncle), Abbot of Winchester (k)
Leofric, Abbot of Peterborough
Aelfwold, abbot
Ansgar the staller, Sheriff of Middlesex
Godric, Sheriff of Fyfield, Berkshire (k)
Thurkill, Thegn of Kingston Bagpuize, Berkshire (k)
Eadric, a deacon from East Anglia
Aelfric, thegn from Huntingdonshire
Skalpi, housecarl
Alwi of Thetford
Ringolf of Oby
Breme, freeman (k)
'Son of Helloc' (k)

(k) = killed in battle

Most modern commentators place the size of the respective armies at around 7,000, i.e. about equal. Marren gives a ballpark split for the Norman army as 4,000 infantry, 1,500 archers and crossbowmen and 2,000 cavalry.

It is impossible to assess casualty figures with any accuracy. It was a hard-fought battle but, judged by aristocratic casualties, Norman losses look light because in their case there was no rout. Only five significant knights were killed. Less is known about the English participants at Hastings but their casualty rate looks much higher. The key outcome however was the death of three Godwinson brothers; Wulfnoth the youngest still lived but was a prisoner in Normandy.

Location and What to See £
The battlefield is accessible through the gatehouse of Battle Abbey, 7 miles north of Hastings up the A2100. This fourteenth-century building dominates the main street of the town at the south-east end. Car parking is nearby and signed. (EH)

The remains of Battle Abbey, the Abbey School and the battlefield itself provide a truly dignified memorial to this most celebrated of battles and to King Harold in particular. The **high altar** of the original abbey, constructed in the twelfth century, is said to mark the spot where the king made his last stand. This is now marked by a modern **memorial stone** on the Serlac Ridge within the abbey grounds, where archaeological excavation has revealed remains of the original church.

*On entry turn right out of the gatehouse shop and follow the anti-clockwise **battle trail** round the site for forty minutes or so. This is most rewarding. Also do not miss the museum, café and bookshop.*

Calbec Windmill, marking the approximate location of the 'hoary apple tree', can be driven past on the minor road from Battle to Whatlington about 1 mile north of the abbey. A visit to the alleged location of the Malfosse is less rewarding.

KINGSTON-ON-THAMES, Coronation Stone **
Town centre on High Street tucked in next to 1930s Guildhall.

The tenth-century Wessex/English kings were crowned in Kingston. Amazingly the **stone** on which they sat during the ceremony has survived. Over the centuries it has been moved a number of times but now resides in a dignified corner of the town centre. The stone is mounted on a more recent plinth which displays each king's name on a side.

The monument celebrates seven kings from Edwin onwards. The two of particular interest are **Edward the Martyr (962–78, king 975–8)**, murdered at Corfe Castle on the orders of his stepmother Aelfthryth, and his step-brother **Aethelred the Unready (968–1016, king 978–1016 with a break 1013–4)**. This is the only historic site commemorating Aethelred. His tomb in Old St Paul's Cathedral was lost in the Great Fire of London in 1666.

LEWES ***

From its inception by the Conqueror in 1067, this township formed the administrative and military HQ for the eponymous rape. Lewes, formerly a Saxon burgh, was entrusted by King William to the energetic William de Warenne, who had been present at the Battle of Hastings. The remains of both the original motte and bailey castle, as well as a splendid priory and other sites, make it a treasure trove for the historian of this period.

Aethelred II was crowned at Kingston; the stone used survives.

Castle £
Upper town centre, north side of High Street.

William de Warenne's castle, built soon after the Conquest, was unusual in having two mottes. By tradition the original castle was erected on the north-easterly motte, now called **Brack's Mount**, probably in timber. This can be viewed beyond the bowling green. However, after a relatively short time, a second motte was constructed to the south-west on which the **shell keep** now stands – possibly because it was deemed necessary to provide more protection to the growing town. Early Norman work survives in the shell keep (but not the thirteenth-century angle towers) and the **second central gatehouse** (overshadowed by the later Barbican).

St John's Church, Southover
Suburb of Lewes, ¾ miles south of castle.

This church originally formed the 'hospitum' at the gates of Lewes Priory (see below). In 1847 a new **south chapel** was constructed to house the recently discovered remains of **William de Warenne, Earl of Surrey** and his wife Gundrada/Gundred (d. 1085). They had been excavated from the ruins of Lewes Priory chapter house, which had been disturbed by the building of the Lewes–Brighton railway the year before. Their remains were found in caskets and were re-buried in the chapel beneath the black slab that had originally covered Gundrada's grave and which, with similar good fortune, had been found the wrong way up in the graveyard of Isfield church in 1775.

Gundrada died in childbirth at Castle Acre Priory in Norfolk, a second Cluniac house founded by her husband. At one time it was thought that Gundrada was one of William the Conqueror's daughters but this tradition has been disproved (see Castle Acre).

Priory of St Pancras

Not easy to find: from the north door of St John's Church, Southover, turn left into Southover High Street. Take first left into Cockshut Road. Proceed under railway arch (low clearance for cars) to Southdowns Sports Club. Turn left by side of tennis courts. Some signposts.

About 1075 **William de Warenne, Earl of Surrey** and his wife Gundrada visited the great monastery of Cluny in Burgundy. Perhaps urged on by Gundrada, William obtained permission from the Conqueror to found the first Cluniac priory in England in 1077 here at Southover. A large stone church was quickly built and consecrated by 1098. The early Norman buildings were extended in the thirteenth century and the monastery prospered until the church was approximately 450ft long. The **remains** can be viewed, with the original eleventh-century work on the left-hand side of the site. William was brought here after he was struck in the leg by an arrow at the siege of Pevensey Castle in 1088, and here he died on 24 June of that year.

St John-sub-Castro Church

North side of town centre, ⅓ miles north of castle down hill.

Lewes really is blessed with survivals from a 1,000 years ago. On the south-east corner of the church exterior, away from the road, the chancel arch of a previous church on this site has been incorporated in the brickwork of the 'new' church (1839) together with a **restored inscription** in Lombardic/Anglo-Saxon script, commemorating Magnus of the Royal Danish line, who chose to be an anchorite and served this church. This monument had been similarly attached to the previous church in 1635 by John Rowe.

Magnus is seen either as a former Danish general of our period who had converted to Christianity or, more interestingly, as the son of King Harold II.

LONDON

Greenwich, St Alfege's Church **
Town centre near the Cutty Sark, *corner of Greenwich High Road and Creek Road. Visit 10–11 a.m. on Saturdays.*

In August 1009 a great Danish raiding army arrived in Sandwich under Thorkell the Tall. The army ravaged almost at will through southern England during 1009–11 defeating the Anglo-Saxons at the Battle of Ringmere. In the autumn of 1011 Canterbury fell to Thorkell through treachery, and the Archbishop of Canterbury, Aelfheah, was captured. The Danes moved up to Greenwich and Danegeld of £48,000 was paid, but the Danes also wanted to ransom the archbishop. Aelfhah refused to allow this and at a feast after Easter 1012 was pelted with animal bones by drunken soldiers in defiance of their leader Thorkell's wishes. Aelfhah was finished off with the blunt end of an axe. This brutal murder represents a truly dismal moment in Anglo-Saxon history – an archbishop being bludgeoned to death by drunken gangsters. From now on it was downhill all the way.

Temporarily however King Aethelred gained some advantage from this dreadful incident. For a Viking commander to be ignored as Thorkell had been was traumatic; so much so that Thorkell gathered up the remnants of his force and changed sides to support the Anglo-Saxon king! Unfortunately it made no difference to the final outcome of the Danish Conquest.

Alfheah (Alphege) was buried in Old St Paul's Cathedral. He was declared a

The Tower of London – icon of the Norman Conquest?

martyr and the focus of a cult, and miracles occurred. However, in 1023, as atonement for the murder of the archbishop, King Cnut ordered that his body be moved to Canterbury in a procession led by Queen Emma and her young son, Harthacnut, with an armed escort. The clergy of St Paul's were none too pleased as relics were big business in the eleventh century.

This church is said to stand on the spot where <u>Archbishop Aelfheah</u> was killed and is a restored Hawksmoor from the eighteenth century. There are two modern stained glass windows and a memorial tablet inside commemorating Aelfheah (Alfege or Alphege) – be sure to visit this church during 2012.

The Tower, The White Tower ***** ££
Tower Hill Tube Station

One of William the Conqueror's earliest acts in England was to construct a wooden motte and bailey castle in the south-east corner of the Roman walls of London (probably before his coronation in December 1066). **King William I** soon wished to replace the wooden structure with stone for greater security. Tradition dictates that the magnificent White Tower was started in around 1078 and completed in the 1090s. Although there have been some modifications, the basic structure survives and surely represents the finest and oldest of royal monuments in England. Probably based on similar buildings in Normandy, the Tower was designed by <u>Gundulf, Bishop of Rochester (d. 1108)</u> who managed to combine much architectural work with piety – he built Colchester and Rochester castles, in addition to Rochester Cathedral. It was intended to impress and intimidate the citizens of London. Somehow this building encapsulates the very essence of the Norman Conquest; its militaristic core and icon.

The early Norman chapel of St John the Evangelist in the Tower.

On your tour do not miss the stark but lovely **chapel** of St John the Evangelist, in the early Norman style. It was here that Elizabeth of York, Henry VII's queen, lay in state in 1503 after her death in childbirth in the Tower. The Tower, of course, contained royal apartments until the Reformation.

Westminster Abbey of St Peter ***** ££
Westminster Tube Station

In around 1050 **King Edward the Confessor** decided he would be buried at Westminster. There had been a small monastery on the riverside island of Thorney since early Anglo-Saxon times. In the late tenth century St Dunstan re-endowed it but by 1050 it was somewhat impoverished despite being the initial burial location for

The funeral of Edward the Confessor in Westminster Abbey, January 1066.

King Harold I (before his successor, his half-brother Harthacnut, dug up his corpse). Rebuilding commenced straightaway in the Norman, Romanesque style, following designs of Jumiéges Abbey in Normandy (see Normandy).

The work had progressed sufficiently for the new abbey to be dedicated on 28 December 1065 during the Confessor's terminal illness. Since he died on the 4/5 January 1066 he was probably not present at the ceremony. He was buried beneath the pavement before the main alter on 6 January and Harold II was crowned the same day. His queen, Edith (Harold's sister), who died in 1075, and Henry I's queen, also Edith or Matilda, who died in 1118, were buried nearby. Edward's abbey church was longer than anything then existing in either England or Normandy. It was the setting for the coronation of William I on Christmas Day 1066.

In the twelfth century two attempts were made at Edward's canonisation. The first in 1140 was unsuccessful, but Henry II's attempt with Pope Alexander III succeeded, resulting in Edward being canonised as the Confessor in February 1161. In October 1163 Edward's remains were translated to a shrine within the abbey.

Henry III, a keen supporter of the Confessor, rebuilt the abbey in the thirteenth century. Little remains of the original Norman church. In October 1269 Edward's remains were translated again to the current **shrine** but retained the base from Henry III's predecessor. The shrine was despoiled at the Reformation but restored during the reign of Mary I. Despite this checked history the shrine surely represents one of the finest monuments to an English monarch of any era and – deserving or not – must be one of the most important sites in this book.

Westminster, Great Hall **** £
Parliament Square next to the Houses of Parliament, Westminster Tube Station.

Edward the Confessor built or rebuilt a royal palace at Westminster in around

1050, commencing building of his abbey at the same time. In 1097 **William Rufus** had the great hall of the palace rebuilt. This is the same structure we see today, although the splendid hammerbeam roof was added in the late fourteenth century by Richard II. The hall's dimensions are 240ft by 68ft, thought perhaps to have been the biggest stone building in Europe at the time. It is likely that Rufus rebuilt many of the ancillary palace buildings at the same time (e.g. chapel, kitchens, stables, etc.).

The king's throne used to reside in this hall. Many important events will have taken place here but none so bizarre as that which occurred in the autumn of 1460, at the height of the Wars of the Roses, when – in front of his so-called supporters – Richard, Duke of York, laid his hand on the empty throne, expecting to be acclaimed king. He was in fact greeted with silence, not accepted as king and killed a few months later at the Battle of Wakefield. There is a **statue** of William Rufus in the hall.

NORTH MARDEN, St Mary's Church *
South side of B2146 Petersfield–Chichester road, 2 miles south-east of South Harting.

The four Marden villages nestle attractively in an unspoilt part of the South Downs inland from Bosham. The manors were held by Earl Godwin in the first half of the eleventh century and by Earl Roger de Montgomery after the Conquest. This beautifully situated church was built towards the middle of the twelfth century and is a rare example of a virtually unaltered, single-apse room incorporating nave and chancel. There is also an elaborate south doorway built in the Norman style with Caen stone. Pevsner dates the door to 1130–40, right at the end of our period.

Rural charm at North Marden.

PEVENSEY, Castle ***** £

South-west end of village, now bypassed by A27 Bexhill–Lewes road. From A27 roundabout head towards Westham on B2191 and you can't miss it. (EH)

One of English history's greatest surviving monuments. It is noteworthy for three reasons:

- Around AD290 the Romans built a chain of forts around the south-east corner of England from Portchester in Hampshire to Brancaster in Norfolk to protect the area from the waves of Anglo-Saxon invaders threatening our coasts. They became known as Saxon Shore Forts. They must have been impressive structures indeed. Pevensey (or Andereida as it was called) today, still has massive walls, 20ft high in places. A fine testimony to Roman engineering skills.
- Unfortunately for Roman Britain the chain of forts eventually succumbed to invasion.

The Anglo-Saxon Chronicle records that by AD491 Andereida had been over-run and the defenders slaughtered to a man. So the fort also celebrates the triumph of the English and the end of the Roman Empire in Britain.

- On 28 September 1066 it was here that William the Conqueror chose to land in England. In the early medieval period sea levels were considerably higher than they are today and thus Andereida stood on a low promontory that jutted out into Pevensey Lagoon (now the levels), an area of inland sea/saltmarsh perhaps similar to Chichester Harbour today. It provided a large area of protected anchorage for William's invasion fleet (at least at high tide). Look south from the castle and you will see that the shoreline is over a mile away today. In 1066 it was right below the **south side** of the fort. It is believed that William's ship landed right by the fort and famously he is said to have slipped as he disembarked.

A diary slip-up perhaps?

What to See

The most amazing thing about Pevensey is that William will have been greeted by the remains of the Roman fort looking much the same as it does today. Make sure you get a good look at the **Roman walls.**

William, in fact, used Pevensey as a staging post before moving his fleet and his army on to Hastings, only a two-hour sail in good winds. He did, however, erect one of the pre-fabricated wooden forts he had brought across the Channel in the north-east corner of Andereida. The remains of the stone medieval castle occupy the site today. At the same time the Normans repaired parts of the Roman walls including the **arch** and herringbone masonry at the **Eastgate.** With these fortifications readily available Pevensey did not need a motte and bailey castle.

Once the Conquest of southern England was secure William was able to make his triumphant return to Normandy in 1067 laden with booty. He chose to embark from Pevensey. Possibly at the same moment he granted the Rape of Pevensey to his half-brother, **Robert, Count of Mortain**. One of the latter's early tasks was to re-fortify the original castle. Within the grounds of the later medieval castle in the north-east corner can still be seen the much battered remains of the late eleventh-century **stone keep and the foundations of the chapel**.

It may have been this keep and its Roman walls that were involved in the siege of Pevensey Castle in 1088, when both the Conqueror's half-brothers, Bishop Odo and Robert, Count of Mortain, rebelled against William Rufus in support of Duke Robert of Normandy, the Conqueror's eldest son. The king personally supervised the siege by land and sea. The castle resisted all assaults but ran out of food after six weeks. Robert of Mortain was pardoned but Odo was exiled

(see Rochester). It was in this action that William de Warenne the elder was fatally wounded (see Lewes).

ROCHESTER ****
City centre signposted. (EH)

Perched above the river Medway the grouping of Norman castle and cathedral provide a truly splendid sight guarding the crossing of Watling Street (the current A2) of the river.

Castle £
The first motte and bailey was wooden and located on Boley Hill just to the south of the current site and outside the city walls. It was probably erected as the Normans moved past on their way towards London in late 1066. During the revolt by Bishop Odo of Bayeux (the Conqueror's half-brother) in 1088 in favour of Duke Robert of Normandy against William Rufus, this castle was used as Odo's base. At the end of the revolt, Odo, Count Eustace III of Boulogne and the three Montgomery brothers were besieged here by Rufus and a force of English recruits. Eventually the defenders surrendered and Odo was exiled.

After the siege the castle was rebuilt on its current site firstly by Bishop Gundulf of Rochester (d. 1108) and then by William de Corbeil, Archbishop of Canterbury, to whom Henry I entrusted the construction in 1127. Over the next twelve years William oversaw the work that produced the splendid stone keep, the tallest Norman building in England. His castle still dominates the town and cathedral. It was the location of another famous siege in 1215 when King John destroyed one of the towers.

Cathedral
This splendidly squat building is a mixture of early and late Norman architecture. In

Rochester: the juxtaposition of church and castle at the Medway crossing.

The late Norman west end at Rochester Cathedral. The crumbling but original statues of Henry I and Matilda are visible on the west door itself.

common with other cathedrals Rochester was re-sited and rebuilt by the Normans from 1083. The work was undertaken by the arch builder <u>Bishop Gundulf (d. 1108)</u> whose tomb lies beneath the high altar. Little survives of his church however as fires in the twelfth century necessitated substantial rebuilding of the structure in the late Norman style. Particular items of interest are:

- **Gundulf's Tower** adjacent to the north transept. Part of the original church, originally free-standing. Its exact purpose is unclear.
- **Statues** of **King Henry I** and **Queen Matilda** (or Maud, formerly Edith, d. 1118). The west end was completed by 1160 and had been sponsored by King Henry. These statues are some of the earliest originals surviving in England.
- In the **pulpitum screen** a statue of <u>Bishop Gundulf</u> with a model of his church in hand.

STEYNING, St Andrew's Church **
¼ mile north of Main Street. Turn away from Downs north at mini-roundabout in Main Street.

Founded by St Cuthman in the eighth century this church was given by Edward the Confessor to Fécamp Abbey in 1047 perhaps as a means of restricting the power of the Godwins in Sussex. It was taken back in 1066 by King Harold, at a time when he was securing the south coast against Duke William's expected invasion. In June of that year William declared that, if his invasion of England was successful, he would restore Steyning to Fécamp. This was a ploy aimed at securing the full backing of the Pope, who would see this dispute as a threat to one of his dominions – it worked!

Following the Conquest the monks of Fécamp rebuilt Steyning church between 1100–70, producing a building with a range of Norman styles from early to late. The **chancel** arch and **nave** arcades are especially splendid. In the eleventh century Steyning was an important port on the Adur (see Bramber) and had been a Saxon burgh.

STOUGHTON, St Mary's Church ***
North side of village centre in elevated position.

This late eleventh-century church is wonderfully complete. It is of cruciform plan indicating that it was probably intended as a college before the Conquest intervened. Most likely built in the time of the Godwins in the last fifty years of Anglo-Saxon England, architecturally the church belongs to the Saxo-Norman overlap. The admirable church leaflet indicates that **Earl Godwin of Wessex** and his wife **Countess Gytha** owned the manor of Stoughton together with nearby Westbourne, Compton and the Mardens. It is likely that Gytha involved herself with these churches local to their principal residence at Bosham. Godwin was certainly not renowned as a churchman at any rate. There is also a fine chancel arch of the period, which is similar to that at Bosham, plus exterior herringbone flint work.

After the Conquest Roger de Montgomery, Earl of Arundel, had the lordship directly. He was succeeded by his eldest son, Robert de Beleme ('a monster of iniquity') who was exiled in 1102 by Henry I for his part in Robert, Duke of Normandy's attempt on the English throne. Savaric Fitz Caine in 1121 gave the church to the Priory of St Pancras founded by William de Warenne, Earl of Surrey, in Lewes. By this time that priory already possessed forty churches (and therefore their income) in the Chichester diocese alone. Situated in beautiful and unspoilt countryside.

THURNHAM, Godard's Castle *

4 miles north-east of Maidstone on spur of North Downs, just north of Pilgrims Way. High above village off minor road from Detling to Hollingbourne. Take cul-de-sac up Downs from village.

At Domesday the castle was held by <u>Ralph de Courbepine</u> from the Bishop of Rochester. A highly impressive motte, originally over 100ft high, using the contours of the Downs escarpment. A stretch of curtain wall survives. Much of the site is delightfully overgrown and unspoilt with great views. An excellent place for a picnic – it will not be overcrowded. Note that it involves a steep climb.

TONBRIDGE, Castle ** £

Town centre on river Medway ½ mile north of railway station.

After the Battle of Hastings the Conqueror granted the 'lowy' of Tonbridge to **Richard Fitz Gilbert** who was present at the battle. This comprised widespread lands in Kent sufficient to support a castle. Richard also received estates in Clare, Suffolk, and adopted the title Richard de Clare, founding the powerful Clare dynasty. Richard was descended from a bastard son of Duke Richard II of Normandy (see Clare).

Richard duly constructed a wooden motte and bailey castle on this site that was certainly completed before 1088 when Richard chose to join Bishop Odo in revolt against William Rufus (in favour of his elder brother, Duke Robert of Normandy). The castle commanded the crossing of the Medway on the main road from the port of Hastings to London. Rufus reacted quickly and besieged the castle with a force comprising many English recruits (only twenty-two years after the Conquest). Within two days the castle had capitulated

and Rufus torched both town and castle. The rebellion was quickly snuffed out; Odo was exiled but de Clare pardoned (see also Rochester).

The splendid **motte** survives, high and round. Remains of a thirteenth-century curtain wall can be seen on the top. The plan of the bailey also survives but nothing from the twelfth century was rebuilt.

THE SOUTH

AVINGTON, St Mark and St Luke Church * KAL

Hamlet is between Hungerford and Newbury in Kennet Valley, 2 miles east of Hungerford. Turn off old A4 on minor road south.

A gem of a church, very simple and almost entirely Norman, probably built towards the end of our period. Founded by either Richard Puignant or Richard de Camville, his successor as lord of the manor. At Domesday Avington was assessed at two hides worth 100*s*. It had a mill and an island.

BREAMORE, St Mary's Church **

Just north-west of village centre, west of A338 Salisbury–Ringwood road. Signposted to house/gardens.

Breamore is lovely. Although considerably altered in later centuries, especially in the chancel, this is still basically a Saxon church dated to around 1000. Many Saxon details are on view both externally and internally: original nave with Saxon windows, pilaster strips and long- and short-quoins, the south porticus and a rood above the south doorway including a rare inscription in Anglo-Saxon on the internal arch.

Baldwin de Redvers acquired the manor in 1100. The south doorway is Norman.

The simple interior of Avington's late Norman church.

The view of the south exterior from the south doorway is impressive, especially the south porticus.

CADNAM, The Rufus Stone ****

½ mile north of A31 Southampton–Bournemouth road, 2 miles south-west of the Cadnam interchange. Accessible off northbound carriageway only, but signposted off both. Located at Upper Canterton on minor road to Minstead.

A nineteenth-century **monument** on this minor road in the New Forest commemorates one of English history's greatest murder mysteries, the death of **King William II**. The known facts are straightforward enough.

William Rufus was killed by an arrow late in the day on Thursday 2 August 1100, while hunting deer from his lodge at nearby Brockenhurst. It most probably pierced his heart and he died without saying another word. He may have fallen on the broken arrow to hasten his own end.

Hunting normally commenced soon after dawn but on this day it did not start until after 'lunch' (probably mid-late morning) as the king had to enact some business first – but there are also suggestions of a royal hangover!

Certainly in the hunting party were: Rufus' younger brother Henry, his favourite Robert Fitz Haimo, Walter Tyrel, William of Breteuil, plus a number of other nobles, probably including Richard Fitz Gilbert of Clare.

At the time of Rufus' death Henry was elsewhere in the forest re-making arrows. Rufus was in the company of Frenchman Walter Tyrel, Lord of Poix and castellan of Pontoise, a royal French castle in the Vexin which was a stronghold protecting the route to Paris from Normandy. Tyrel was married to Adelaide, daughter of Richard Fitz Gilbert as mentioned earlier. Tyrel is said to have become one of Rufus' closest friends by the

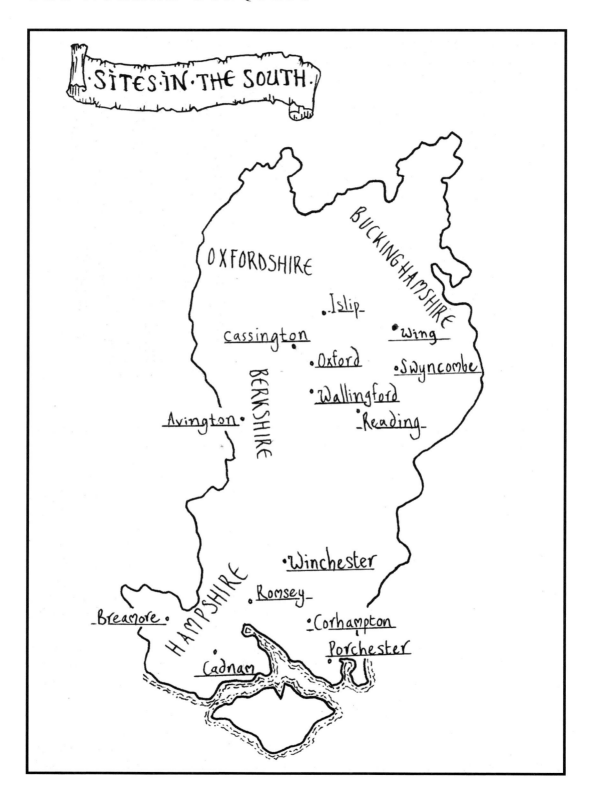

summer of 1100. Most sources made Tyrel the huntsman whose arrow struck Rufus, although later in life he denied the fact under oath more than once.

Confusion reigned after the king's death. Most of the hunting party departed the forest in great haste to safeguard their own interests and it was left to a few ordinary folk to transport the body to Winchester. So far so good – but there are a number of other events that raise the ugly spectre of conspiracy.

After the 'accident' Tyrel mounted his horse and fled directly to France. He was not pursued by any of the royal party. Henry similarly rode hard for Winchester to secure the royal treasure which was still held there. With drawn sword to discourage opposition Henry achieved this and immediately departed for Westminster. Just three days later, on Sunday (the traditional day for coronations in that era) 5 August he was crowned King of England, despite the fact that in 1091 Henry and the English barons had acknowledged Robert Curthose, Henry's eldest brother, as William II's heir.

There were two strategic considerations which were pertinent at this time. Brother Robert, the Conqueror's eldest son, was known to be on his way back from the First Crusade with an enhanced chivalric reputation, a new wife and large dowry. In fact he arrived in Normandy in September 1100. In order to finance his crusade Robert had mortgaged Normandy to Rufus. Was Rufus going to hand back the duchy to his hitherto ineffective and spendthrift older brother? Where would this leave brother Henry's lands in Normandy?

Rufus was known to be planning a major military expedition to Normandy and, if negotiations went well, to Poitou and perhaps Aquitaine – the kingdom of France itself might be threatened through the Vexin.

Cadnam, the nearby pub.

By June 1100 Rufus was assembling an invasion fleet on the south coast.

Unfortunately all these facts and considerations taken together are not sufficient to judge the mystery definitively. Walter Tyrel, even if he had killed Rufus accidentally, would have been wise to flee the country to protect himself against kin-vendetta. Additionally, Henry's actions display no sign of pre-knowledge; he would have acted the same way whether it was murder or accident given Duke Robert's imminent return from crusade. Furthermore, no contemporary or close contemporary source raised the possibility of conspiracy. Most modern authorities thus conclude that it was all an accident – even if it is a big coincidence that the fatal arrow happened to hit Rufus full in the breast and was not a mere glancing blow.

In her recent book on William Rufus, Emma Mason takes a different approach.

She argues that Tyrel may have been a French double agent. A key question surrounding Rufus' death is why Tyrel, a Frenchman, should have been present in the hunting party. Firm evidence is again scarce but most writers assume that, given the key location of Tyrel's castle at Pontoise in relation to the Vexin, he had defected to Rufus' cause ahead of the king's forthcoming expedition to France, perhaps seduced by the king's bounty.

Mason casts doubt on this thesis by pointing out that, on his return to France, Tyrel continued to serve as Castellan of Pontoise – where he entertained Prince Louis of France in 1102, hardly the reception likely to have been given to a returning traitor. If it was a conspiracy it was a very clever one. Could Tyrel have been purely the bait to get Rufus in the forest on his own? Personally it seems much more likely that the chief conspirator was Henry. He was highly intelligent, utterly ruthless (the Conqueror's sons were completely dysfunctional as a group; look at Henry's treatment of brother Robert after 1106) and had so much to gain. It is certainly interesting that Prince Louis visited Henry's court as early as Christmas 1100.

Rufus was buried the next day, Friday 3 August, in Winchester. But in death he was again unlucky: the tower of the cathedral collapsed above his grave in 1107. Yet further divine disapproval of him?

CASSINGTON, St Peter's Church **

Village centre, east side. 5 miles north-west of Oxford north of A40 Witney road.

Inside a fine, largely Norman church, with good tower arches and doorways. Outside a splendid corbel table of carved heads. It was built from around 1120 by <u>Geoffrey de Clinton</u>, Henry I's chancellor of the exchequer.

CORHAMPTON, Church **

Village centre on A32 Fareham–West Meon road. Do not confuse with St Andrew's Meonstoke, ¼ mile south.

A charming Saxon church dated to the first quarter of the eleventh century. Externally, pilaster strips, long- and short-quoins, a blocked north doorway and a Saxon sundial are visible. The fine Saxon chancel arch dominates the lovely interior. The chancel contains Norman wall paintings dated to the end of our period, 1125–75. Don't miss the great yew tree, which has a girth of 23ft and may thus pre-date the church.

ISLIP, St Nicholas Church ***

Village centre, 1 mile south of A34 Oxford–Bicester road.

Details of medieval births are scarce. The birthplaces of only two Anglo-Saxon kings are known to us: appropriately of Alfred the Great at Wantage and of St Edward the Confessor at Islip. Edward's is known because a charter of his mother, Queen Emma, survives, which granted him Islip as a birthday gift. Actually the gift was nearby Launton (east of Bicester) and the charter's provenance somewhat suspect. In 1065 this 'manor' was included in the grants of land and church livings by King Edward to his new Abbey of St Peter at Westminster.

Edward was born in around 1004 at the height of the Viking incursions in southern England. Quite what Queen Emma was doing in a Wessex/Mercia border village in such times we do not know. Winchester would have been the normal lying-in location for such an important first birth. Perhaps Aethelred had sent her away to a safe haven? Or perhaps she was required to stay close to the king, who may have been hunting at nearby Kirtlington or Woodstock?

Nevertheless, the church provides a fine memorial to **St Edward the Confessor**. The structure is thirteenth or fourteenth-century and includes statues and paintings of the saint and St Peter, an appropriate commemoration for a religious man and aesthete. There is a nice green outside for a picnic and two pubs in the village. If you are stuck in heavy traffic on the nearby A34 or M40, stop by for a break.

OXFORD **

Castle £
Western edge of city centre between New Road and Tidmarsh Lane.

By the early eleventh century Oxford had established itself as a significant border town between Wessex and Mercia. In 1036 it was the location for a key council meeting held to resolve the succession crisis which followed Cnut's death. Not surprisingly by 1071 the Normans had established a royal castle here. The hereditary constables were initially the d'Oillys. The fine **motte** survives to over 60ft, but only **St George's Tower** survives of the original masonry. The tower may even have been a keep at first; later it became a prison. In 1074 Robert d'Oilly founded the **Chapel of St George** south of the motte. The **crypt** survives.

PORTCHESTER, Castle and St Mary's Church ** £
South of village centre, at edge of Portsmouth Harbour. Signposted from A27. (EH)

Portchester is a Norman castle built within the protective walls of a Roman fort, probably of the Saxon Shore type (see Pevensey). The fort dates from the late third century. In late Saxon times it became a burgh. After the Conquest Portchester was granted to William Maudit, who probably created the inner bailey, protected by a ditch and wooden palisade. In 1100 his son Robert inherited but was drowned in the *White Ship* disaster in 1120. Eventually the castle passed to William Pont de l'Arche, Robert's son-in-law. William is credited with rebuilding the keep and inner bailey in stone, both of which still stand today. Two extra floors were added to the keep in around 1150. After the death of William in 1148 the castle became royal under Henry II. Portchester in medieval times acted as a port of embarkation from southern England to Normandy.

St Mary's church now serves the local parish but was originally part of an Augustinian priory founded in 1128 by William Pont de l'Arche. This splendid building was constructed in the 1130s and is seen by Pevsner as an 'outstanding Romanesque church of moderate size'. Note especially the **west door**. Strangely, the priory moved to nearby Southwick possibly as early as 1150, so the church survived the later Dissolution of the Monasteries as a parish church.

READING, Abbey ****
Just east of town centre beside Forbury Gardens and the Crown Court. Car parking is difficult so use Queen's Road multi-storey.

This important medieval institution was founded by **King Henry I** in 1121 in the aftermath of the *White Ship* disaster (see Barfleur). It was dedicated to Henry's son William, drowned in the disaster, his brother William Rufus, and his parents. It was extremely well endowed by Henry and followed Cluniac rules. At its height it comprised over 100 monks. The abbey church was said to be bigger than St Paul's. Henry was buried here in early 1136. Stephen, his successor as king, was a pallbearer. Henry's second queen, <u>Adeliza (1110–51)</u>, who married William d'Albini after Henry's death, may also have been buried here.

Time has not been kind to Henry – and there is no reason why it should be. The Dissolution hit Reading hard, with the last abbot being hanged outside the abbey. Henry's tomb and effigy have been completely lost and only a modern **plaque** marks the spot. The abbey remains are sparse, though well landscaped and maintained.

ROMSEY ABBEY **
Town centre, signposted.

A convent of 100 nuns was established here in the early tenth century by King Edward the Elder. This was re-founded in 967 by King Edgar as a Benedictine establishment and continued to the Dissolution in the 1540s. A stone church was built before the Conquest, the foundations of which can be seen in the north transept. Building of the Norman abbey commenced in 1120, with the chancel located to the east of the Saxon church and remaining in use for some time. Of special interest today is the straight east wall of the chancel in the Saxon style. The whole rebuilding took over 100 years, so Romsey provides a master class in the three architectural styles of early Norman, late Norman and early English Gothic.

The altar in the **south chancel aisle** chapel is a beautiful Saxon rood, perhaps a gift from King Edgar on the abbey's re-foundation. Another rood from the old church can be found outside the church on the **west wall of the south transept**, believed to be eleventh century.

The guidebook links Romsey to an important diplomatic episode in the late eleventh century. Convents were, of course, used to educate young women. **Edith** (later

Regal lack of splendour for Henry I at Reading. Even a control-freak is powerless after death.

called **Matilda**), the daughter of Queen Margaret of Scotland, had been placed in a convent under the direction of Margaret's sister, Christina, who was a nun. The sources are confusing regarding which 'West Saxon nunnery' she lived in, but Wilton (near Salisbury) and Romsey are the candidates. Edith's political importance derived from the fact that Queen Margaret and Christina were among the last surviving members of the Anglo-Saxon royal family. Edith was the granddaughter of King Edmund Ironside, Aethelred's eldest son by Aelfgifu. King Malcolm, Edith's father, wanted to marry her to the elderly Alan the Red of Brittany. But in 1093, when Alan visited the nunnery to inspect her, he was instead smitten by another nun, Gunhild, youngest daughter of Harold Godwinson, whom he abducted and persuaded to live with him! Next to visit Edith later that year was King William Rufus, at a time when marriage to the daughter of the King of the Scots had diplomatic appeal. Once again however the king was unimpressed. No need to blame Edith in this case though: a counter story runs that Christina found Rufus so appalling that she ensured her niece was wearing a veil and insisted that she had already taken holy vows.

Finally however, in 1100, the newly crowned Henry I married Edith, thus bringing about the union of the Norman and Saxon royal lines. The awesome Henry was surely not the sort of king to have worried about the physical attraction of his queen. His tally of twenty-five known royal bastards is a clear record for English kings (not even approached by Charles II). Many were born after Henry and Edith's marriage but Edith hung on in there however, taking the Norman name Matilda and, through her daughter, also Matilda, becoming the ancestor of all English kings.

SWYNCOMBE, St Botolph's Church **

About as 'far from the madding crowd' as you can get in the south. Hamlet is 3 miles north-west of Nettlebed. Turn left off B481 Nettlebed–Watlington road at Cookley Green on minor road. After 1 mile turn left again to Swyncombe House.

Set in glorious countryside, this is a fine example of the juxtaposition of manor and church. The small church dates back to the early post-Conquest years (with hints of Saxon); the present house on the other hand dates to around 1840 (an Elizabethan predecessor had been destroyed by fire). Unfortunately the church was partially restored at this time, but the work has not destroyed the fine simplicity of the early Norman structure. The church was probably built by Robert d'Oilly, who married the daughter of a Saxon leader, Wygod of Wallingford, or by his son-in-law Milo Crispin, Constable of Wallingford Castle. At Domesday the manor was held by the monks of the Abbey of Bec in Normandy. The excellent guidebook suggests Milo may have gifted the estate to Bec. There were 10 acres of meadow valued at 60*s*. It never paid geld (tax).

WALLINGFORD ***

Best approach is on A4130 from Henley. Proceed through Crowmarsh Giffard to river Thames. Park by bridge. Town provides opportunity for walk to view some interesting survivals.

The Bridge

Wallingford occupies a special place in our story because it was here in late autumn 1066 that the Conqueror's army finally crossed the Thames from west to east, and headed for Berkhamsted where the English leaders surrendered. The geography of the town suggests any ford would have been situated at or near the line of the bridge, so the Conqueror definitely passed this way. **Stigand, Archbishop of Canterbury** chose the moment to throw in his lot with the Normans, thus not only weakening the English cause but also probably saving his own life (the Normans regarded his appointment as uncanonical). Wallingford was a large Anglo-Saxon burgh. Scant remains of the burgh's outer defences in the form of **ditches** can be seen on the eastern bank close to the river bank where the Norman army camped.

Burgh Ramparts

Wallingford and Wareham demonstrate the two best survivals of a Saxon burgh first developed by Alfred in the eighth century and re-fortified in the tenth. These earthworks enclosed the whole town in an attempt to save it from the Danes. The **ramparts** have survived on the western, northern and southern sections (it is unlikely the eastern, i.e. river side, was similarly fortified). While viewing the banks do visit the local **museum** and the Coach and Horses, which are situated in **Kinecroft** – an ancient open space within the walls in the south-west corner.

St Leonard's Church
Thames Street/St Leonard's Lane at south-east corner.

In the thirteenth century Wallingford boasted fifteen churches. However since the Black Death and the decline of the royal castle the town's population has declined and the number of churches shrunk. By 1439 there were only four, and now there are three.

William the Conqueror crossed the Thames here.

St Leonard's is the oldest of those. Although quite heavily restored in the nineteenth century, this remains an impressive example of a Norman church with herringbone masonry and splendid internal arches.

Castle

It is the north-west quarter of the town. There is limited car parking in Castle Street.

In terms of masonry the remains of this once-important royal castle are scant indeed. What in effect survives are the earthworks of a large motte and bailey structure. It is very likely that the Conqueror immediately ordered the construction of such a castle to protect his supply lines from the Channel ports. This may have been done by Robert d'Oilly. It remained a royal castle. The very large, tree-lined **motte** can still be seen north of Castle Gardens (better in winter). The bailey also occupied a large area. The construction of the castle here provides a stark contrast with that of the Saxon burgh. For the castle the Normans demolished a large portion of the town. They were not intent on defending the whole town but defending only themselves, the new ruling elite in a potentially hostile land.

The castle saw much action during the civil war of the twelfth century, known as the Anarchy, and again in the Civil War. It also served as a prison for important royal captives in the Middle Ages (e.g. Queen Margaret of Anjou in the 1470s).

WINCHESTER *****

By late Anglo-Saxon times, Winchester was well established as the capital of Wessex and of England – both Cnut and Edward the Confessor were crowned here, as indeed was William the Conqueror in a second ceremony in early 1067. The king had a palace in the city and kept his treasure here. After the Conquest the treasury remained here and the king wore his crown at Easter. However, from early in Henry I's reign, the centre of power switched irrevocably to London; later in the reign the treasury also moved.

Cathedral

City centre south side.

A Saxon cathedral, the Old Minster, was established here as early as the mid-seventh century. St Swithin was buried outside its west door in the ninth century. The Old Minster was rebuilt 971–94 at the instigation of King Edgar; during this period the bones of St Swithin were ceremoniously transferred to the new church. On the exact day this occurred, 15 July 971, a violent storm broke out creating the legend. The **foundations** of this church were excavated in the twentieth century and can be seen today to the north of the current cathedral. Alongside the Old Minster the Saxon kings had also established a New Minster in 903, built so close that singing in both churches together would intermingle and caused confusion. A convent also existed nearby called Nunnaminster, making Winchester a religious Saxon centre without parallel in England.

The Normans, of course, could not let this situation rest. Bishop Walkelin (bishop 1070–98) replaced the Anglo-Saxon Bishop Stigand and began work on a new and much larger church in 1079. The relics of St Swithin were transferred to the new church in 1093. This church has been much altered in later centuries, but the **transepts** do remain from Walkelin's original church.

For the medievalist, the thrill of Winchester lies in the **mortuary chests** high up on the wooden screens in the **presbytery**. These chests contain the bones of nine individuals dating from the earliest Saxon times. Our interest focuses on:

- **King Cnut** (995–1035, reigned 1016–35) and his **Queen, Emma** (985–1052)
- **King William II 'Rufus'** (*c*. 1058–1100, reigned 1087–1100)
- **Stigand, Bishop of Winchester** (bishop 1047–70 and Archbishop of Canterbury 1052–70)
- Alwyn, Bishop of Winchester (bishop 1032–47)

These remains were transferred to the wooden chests in 1525 by Bishop Fox. However during the Civil War they were re-opened and the bones were used by Parliamentary soldiers as missiles to break the stained glass in the cathedral. The bones were eventually re-gathered and returned to the chests but not necessarily to the right ones. So we have more of a communal memorial, but nevertheless a splendidly unique survival, containing four of the major characters in our story.

It was thought at one time that the **tomb chest** in the middle of the **presbytery** was that of William Rufus, but recent investigations suggest it is that of Bishop Henry of Blois (bishop 1127–71), the brother of King Stephen, who originally exhumed the medieval royal remains in the mid-twelfth century and brought them into Walkelin's cathedral.

King Harthacnut (*c*. 1018–42, reigned 1040–2) was also reburied here and his tomb chest resides alone on the **north side** of Bishop Fox's **presbytery screen**.

Little else survives of early medieval Winchester. At the top of the **High Street (west)** information boards indicate the location next to the council offices of the castle, now demolished. Very early on after Hastings the Normans erected a wooden motte and bailey castle that later received stone fortifications. Lower down the pedestrianised street on the opposite side (north) do look out for **Godbegot House**, now a restaurant. This building stands on the site of the eponymous manor which in the eleventh century was the principal residence of the awesome **Queen Emma**.

The tomb of King Harthacnut in Winchester Cathedral.

It is very likely that Edward the Confessor – accompanied by his three principal earls, Godwin, Leofric and Siward – rode to this spot straight from London in 1042, in order to arrest his mother and dispossess her of the royal treasury which she had held onto after the death of her other son, Harthacnut.

WING, All Saints Church *
Western edge of village, ¼ mile north of A418 Aylesbury–Leighton Buzzard road.

This much-celebrated church is described by Pevsner as 'one of the most important Anglo-Saxon churches in England'. The apse and crypt are dated as early as eighth or ninth century. The rest of the Anglo-Saxon work in the nave and the north aisle are late tenth or eleventh century. In the Domesday Book, Wing was a large manor assessed at five hides or forty ploughs. It was held by Robert, Count of Mortain, the Conqueror's step-brother.

THE WEST COUNTRY

AVENING, Holy Cross Church ***
On south side of B4014 Nailsworth–Tetbury road at north-west end of village.

This surprisingly elegant church celebrates what perhaps constitutes the most unlucky lover of the eleventh century. Domesday book records that one <u>Beothric</u>, son of Earl Aelfgar of East Anglia, held the manor before the Conquest, as well as being Lord of Gloucester. Beothric was one of Edward the Confessor's courtiers and was sent on an embassy to Flanders where he met Matilda, daughter of Baldwin V, Count of Flanders. Matilda is said to have fallen in love with him but he rejected her advances.

In 1051–2 Matilda married Duke William of Normandy. After the Conquest, Beothric

Godbegot House, Winchester, on the site of Queen Emma's manor.

was, like so many other Anglo-Saxon thegns, dispossessed of his lands but, perhaps urged on by a vengeful Matilda, William had his 'rival' thrown into Worcester Prison where he died. The story as told doesn't really add up. Even in those times Matilda's response seems disproportionate for a 'turn down' nearly twenty years before. Perhaps a more realistic interpretation would be that Beothric enticed Matilda as a young woman into bed with promises, and then rejected her. Whatever, as a penance for this unmitigated act of revenge, **Queen Matilda** is said to have rebuilt the existing Saxon church here into the early Norman cruciform structure we see today (see William I). A magnificent memorial indeed. In 1082 this

Fine capitals in Avening church hint at the intriguing royal connection.

church and other lands around it were given to the Abbey of Holy Trinity, Caen, one of the two religious foundations established by William and Matilda as penance decreed by the Pope for irregularities in their marriage. There is surely a connection here.

BICKLEIGH, Chapel *
Part of the Bickleigh Castle leisure complex ¾ mile west of village centre across the river Exe. From A3072 Crediton road take first minor road left for ⅓ mile. Chapel is on east side of road next to river.

A really delightful twelfth-century thatched chapel all of apiece. If you want to get married with a Norman theme this is the place – the complex specialises in it. At Domesday, Bickleigh was part of the massive holdings of Robert, Count of Mortain. A castle

probably existed here in Norman times but nothing remains.

BRADFORD-ON-AVON, St Laurence's Church **
Town centre, south side of river, just off A353 Trowbridge road right next to parish church (Holy Trinity).

This ancient church was only rediscovered in the 1800s after centuries of neglect. Since a monastery is mentioned here in a deed of 705 when Aldhelm was abbot, the structure was initially thought to be of that period. Debate still exists but most authorities plump for late Saxon. Whatever the outcome it is a truly delightful building, unusually tall in relation to its width. What makes it particularly exciting is that the years of neglect have ensured that no alterations have been made and the building remains entirely early eleventh century. A fine, small-scale example of what the Anglo-Saxons could do.

CORFE CASTLE **** £
Impossible to miss.

The superb natural location of this daunting fortress ensures a really enjoyable family day out. There was no need to construct a motte here. By Domesday the castle was in royal hands and stonework survives from an early castle. There is also a fine example of a **tower keep** built by **King Henry I** in 1105. Initially Henry imprisoned his elder brother, Robert, here in 1106, after their clash at the Battle of Tinchebrai in Normandy. Within a few months however he had moved him to Devizes Castle.

It is, however, the **West Bailey** that holds our main interest here. Post-war excavations have confirmed the existence of the postholes of a Saxon hall in this area. The Isle of Purbeck was already a royal hunting forest

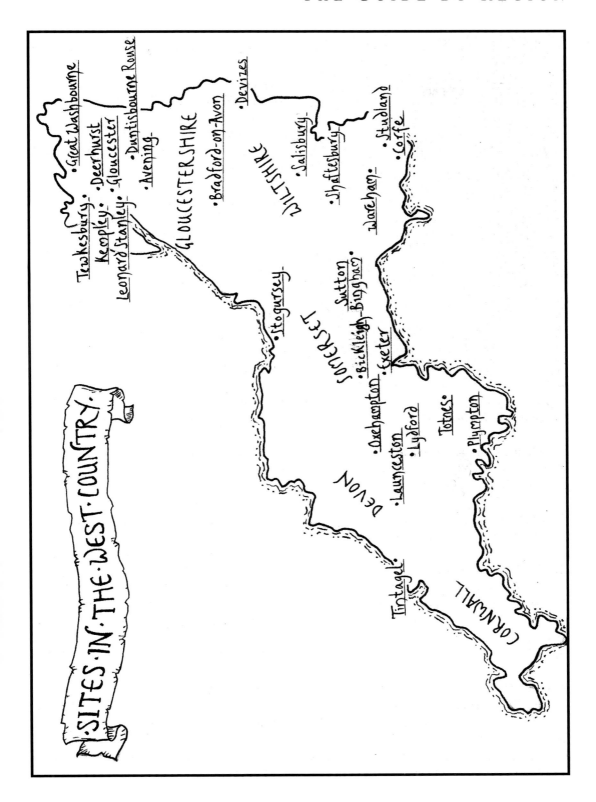

SITES·IN·THE·WEST·COUNTRY·

Tewkesbury·
·Great Washbourne
Kempley·
·Deerhurst
Leonard Stanley·
·Gloucester
·Duntisbourne Rouse
·Avening·
GLOUCESTERSHIRE
·Bradford-on-Avon
·Devizes

WILTSHIRE
·Salisbury
·Shaftesbury
·Studland
·Corfe
·Wareham·

·Togarsey·
Sutton
Bingham·
·Bickleigh
·Exeter
SOMERSET

·Okehampton
Launceston
·Lydford
Totnes·
·Plympton
DEVON

·Tintagel·
CORNWALL

125

Henry I's tower keep at Corfe Castle.

in Saxon times with a hunting lodge on this hill. It is therefore fairly certain that this delightful spot is in fact the location of the murder of **King Edward the Martyr** in 978, the foul and inauspicious deed that allowed Aethelred Unrede to accede to the throne of England aged 9 years. Our story starts here.

Political Background

The death of King Edgar in 975 led to a contested succession – not unusual in Anglo-Saxon England. Edgar, though only 31 or 32 years old, had had three wives and two surviving sons, or aethelings: one son, Edward, by his first wife, Aethelfaed, daughter of Ordmaer, and one son, Aethelred, by his third wife, Aelfthryth, daughter of Ealdorman Ordgar from Devon. In 975 Edward was 12 or 13 years old. Edgar had married Aethelfaed before he became king and it is thought that he intended the succession to pass to the son of his crowned queen, Aelfthryth. Unfortunately for the latter there was a problem caused by the fact that Edgar's second wife, Wulfthryth, was still alive and occupying the post of Abbess of Wilton near Salisbury. Wulfthryth withdrew to Wilton in around 965, having borne a daughter, Edith, for Edgar. This situation brought clerical censure, especially from Archbishop Dunstan.

The English political community split into two camps. Behind Edward lined up Dunstan, Ealdorman Aethelwine of East Anglia, Ealdorman Bryrhtnoth of Essex and Bishop Oswald of Worcester. Behind Aethelred, aged only 10 years old at the time, were Ealdorman Aelfhere of Mercia, the most powerful ealdorman, and Bishop Aethelwold of Winchester. Initially Edward's faction gained the upper hand and he was crowned at Kingston-upon-Thames in 975. However over the next three years Edward's faction lost support of both lay aristocracy and clerics. In early 978 the royal council suffered the collapse of a room in which it was meeting at Calne, causing death and injury. The scene was set for regicide.

The Foul Deed

On 18 March 978 King Edward, now aged 15 or 16 years, had come to Purbeck to hunt. Perhaps returning to the Corfe hunting lodge the sources are clear that he was murdered at this spot, perhaps on the orders of his stepmother, Aelfthryth, mother of his rival and half-brother Aethelred. William of Malmesbury, a contemporary historian, went further and involved her in the act of murder. While Edward was still on horseback she: 'allured him to her female blandishment and made him lean forward, and after saluting him, while he was eagerly drinking from the cup which had been presented, the dagger of an attendant pierced him through' – heavy stuff indeed.

At that Edward's horse galloped away and the dying man slipped from his saddle. One of his feet became entangled in its stirrup and he was dragged towards Wareham and through a wood. Thus was his body found and hurriedly buried in St Mary's church, Wareham (see Wareham). A **cottage** on the north-east side of the Corfe–Wareham road, the A351, commemorates this unfortunate end. It is named St Edward's Cottage and is 1 mile from Corfe.

Aftermath

This squalid murder brought to the throne one of the most notorious of English kings, Aethelred Unrede, at the age of 10. In the years before, around 984, his mother, the redoubtable but controversial Aelfthryth, held the reins of power on his behalf. Regicide was not unknown in tenth-century England but was a rare event. It somehow set the tone for Aethelred's reign. The weakened and

King Edward the Martyr died here near Corfe.

onto B4213 to Tirley. After ½ mile go straight on minor road to hamlet of Deerhurst.

There are four good reasons for visiting Deerhurst, but taken together the case is overwhelming:

- The priory church of St Mary is a fine example of a Saxon abbey church.
- Odda's Chapel, built in 1056, lay hidden beneath plaster until discovered in the nineteenth century and celebrates a major late-Saxon ealdorman.
- Deerhurst was the location chosen in October or November 1016 by King Edmund Ironside and Cnut when they met, it is said, on an island in the river to conclude a treaty and pact of friendship and divide the kingdom.
- It is a splendid setting on the banks of the river, ideal for a picnic.

divided government in the country opened the way for renewed and enlarged Viking attacks on England, which recommenced in 980. During the reign of Edgar the Peaceable between 959–75 few if any of these attacks occurred, no doubt deterred by a strong king and considerable fleet defence. Edgar is said to have put to sea over 3,000 ships each season. Such activity did not happen during Aethelred's troubled reign.

After a year Edward's body was moved to Shaftesbury Abbey (see Shaftesbury). His relics were enshrined there and miracles began to occur. In 1001 he was canonised and Shaftesbury became a major centre of pilgrimage. He had no children.

DEERHURST ✳✳✳✳

On river Severn, 2½ miles south of Tewksbury. Turn west off A38 Tewksbury–Gloucester road

St Mary's Church

Though modified in the fourteenth century, the tall dimensions of this superb building are unmistakably Saxon and much remains from that period: doors, blocked arches and windows, carvings, sculpture and double-headed windows, herringbone work and a ruined apse. Most of this dates from the ninth and tenth centuries – a monastery existed here by 804, which had become the pre-eminent religious house in this part of Gloucestershire by the time of the Conquest.

It was for this reason no doubt that Deerhurst was chosen for the landmark meeting between **King Edmund Ironside** and **Cnut**, son of Sweyn Forkbeard and King of Denmark, in the autumn of 1016, which occurred after Cnut's victory over the English forces led by Edmund at the Battle of Ashingdon in Essex. Previously, in 1016, the two men had fought a number of inconclusive battles in the south-west, but matters came

1. Frontispiece to King Edgar's charter for the New Minster, Winchester.

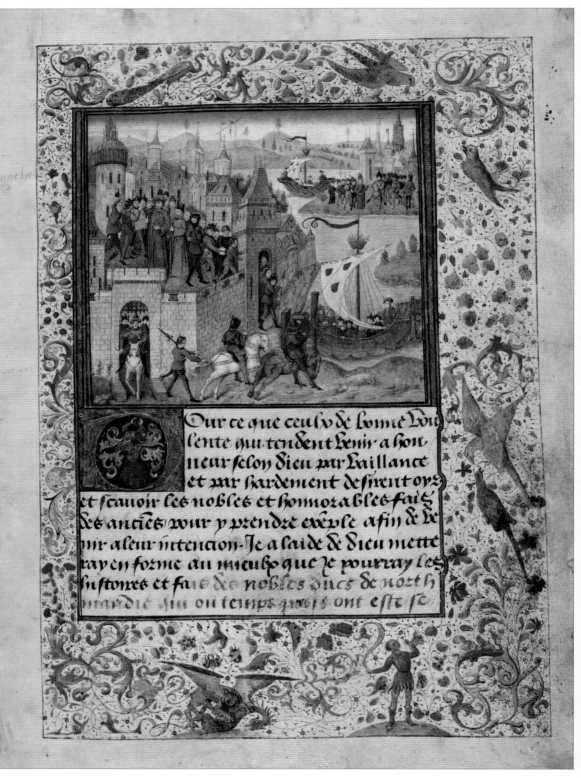

2. Rollo, founder of the Norman dynasty, arriving at Rouen from the Chroniques de Normandie.

3. *Cnut and Queen Emma present an altar cross to the New Minster, Winchester.*

4. *St Edward the Confessor in a 'Last Supper' depiction.*

5. Cnut and Queen Emma present an altar cross to the New Minster, Winchester.

6. *The Dreams of Henry I with an allusion to the* White Ship *disaster, as recounted by John of Worcester.*

7. *The delightful setting of Bosham church and quay in Chichester Harbour.*

8. *Guildford Castle has a high motte and a keep, now thought to have to have been built by Henry I.*

9. *The shrine of St Edward the Confessor, the centrepiece of Westminster Abbey.*

10. The death of Harold as per the Tapestry. Most scholars now favour the king being cut down by Norman knights as on the right.

11. Duke William landed here or hereabouts at Pevensey Fort.

12. *Norman might at Portchester.*

13. *Mortuary chest in Winchester Cathedral containing the bones of Cnut and Queen Emma, among others.*

14. If you are getting married and enjoy history, what better place to choose than Bickleigh?

15. Majestic Corfe Castle, scene of a dark deed in 978.

16. Fabulous wooden effigy of the unfortunate Robert, Duke of Normandy, who was buried in Gloucester Cathedral.

17. Fine twelfth-century wall paintings at Copford.

18. Southwell Minster west front.

19. The stylish Anglo-Saxon tower at Barton on Humber.

20. Winter sunset at Kirkdale Minster in North Yorkshire.

21. *The glory of Durham Cathedral's Norman nave. (By permission of Durham Cathedral)*

22. *Barfleur Harbour whence sailed the* White Ship *to disaster.*

23. *Even today the Normans make much of their king and queen!*

24. The powerful Abbey aux Hommes in Caen, built by the Conqueror and where he was buried.

25. The dawn of the Norman Conquest: the mouth of the river Dives, which acted as the concentration point for Duke William's fleet.

26. The impressive border fortress of Gisors Castle.

The fabulous Saxon Abbey church at Deerhurst.

Odda's Chapel, Deerhurst.

to a head at Ashingdon on 18 October as Edmund sought to prevent Cnut raiding into Mercia. The Anglo-Saxon Chronicle tells us emphatically that Edmund's forces were betrayed by Earl Eadric Streona during the battle but that Edmund managed to escape. Perhaps surprisingly, he retreated to Gloucestershire, Eadric's west-Mercian earldom. It is believed that Edmund had in fact been badly injured in the battle (although there may have been a subsequent one in the Forest of Dean).

Unexpectedly, Eadric brokered a deal between the two leaders and they met near Deerhurst on an island in the Severn. This could have been the monastery itself, an island itself at high tide on the flood plain. The two rivals affirmed their friendship, both with pledge and oath, and set the payment for Cnut's raiding army; they then divided England up between themselves: Edmund kept Wessex, smaller but politically more important, while Cnut took Mercia and the rest. A truly awesome historical moment in our story. They may have met alone – there was talk of one-to-one combat in heroic style. Within weeks Edmund was dead and Cnut became King of all England. No other candidate from the English ruling House of Cerdic succeeded in challenging Cnut; Edmund's sons were babies, while his brother, Eadwig, probably lacked sufficient landed wealth and resources. A revolt in favour of Eadwig was put down and Eadwig fled abroad in 1017. England had been conquered by the Danes and became a part of Cnut's Anglo-Scandinavian empire for twenty years.

Odda's Chapel lies 200yds past St Mary's church to the left. This virtually intact survival was dedicated by Bishop Ealdred of Worcester on 12 April 1056. It was built by **Earl Odda** to commemorate his brother <u>Aelfric</u>, who died here in 1053.

DEVIZES, St John's Church ***
On south-western edge of town centre just off A360 road to Salisbury.

A large Norman church with splendid crossing tower. Internally, the tower arches and particularly the chancel decoration with arcading, are noteworthy. The church with all its fine decoration was built in around 1130 by **Bishop Roger of Salisbury**, chancellor to Henry I. The remains of the nearby **castle** can be viewed from the west end of the churchyard. It is now a private house. It was rebuilt by Roger at the same time as the church but destroyed by Cromwell. Roger was one of the great Norman builders. After the Battle of Tinchebrai in 1106 Henry I incarcerated his elder brother Robert 'Curthose', Duke of Normandy, in this castle under the care of Roger (see Tinchebrai and Cardiff).

DUNTISBOURNE ROUSE, St Michael's Church **
1½ miles west of Cirencester–Gloucester road. Turn off A417N signposted to Duntisbourne Abbots and Duntisbourne Leer. In Leer turn left on minor road. After ¾ mile the church gate is seen on the right.

Gloucestershire specialises in hidden or tucked away places but this is one of the best. The delightful church is built on a slope leading down to the Dunt stream (named after a Saxon chief who lived at nearby Brimpsfield). The age of the building is uncertain. Although the nave is Saxon in style, a recent assessment puts the date no earlier than the twelfth century. The chancel and unusual crypt are early Norman in style, so we find ourselves in the Saxo-Norman overlap.

In the time of Edward the Confessor a Saxon named Ulward (or Alwead) held the manor. At Domesday it was held by durand, Sheriff of Gloucestershire, who

Duntisbourne Rouse – no windows on the north side of the nave!

'sub-let' to Ralph. The manor had two ploughs in demesne, three villains and one bordar with one plough, four slaves and 2 acres of meadow, all valued at 40*s* – not the wealthiest manor in the county. No wonder the church hasn't been much altered since.

EXETER, Rougemont Castle ***
City centre in north corner of old walled city next to Law Courts and Rougemont Gardens.

By the time of the Norman Conquest, Exeter had long been a regional centre in both Roman and Saxon times. Despite being a fully fortified Saxon burgh the city was sacked by the Danes in 876 and 1002, at which later time the city was held in dower by the recently married Queen Emma, second wife of Aethelred Unrede. In the winter of 1067–8 an uprising against the Normans was orchestrated by **Countess Gytha**, widow

of Godwin and mother of Harold II (see Bosham). The 'rebels' were besieged in the burgh by the Conqueror and his forces (which for the first time included Englishmen). They held out for eighteen days before mining weakened their defences. William granted the defenders terms and famously prevented looting by his troops by his 'international' force (at this stage he was still trying to be kind to the natives). Gytha took refuge on the Isle of Flatholme in the Bristol Channel.

Almost immediately William ordered the construction of a castle on this location, which we can therefore take to commemorate the only real attempt of any size to defy William in southern England. A few months later in 1068 the sons of Harold II attempted to overrun Bristol but were repulsed by Somerset thegns acting alone. Perhaps they had originally intended to co-ordinate with Gytha's uprising.

Rougemont Castle, Exeter, a Norman gatehouse keep.

The centrepiece of this castle was not a motte but the **gatehouse keep**, which survives. Interestingly the structure incorporates a number of Anglo-Saxon features, indicating that local Anglo-Saxon masons were employed in the construction. The bailey and some later stonework can be enjoyed in the adjoining Rougemont Gardens.

GLOUCESTER ****

Gloucester was for a long time an important stop in the annual royal itinerary. Kings undertook crown-wearing ceremonies here at Christmas.

Cathedral
City Centre.

This church only became a cathedral at the Reformation. Previously it had been a monastery of St Peter founded in around 681. In 1022 Benedictine rule was introduced and in 1072 the Norman Serlo was appointed abbot. He must have been an energetic and capable leader, for despite this still being front-line border country for the Normans, he built up the number of monks to 100 by the end of the century. Serlo began rebuilding his church in 1089 and it was consecrated in 1121. Much of it survives, especially the nave and piers, but note that the tower is fifteenth-century. The abbey quickly became the most important in the area.

The focus of our interest is the marvellous painted wooden effigy of **Robert 'Curthose', Duke of Normandy**, eldest son of the Conqueror and brother to kings William Rufus and Henry I. Robert was buried here because he had been captured by his younger brother Henry at the Battle of Tinchebrai (1106) in Normandy and then held prisoner in England at various locations, but latterly at Cardiff Castle under the protection of Robert, Earl of Gloucester, Henry's eldest bastard son (he had a few others). The effigy was made in Bristol in the thirteenth century and is now located in the **south side of the presbytery**. Note also the thirteenth-century stone effigy said to represent <u>Abbot Serlo</u>, founder of the abbey.

On the east walk of the cathedral cloister is the **chapter house**. Fire destroyed the original Norman building in 1102 but parts remain. Here the Conqueror gave the order to compile the Domesday Book at Christmas 1085. Robert Curthose is buried here but nothing remains.

St Oswald's Priory
City Centre north of the cathedral outside St Mary's Gate.

An Augustinian house that was rebuilt in the first half of the twelfth century. At the Reformation the north aisle was converted into a parish church, the ruins of which remain, including an arcade of Norman arches.

GREAT WASHBOURNE, St Mary's Church *

3 miles east of M5 J5. Take A46 east towards Evesham. After Beckford village (3 miles) take a right to Washbourne and Alderton. Village is on the right down a cul-de-sac.

The Domesday Book entry reads: '3 hides. There are 2 ploughs and 6 villains with 3 ploughs and 1 bordar and 9 slaves with a female slave.' It was worth 60*s*. As you turn into it, this small village appears to have changed little since 1086 (apart from the slaves and the valuation of course) – certainly the early Norman church hasn't. It is an absolute delight, and note the tympanum. The land belonged to Tewkesbury Abbey.

KEMPLEY, St Mary's Church **

1½ miles west of Dymock. Take B4221 west off J3 of M50. After 200yds, turn right to Kempley through Fishpool. By 'new' church on right, turn left in village and follow road and signposts to 'old' church on right.

At some stage this church lost its village which then built itself a 'new' and closer structure in 1903. The 'old' church may be redundant but provides us with something special. You are unlikely to encounter a 'madding crowd' here, which is a shame because this church contains some of the very finest Norman **wall paintings** in England (see also Copford, Hardham and Coombes).

In both the chancel and nave the paintings (frescoes) have been restored and dated to the 1120s. They include figures of a bishop (most likely the Bishop of Hereford) and of two lay figures usually interpreted as the church's founder, Hugh de Lacy, and his father Walter. The family came from Lassy in Normandy. Both are said to have fought at Hastings, as did Walter's eldest son, Roger. Walter died in 1085 after a fall from the tower of his newly built church of St Peter in Hereford. Roger inherited and is shown in Domesday Book as lord of the manor of Kempley. In 1095 he joined an unsuccessful rebellion against William Rufus, and the family lands, which stretched along the Welsh border and included castles at Weobley and Longtown, passed to his brother, Hugh. Hugh unfortunately died in 1121 before the church was complete. He also founded Llantony Priory in Monmouthshire in 1108.

Recent work has revealed another surprise in this building. The seventeenth-century ceiling in the nave has been removed to reveal the original roof timbers. These have been dated to the late 1120s and are made from trees from a single wood. They currently constitute the oldest dated, open roof without tie beams in north-west Europe. The west door is also original. The rest of the church, with the exception of the tower and south porch, is largely original and dates from the 1120s. It has a splendid chancel arch. Not to be missed.

LAUNCESTON, Castle ** £
Town centre. (EH)

This castle dominates not only the town but the surrounding countryside too. Although there is plenty of later masonry the outstanding feature of the remaining structure is the very high motte, set on the end of a rocky spur. The motte supports a late Norman shell keep. A castle existed here by 1076. It may have been constructed in the immediate aftermath of the Exeter revolt of 1067–8 by the Conqueror himself or, more likely, by his half-brother **Robert, Count of Mortain**. At any rate it is referred to in Domesday Book as 'the Count's castle'. Robert, being one of William's main supporters, was granted vast estates in the West Country. He was easily the dominant landowner in Cornwall.

The castle protects what was the main route into Cornwall (before the Saltash bridge was built), where it crosses the river Tamar at nearby Polson – originally as a ford. The river Kensey, a tributary of the Tamar, provides defensive protection for the castle's north flank. The Tamar forms the county boundary so Launceston is only just in Cornwall. It is a Norman town that grew up around the castle. Perhaps surprisingly, it was the county town until the nineteenth century.

Robert's son, William of Mortain, forfeited the castle in 1104 after siding with Robert Curthose against Henry I. The castle passed through subsequent Earls of Cornwall to the Duchy. Go on a fine day to ensure you don't miss the view.

LEONARD STANLEY, St Swithin's Church **
1½ miles south of A419 Stroud–M5 J13 road. Take minor road south out of Stonehouse to Leonard Stanley and Frocester. Church is at south end of village off the minor road.

This is Berkeley country and has been since the Conquest (with one interruption). The church and other remains form part of an Augustinian priory founded by Roger de Berkeley (d. 1131) between 1121 and 1129. The crossing tower survives, providing a real Norman atmosphere within. The Norman capitals in the chancel are exceptionally good. To the south-west of the church can be found the remains of an eleventh-century chapel, now on private land within a farmyard. Herringbone masonry is visible.

LYDFORD, Castles and Ramparts **
Lydford is ¾ mile west of A386 Okehampton–Tavistock road. Turn off on minor road to the village, which now covers but a fraction of the area originally occupied in Anglo-Saxon times.

In Anglo-Saxon times Lydford became a burgh and mint. Domesday Book indicates that it was in royal hands in the eleventh century and generated considerable revenues for the Crown from tin mining. By 1086 it was one of the four main towns of Devon after Exeter (Totnes, Barnstaple and Okehampton were the others). Much has changed in the intervening 1,000 years.

Town Ramparts
The layout of Lydford remains as laid out by King Alfred in the 880s. It formed part of his Burghal Hideage and was one of four such towns in Devon. The earthwork walls of his burgh are perhaps best seen at the north-eastern edge of the village on both sides of the 'main street'. A royal mint began operation in the reign of Edward the Martyr (975–8). A small collection of coins from the mint is kept in the Castle Inn, so a pint or two is a must here. Lydford was the birthplace of Aelfthryth, Edgar's queen. She was the daughter of Ordgar, a Devon landowner born around 945, and the mother of Aethelred Unrede. Notoriously she probably organised the murder of Aethelred's half-brother, Edward the Martyr at Corfe (see Corfe). Despite the burghal defences the Anglo-Saxon Chronicle records that Lydford was attacked and burned by the Danes in 997, during the traumas of Aethelred's reign. A small **monument** was erected in 1990 to commemorate this and stands opposite the

church gate at the south-west end of the main street.

Ringwork Castle (the Norman Fort)

South-west edge of main street behind and beyond the parish church. N.B. This is not the stone keep by the side of the church.

Probably erected soon after the Conquest, this fortification utilised both the existing burghal ramparts and the natural steepness of the slope down to the river Lyd. A spectacular defensive location especially in winter. In the late twelfth century this site was abandoned and the new castle was built next to the church. Although this has the look of a motte and bailey, in fact the earth was piled up above the original ground floor of the keep. For many centuries the new castle served as a prison. The adjoining church is of the later Middle Ages and very pleasant to visit. Altogether Lydford offers much of historical interest for the visitor.

OKEHAMPTON, Castle * £

1 mile south-west of town centre on B3260 Okehampton–Holsworthy/Tavistock. (EH)

Okehampton was a Norman plantation town founded by Baldwin de Brionne who was made Sheriff of Devon after its conquest in 1068. Unusually the major streets followed a linear pattern of High, West, Fore and East Streets along the old A30 route now bypassed. The castle is also attributed to Baldwin de Brionne, who chose a fine location. Although somewhat dominated by later masonry from the Courtenay Earl of Devon era, the original motte with a small keep (eastern half) survive from the early Norman era together with a defensive bank to the west of the motte.

Baldwin de Brionne or Meules was the younger son of Gilbert, Count of Brionne who himself was an illegitimate son of Duke

Robert I of Normandy and became tutor to the young Duke William in 1040. He lasted only a few months in this dangerous position before being murdered, the family then losing possession of Brionne. Baldwin was thus a kinsman of the Conqueror and one of a number that William placed in key positions. He also held Exeter Castle. Baldwin's elder brother was Richard Fitz Gilbert who founded the Clare dynasty from the name of their principal residence in Suffolk (see Clare).

PLYMPTON, Castle *

In old Plympton village near the church (St Maurice), just 1 mile north of A38 Exeter–Plymouth road but actually not straightforward to find. Turn right off A38 west at large roundabout by the river Plym onto B3416 Chaddleswood road. After 1½ miles turn right through Plympton to Old Plympton. Castle is west of medieval church.

Plympton was once a port in its own right and certainly in the mid-twelfth century a much more important town than Sutton, its offshoot across the Plym and the forerunner of Plymouth. Plympton was a royal manor in Domesday Book but early in the reign of Henry I was granted to Richard de Redvers (d. 1107), one of Henry's inner circle. Redvers held land in various parts of Normandy, near Caen, at Vernon in the Vexin and at Nehou in the Cotentin, and was one of Henry's very early and most loyal supporters – going back to Henry's early days in the 1090s in the Cotentin. On Henry's accession Richard received a lavish grant, including lands throughout Devon and in Hampshire and the Isle of Wight. Richard built this castle. Later Richard's son Baldwin was made Earl of Devon by Henry. During the Anarchy Baldwin sided with Matilda. King Stephen duly besieged the castle and seriously damaged/

destroyed it. It was rebuilt so the imposing motte may not be the original early twelfth-century version. Nevertheless the unimpeded site gives a fine indication of the layout and extent of a typical motte and bailey.

SALISBURY (OLD SARUM), Ruins of Castle, Cathedral and Royal Palace *** £
2 miles north of Salisbury on A345 road to Amesbury. (EH)

This site has everything for the medievalist. The natural hilltop site lies at the junction of three Roman roads and the outer defences go back to the Iron Age. In the late Saxon period defences were strengthened against the Danes. A **castle** was established in the early years after Hastings, certainly before the Conqueror chose this as the location to pay off his army in 1070 with Anglo-Saxon treasure acquired during the Conquest. The geographic location and the size of the site must have been the attractions. The royal castle was enlarged by **Roger, Bishop of Salisbury** in the early twelfth century, including the stone keep or **Great Tower**. Unfortunately the masonry remains are scanty.

Bishop Roger also built a **Royal Palace** for Henry I during the same period. The remains also lie within the **Inner Bailey**. In 1075–8 the Anglo-Saxon see was transferred from Sherborne to Old Sarum and work begun on a Norman cathedral here by Bishop Hereman and his successor St Osmund. That prodigious builder, Bishop Roger, greatly extended the building. However by 1220 the cathedral community had fallen out with the military personnel in the castle and water supplies were proving a problem, so the decision was taken to move the cathedral 2 miles south to the banks of the river Avon. Old Sarum was never the same again and all that remains of Hereman's **cathedral** are the foundations,

painstakingly excavated so that one can still appreciate the sheer size of the structure.

SHAFTESBURY, Abbey ** £
Town-centre hilltop, signposted.

In 979, a year after his murder at Corfe, the body of **King Edward the Martyr** was moved from St Mary's church, Wareham, to this nunnery. His presence very quickly attracted pilgrims and miracles and in 1002 he was canonised. His bones were enshrined in the abbey. Although little remains standing, the plan of the old structure is clear and the probable location of Edward's relics is indicated on the north side of the altar. A modern **altar** has been built in the ruins of the chancel in his honour (see Corfe Castle). Edward's relics were hidden at the Dissolution and re-discovered in 1931. However when the abbey was sold in the 1950s the relics were bizarrely relocated to Woking and are now kept in a Russian Orthodox chapel. Cnut died in this abbey in 1035 but was buried in Winchester.

STOGURSEY, St Andrew's Church *
East end of village centre.

A church with much Norman work but of two distinct periods. The original church was built around 1080 by William de Falaise and survives as the crossing tower and transepts. Between 1100–7 William's son, also William, presented it to the Benedictine Abbey of Lonlay, 30 miles south-west of Falaise in Normandy. It became a priory. About 1180 the chancel was extended eastwards to form a choir in the late Norman style. In 1414 this foundation was sequestered by Henry V as an alien priory during the Hundred Years War with France, then given to Eton College by its founder Henry VI. Eton still possesses the original

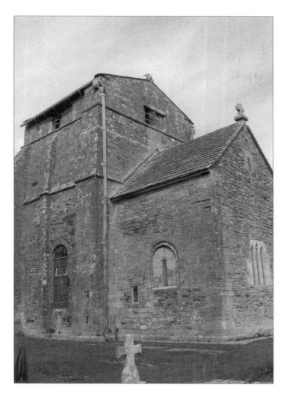

The angular lines of Studland church.

Chantry chapel commemorating Robert Fitz Haimon, Tewkesbury.

grant by William de Falaise, which was witnessed by Henry I himself.

STUDLAND, St Nicholas Church **

4 miles by road north of Swanage. Just east of crossroads on B3351 Corfe–Sandbanks ferry road. Take minor road east off B3351, church on left.

A virtually complete Norman church with only a few later windows and the south porch. Both the exterior and the dark interior are as genuinely Norman as we encounter in England. Precise dating is difficult but most authorities plump for early Norman (possibly 1090–1120) because of the lack of zigzag decoration. At Domesday, one Hamo held Studland from Robert, Count of Mortain, the Conqueror's half-brother, who

held vast tracts of land in the West Country. A great site with marvellous views of both the sea and surrounding countryside.

SUTTON BINGHAM, All Saints Church *

Next to eponymous reservoir 4 miles south of Yeovil. Turn right off A37 south Yeovil–Dorchester road 3 miles out of Yeovil onto minor road to Sutton Bingham and Halstock. Cross reservoir, church is on left down leafy lane.

Dated to 1111 in the guidebook, the church may have been built by Roger Arundel, who was lord of the manor in Domesday Book and a substantial landowner in the county. A fine small church, just nave and chancel and no tower, in lovely surroundings. Norman doorways and windows plus unexpectedly large chancel arch (dated by Pevsner to late Norman). Impressive wall paintings from around 1300.

TEWKESBURY, Abbey ***
South end of town centre on A430 road to Gloucester.

Many people's favourite Norman church. The original tower, the nave and piers and the magnificent west end of this most aristocratic of churches all survive. An abbey has been on this site since 715. In 1087 **Robert Fitz Haimon**, a favourite of William Rufus, became lord of the manor and set about rebuilding the Benedictine house. On the **north side of the choir** is a **chantry chapel** for Robert, built around 1400. The new church was finally consecrated in 1121, by which time Robert had died and his son-in-law, **Robert, Earl of Gloucester**, had become patron. Robert was the eldest bastard son of Henry I and very much in favour with Henry, especially after the *White Ship* disaster in 1120 when his legitimate son was drowned.

The church is a treasure trove of later medieval monuments and also of memorials from the Battle of Tewkesbury (1471), a crucial encounter in the Wars of the Roses.

TINTAGEL, St Merteriana's Church **
½ mile west of village centre above Glebe Cliff. Signposted.

Built from 1080 by **Robert, Count of Mortain**, his son William, and Reginald de Dunstanville, one of Henry I's many illegitimate children. Its cruciform shape survives together with north and south doors, Norman windows in the nave and chancel, plus the chancel arch. Reginald probably built the first elements of Tintagel castle later in the twelfth century. Gets very busy in August.

TOTNES, Castle * £
Town centre, north-west side – still dominates town to north and east. (EH)

Totnes was one of the four main burghs of Devon in Anglo-Saxon England and the central streets still follow that pattern (see North and South Street). The castle was most probably built sometime in 1068–9 after the Norman campaign against the Exeter revolt. It was almost certainly erected by Judhael de Totnes (d. 1123), a Breton who was given over 100 manors in south Devon by the Conqueror. The original early Norman motte and bailey still survives, though a later shell keep sits upon the motte. The motte truly imposes itself on the surrounding Dart Valley, of which it provides great views.

Totnes flourished and by 1086 was the second-largest town in Devon. Judhael seems to have fallen out with William Rufus soon after the latter's succession – perhaps because he supported Duke Robert in the 1088 revolt. At any rate, Judhael lost possession of Totnes, which Rufus gave to one of his favourites, Roger de Nonant, in 1089. On Henry I's accession Judhael was back in favour and compensated with the grant of Barnstaple.

WAREHAM **

The Walls
Surround the old part of the town situated between the rivers Frome and Piddle.

Wareham was one of Alfred the Great's burghs, which he fortified to oppose the Danes in the ninth century. In the Tribal Hideage list there are more than sixty such towns in Wessex. The fortifications were of course designed to keep marauding invaders out of the town, offering protection for the townsfolk and those of the surrounding countryside. Their function contrasts starkly with that of Norman castles designed to protect the castle garrison and were, more often than not, located in the countryside. Wareham's fortune is to have inherited the earth ramparts of virtually all its **town walls**, which date back to Alfred except on the south side. They make a very pleasant walk.

St Martin's Church KAL

Situated at the north entrance to the town east of North Street (B3075), next to the walls.

A delightful Anglo-Saxon church which was founded in around 1020 and has twelfth-century wall paintings. Its main point of interest, however, is that **King Edward the Martyr** was buried here after his murder at nearby Corfe in 978. He rested in these modest surroundings for a year before his body was moved to Shaftesbury Abbey.

EAST OF ENGLAND

ANSTEY, Castle *

This small village lies in delightful countryside 10 miles north-west of Bishop's Stortford. The castle remains lie behind the church at the west end of the village, accessible off the B1038 Buntingford–Clavering road on minor roads 2½ miles north from Brent Pelham or Great Hormead.

The motte and bailey makes a fine group with the late Norman church and surviving moat. The latter is unusually well preserved and still holds water. Pettifer tells us that the castle was most probably first constructed by **Count Eustace of Boulogne** soon after the Conquest. In 1944 a wayward American bomber crashed into the motte, which has survived.

The walls of the Anglo-Saxon burgh of Wareham.

THE BATTLE OF ASHINGDON (18 October 1016) ++

Strategic Background and Campaign

The Battle of Hastings is universally known as the date when the Norman Conquest of England began, but there was another battle almost exactly fifty years earlier, which ushered in the Danish Conquest of the country. After nearly twenty years of raiding, Sweyn Forkbeard, King of Denmark, drove out Aethelred Unrede in the summer of 1013 and became King of all England. He died little more than six months later however, in February 1014 at his headquarters in Gainsborough, Lincolnshire. Aethelred returned from exile in Normandy but died in April 1016.

Sweyn's eldest son, Cnut, was unable to command the allegiance of all the English nobles; many in Wessex and London now preferred Edmund Ironside, Aethelred's eldest surviving son by his first marriage to Aelfgifu of Northumbria, as king, and so he was duly proclaimed in London. Cnut first attacked London without success and then struck westwards to engage Ironside in battle at Penselwood (Dorset) and at Sherston (Wiltshire) but was defeated. This resulted in Edmund being able to go on the offensive. He relieved the Danish siege of London and Cnut retired to winter positions in Sheppey, Kent. As Ironside advanced towards Cnut his fortunes were seemingly boosted by the defection of Eadric Streona (the Greedy), once Aethelred's right-hand man. Cnut responded by raiding towards Mercia, presumably ferrying his men by ship to the Crouch estuary in Essex. According to the Anglo-Saxon Chronicle, he was confronted by an English army led by King Edmund Ironside at a hill called Assandun, Essex.

The Battle

Edmund's troops included elements from Wessex, East Anglia and Mercia. Some were no doubt local levies but it is thought he may have had the larger army. Opinion differs as to whether the battle was fought on the hill or whether Cnut drew up his forces on the lower ground midway between nearby Canewdon and Ashingdon. I prefer the hill as the lower ground could well have been marshy in medieval times.

Edmund probably drew up his own forces in the centre, with Ulfcetel of East Anglia and Eadric of Mercia on the left and right flanks respectively. Edmund may have attacked first and his left and centre advanced more quickly than Eadric on the right. In fact the Anglo-Saxon Chronicle suggests Eadric's force remained uncommitted and retreated from the field. The Danish left was thus able to roll up the English flank and envelop the rest of the Edmund's army. The English resisted stoutly until late afternoon. Perhaps surprisingly, Edmund was able to escape the field but his army suffered heavy casualties amongst the nobility: killed were Ulfcetel, Aeltric Ealdorman of Hampshire, Godwine of Lindsey, Aethelweard and the bishops of Dorchester and the Abbot Ramsey. However it is probable that the most significant event to occur that day was the serious wounding of King Edmund.

Aftermath and Commentary

The traditional account of Eadric's treachery in battle given above is called into question by Edmund's destination after the battle. He headed for Gloucestershire to the heartland of Eadric's support. Here Eadric and the council brokered a peace between the two kings. A week or two after Assandun they met on an island in the Severn near Deerhurst (Ola's Island) where they divided the kingdom: Edmund retaining Wessex and

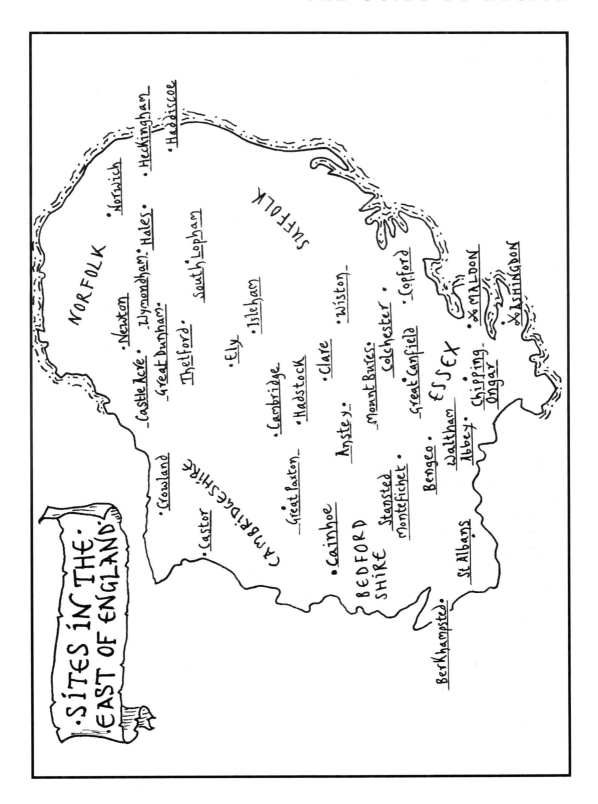

·Sites in the·
East of England

NORFOLK

SUFFOLK

ESSEX

CAMBRIDGESHIRE

BEDFORD-
SHIRE

·Heckingham
·Haddiscoe
·Norwich
·Newton
·Wymondham·Hales·
·Great Dunham·
·South Lopham
·Isleham
·Ely
·Thetford·
·Wiston·
·Clare
·Hadstock
·Cambridge
·Copford
Mount Bures·
·Colchester
·Great Canfield
·MALDON
·ASHINGDON
·Chipping-
Ongar
·Crowland
·Anstey·
·Great Paxton
·Bengeo
·Waltham
Abbey·
·Castor
·Stansted
Montefichet·
·Cainhoe
·St Albans
·Berkhampsted·

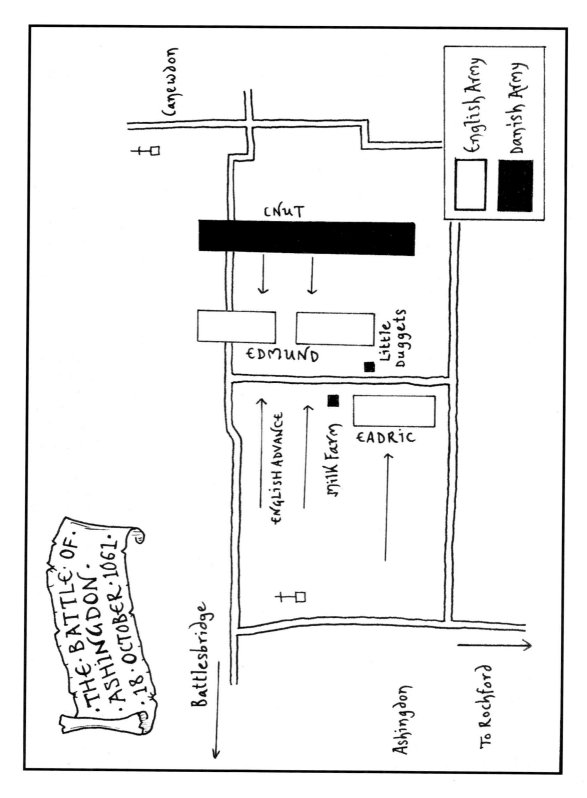

THE · BATTLE · OF · ASHINGDON · 1061 · 18 · OCTOBER ·

Canewdon

English Army

Danish Army

CNUT

EDMUND

Little Duggets

English Advance

Milk Farm

EADRIC

Battlesbridge

Ashingdon

To Rochford

Cnut gaining Mercia, to add to his rule of the north (see Deerhurst). After Assandun Edmund's activity seems to have slowed down (although there may have been a further confrontation with Cnut in the Forest of Dean), perhaps because he was now incapacitated from his wound. At any rate he died on 30 November 1016 in London, leaving the field open for Cnut.

Although with hindsight the Danish takeover of England may look to have been somewhat inevitable, at the time it certainly didn't seem that way. Cnut was barely 20 years old and had little experience of military leadership. To quote Higham (*The Death of Anglo-Saxon England*, p. 76): 'By the eve of the Battle of Ashingdon, Cnut had lost the support of all significant sections of the English elite and was nothing more than a Viking war-lord facing the prospect of imminent defeat at the hands of superior forces closing in on him under resolute leadership.' A recipe for battlefield treachery. What price the Norman Conquest (and indeed the next 500 years) if Edmund had been victorious and lived? Old England died here.

Location and What to See
The location of the battle, the hill at Assandun, is interpreted by most modern commentators as Ashingdon near Rayleigh in southern Essex, and close to the Crouch estuary where Cnut's ships may have been moored. However, Ashdown in northern Essex near Saffron Walden also lies on an elevated plateau and has been championed as the likely site. In strategic terms it has some advantages as a place where Edmund could have confronted Cnut (raiding into or returning from Mercia) with a predominantly Mercian/East Anglian army. It is known that Cnut built a minster in commemoration of the battle that was founded in 1020 with Stigand as priest (later to be Archbishop of

Canterbury). The existing churches at both alternative locations offer no suggestion of such antiquity, but the fine church at Hadstock, 5 miles from Ashdon and on the same plateau, is of sufficient size and age to have perhaps fulfilled that role (see Hadstock).

*Here at Ashingdon St Andrew's Church is situated on the **hill** on which the battle may have been fought. Looking north-east, the village and church at Canewdon can be seen across the valley. The land between the villages is the other possible location for the action. Church is open summer afternoons at the weekend.*

BENGEO, St Leonard's Church *
1 mile north-east of Hertford town centre over river Lea. Travelling northwards turn right off B158 Hertford–Thundridge/ Buntingford road at Holy Trinity church (Victorian) into New Road and proceed ½ mile before turning right into St Leonard's Road. Open summer afternoons at weekends.

A splendid example of a virtually intact Norman village church, comprising nave, chancel and apse. Good windows. At Domesday the parish/village was held by no fewer than five members of the Norman aristocracy, the largest landowner being Hugh de Beauchamp. Pre-Conquest, two of the Anglo-Saxon landowners were housecarls to King Edward.

BERKHAMSTED, Castle ***
Just north of railway station on the Ashridge road.

With the grand remains of this motte and bailey castle we are doubly blessed. Firstly the motte is one of the most impressively situated in England – and a high one. It is surrounded by the remains of the bailey and later developments of the castle. It is unclear exactly when the castle was first built, but it is mentioned in Domesday Book and attributed to **Robert Count of Mortain** (the Conqueror's half-brother). However there is good reason to assume that it was built twenty years earlier in the first days of the Conquest.

In late November 1066 the Normans fired Southwark but turned away from London, initially heading south. In a huge sweep they eventually crossed the Thames at Wallingford. Here they turned east and at Berkhamsted met with a delegation of the remaining English leaders (there is a school which claims this was at Little Berkhamsted but most scholars plump for the former location). These leaders included **Edgar Aetheling**, nominally King of England; Earls Edwin and Morcar; Ealdred, Archbishop of York; and Bishops Wulfstan and Walter (Archbishop Stigand of Canterbury had already submitted at Wallingford). The party submitted to Duke William here and offered him the crown of England. This castle serves as a monument to that inglorious day.

After Count Robert's son, William of Mortain, sided unsuccessfully with Duke Robert of Normandy against King Henry I in 1104, the castle became royal property. It was a popular residence for medieval queens like Margaret of Anjou, Henry VI's queen.

CAINHOE Castle (near Clophill) **
West of A507 Ampthill–Baldock road on bend 1 mile east of Clophill roundabout. Road is fast-flowing at this point so park on minor road to Upper Gravenhurst and take footpath north, earthworks are on right-hand side.

A hidden gem, this motte and bailey castle occupies a fine site above the river Flit. A steep motte dominates the site which also accommodated no less than three bailies. The earthworks are well preserved but no stonework remains. The castle was built by Nigel d'Albini, brother of Richard, Abbot of St Albans, and uncle to William, of the same name, and chief butler (see Wymondham). Nigel was described as a 'vigorous knight' and was sent by William Rufus to invade Scotland with a strong force of knights in around 1092, to revenge a raid on Northumberland and Durham carried out by the Scottish king, Malcolm.

CAMBRIDGE **

Holy Sepulchre Church £
City centre west side, corner of Bridge Street and Round Church Street.

This round church was built some time after 1130 by the Fraternity of the Holy Sepulchre, an order probably of Austin canons associated with guarding the Holy Land and the Holy Sepulchre after the First Crusade. Its design mirrors the Rotunda of the church of the Holy Sepulchre in Jerusalem. It is one of only four round churches still in use in England. The church was extensively restored in 1841, thus ensuring the interior of the circular church is wholly Norman.

St Mary Magdalene Church (Barnwell) KAL
In the eastern suburbs of the city located right on the A1303 Cambridge–Newmarket road between a bend at the eastern end of the dual carriageway and the disused Barnwell railway station. 1¼ miles east of the ring road.

Formerly a chapel for a leper hospital, this is an unexpected delight in run-down surroundings. Virtually complete and unspoiled, this building gives a real flavour of the mid-twelfth-century Norman style.

St Mary Magdelene church at Barnwell, Cambridge.

It was restored by Sir Giles Scott in the nineteenth century.

Castle
West side of river Cam on Castle Street, next to County Council offices.

William the Conqueror erected a motte and bailey castle here in 1068, one of the early castles in England. Only the motte remains, about 40ft high and impressively steep. It was built on the site of the Roman/Saxon town, forcing the locals to migrate to the present city location on the east bank of the Cam. The stonework of Edward I's later defences was stripped in the later Middle Ages for use in building the university colleges.

CASTLE ACRE, Priory and Castle ***
£

Priory at south end of village, castle at north end. (EH)

Immediately after the Battle of Hastings the Conqueror created four units of land area to secure the defence of the Sussex coast and hence the crossings back to Normandy. In 1073 William carved out a fifth unit based around Bramber near Steyning, taking land from both William de Warenne and Roger de Montgomery (see Bramber). In compensation Warenne was given extensive lands in west Norfolk. Here at Castle Acre, Warenne is thought to have initially constructed a stone country house/hunting lodge on the banks of the river Nar, which gave access to the sea at Lynn at the time.

In 1085 Warenne's wife Gunnhilda died in childbirth here. Over the centuries historians have tried to prove that she was

145

The magnificent west door of Castle Acre Priory in the late Norman style.

in fact a daughter of the Conqueror. A foundation charter for a Cluniac **priory** at Castle Acre was issued between 1087 and 1089, probably to commemorate Gunnhilda. After his father's death in 1088 **William de Warenne II, Earl of Surrey**, confirmed the foundation, added a further grant of land and continued the building work. Finally consecrated in 1146–8, the priory survives today as a fabulous late Norman ruin in delightful surroundings. Around 1140 the second or third William de Warenne gutted the hunting lodge and fortified the site as civil war loomed. Much of the **castle** ruin dates from this time but the site of the hunting lodge also remains.

CASTOR, St Kyneburga's Church *

Village centre ½ mile south of A47 Peterborough–Uppingham road, 3 miles west of Peterborough.

St Kyneburga has quite simply the most impressive Norman tower of any parish church in England. Its prominent position above the village serves to enhance the effect. Only the spire is later. Inside the church the tower arches and capitals are equally impressive. Note the fine south doorway and the inscription above the priest's door on the south side of the chancel which indicates that the church was dedicated in 1124. A Saxon minster had existed here and there are one or two Saxon elements in the church. At Domesday the church belonged to Peterborough Abbey (now Cathedral).

CHIPPING ONGAR ***

Castle
Town centre, east side of High Street Park by library.

Chipping Ongar was the centre of a Saxon hundred, which in the Domesday Book contained twenty-six villages and 147 estates; first recorded in 1015. At the Conquest the hundred was given to **Count Eustace of Boulogne**, William I's brother-in-law and a big player in the Norman invasion. Although a castle is not recorded here until Henry II's reign, when it was owned by Richard de Lucy; we can be almost certain that the splendid remains of the motte and bailey castle date from Eustace's time because he retained the town as the principal residence of the hundred. There are also fragments of a town enclosure west of the castle which are thought to relate to a Norman plantation town which may have failed. On the eastern side of the castle are fragments of an outer moat which can be observed on an interesting circular walk around the outside of the castle.

Chipping Ongar was given by Eustace in dowry to his daughter, Matilda, when she married Stephen of Blois sometime before 1125. On Stephen's usurpation of the throne in 1136 this Matilda thus became Queen of England.

St Martins of Tours Church
¼ mile south-west of the castle.

The building has a surviving Norman nave and chancel built in about 1080 as part of the Norman plantation town. Note the small windows and liberal use of Roman bricks.

CLARE, Castle **
Town centre, adjacent to car park for Clare Country Park. If you are a railway enthusiast combine two interests and enjoy the old railway station preserved in the park.

The Honour of Clare was awarded to **Richard Fitz Gilbert** after the Norman Conquest. A motte and bailey castle was erected as Richard's principal residence (first mentioned in 1090). The high conical **motte** survives and can be explored. The surviving masonry on the motte is of a later date. A disused railway station occupies the site of the inner bailey. Fitz Gilbert's descendants took the name de Clare.

COLCHESTER ***

Castle £
Town centre, north of High Street at east end.

There is perhaps a surprising reason to visit Colchester: it possesses the largest Norman building in England. Begun by 1076 this hall keep is similar to the more famous White Tower in London and thus was probably designed by the same architect, Bishop Gundulf of Rochester. Its size probably reflects the strategic importance of the town and the continuing threat of Danish raids at that time. This keep is now a museum and contains interesting Norman features inside, such as windows, fireplaces and garderobes. Note also the 'sheila-na-gig', a twelfth-century fertility symbol from nearby Easthorpe church. Like Norwich this was a royal castle whose first steward was Eudo Dapifer.

Holy Trinity Church
Trinity Street within a limited-access town centre.

Statue of Eudo Dapifer on Colchester Town Hall.

The west tower is the only Anglo-Saxon survival in the town. Note the windows, the small doorway with a triangular head and the use of Roman bricks. It dates from around 1000.

St Julian and St Botolph's Church

Priory Street on the east side of Queen Street and the town centre.

The splendid remains of the first Augustinian priory in England, founded in 1103. The nave and the west front survive, though the latter is in the late Norman style.

Town Hall

North side of High Street.

Fronting the **High Street** is an early twentieth-century **statue** of <u>Eudo Dapifer</u> amongst others. His full name was Eudo Fitz Hubert of Ryes (d. 1120) and he was the son of the Hubert who had given sanctuary to Duke William of Normandy in 1047 when an attempt had been made on his life. After the Conquest Eudo became a household steward (dapifer) to the Conqueror. He became wealthy and held land in ten counties in the east of England as well as the castle and Honour of Preaux in Normandy. William made him constable of Colchester Castle and the first Sheriff of Essex. About 1088 he married Rohese, daughter of Richard Fitz Gilbert of Clare and Tonbridge.

He was a financial man who, as a member of Ranulph Flambard's coterie, rose to be chief steward or seneschal under William Rufus and achieved the status of baron – he was in fact a proto-baron of the exchequer. He was in regular attendance on the king and witnessed many royal writs. He was present in the New Forest on the day Rufus was killed and would surely have an interesting tale to tell there. Eudo appears to have continued in favour with Henry I. He founded St John's Abbey in Colchester (nothing remains) while a daughter married William de Mandeville.

COPFORD, St Michael and All Angels Church **

1½ miles south-east of A12 Colchester–London road next to Copford Hall but not easy to find. Exit at Marks Tey. Take B1408 back towards Colchester. After ½ mile turn right to Copford Green. Take minor road for church.

A virtually complete (except for the south aisle) Norman church, comprising nave, chancel and apse dated to around 1130. It was built as the chapel next to the manor house (the site is now occupied by Copford

Hall) by the bishops of London, who had owned the manor since 995 as their summer residence. The glory of Copford are the original **wall paintings** (also dated to 1130), which occur throughout the original church. The apse in particular remains exactly as built. These Norman wall paintings are among the best in England. During the Reformation the bishops were dispossessed.

CROWLAND (OR CROYLAND)
Abbey ***
6 miles north-east of Peterborough. East side of town centre.

This important abbey was founded by St Guthlac at the end of the seventh century. During its long history its buildings suffered two disastrous fires and an earthquake. In 1109 Abbot Joffrid of Orleans laid the foundation stone of the third abbey to be built in the Norman style. A fire in 1143 destroyed most of this work however – only the splendid **dogs tooth arch** at the east end of the Old Nave and a font survive. The arch was part of Joffrid's central tower which indicates how much larger the Norman church was. Hereward the Wake and his wife Torfrida are said to have been buried in the Anglo-Saxon abbey that burned down in 1091, together with his mother Countess Godifu (Lady Godiva). Nothing survives.

The star of the show is **Waltheof, Earl of Huntingdon**, who was brought here by the monks after his execution by the Conqueror following his part in the 1075 revolt in East Anglia. The charges against Waltheof were largely trumped up or exaggerated. He was the only Anglo-Saxon of note to be executed by William. His **statue** can be seen on the fourth tier down (third from left) on the **west front** of the Old Nave. The statues, originally brightly coloured, are thought to be fifteenth century. On the third tier down,

Statue of Waltheof, Earl of Huntingdon, at Crowland Abbey.

left-hand side, is **William the Conqueror** with **Queen Matilda** on the right. The statue of **Archbishop Lanfranc of Canterbury** lies on the fourth tier down, first on the left. Lanfranc, a renowned scholar on the European stage, was a close confidant of King William. Interestingly, after Waltheof's involvement in the revolt he sought the advice of Lanfranc on what to do. Lanfranc recommended he told all to the king. Waltheof followed this advice but his life was not spared. Do these statues send a message?

ELY, Cathedral ***
City centre.

Ely has been a major religious site at least since 673. After the Norman Conquest work began on a new minster in 1081. In 1106 the relics of St Etheldreda (who had built the first church) were translated to Ely and three years later it became the see of a bishop – a monastic cathedral like Canterbury. The Norman building was probably finished by the early thirteenth century. Disaster struck in 1322 when the crossing tower collapsed. The subsequent rebuilding has provided us with one of the glories of English medieval architecture but actually a most un-English exterior. Inside, the nave remains a classic example of early Norman architecture and is typically austere. The north, south and west transepts should also not be missed.

Ely however has an extra fascination for the student of the demise of Anglo-

Tablet commemorating Byrhtnoth, Earl of Northumbria, killed at the Battle of Maldon.

Saxon England. In Bishop West's **chantry (south aisle east end)** is a monument to a number of early medieval worthies. One **tablet** commemorates Byrhtnoth, Earl of Northumbria (d. 991), who was killed at the Battle of Maldon while leading the English army against the Vikings. He was apparently decapitated in the battle and his death led quickly to the defeat of his army. Byrhtnoth had established connections with Ely and is said to have called at the minster for succour on his way from the north to Essex prior to the battle.

The most celebrated person to have been laid to rest in this church is none other than Alfred Aetheling, younger brother of Edward the Confessor, but there is no monument. At the instigation of their mother, Dowager Queen Emma, Alfred and Edward separately returned from exile in Normandy with armed retainers after Cnut's death in 1036. Edward quickly retreated back to Normandy but Alfred was captured in Guildford while ostensibly being entertained by Earl Godwin. Alfred was brought to the Isle of Ely on the orders of King Harold I (Harefoot). Here, while attempting to blind and castrate their captive in the Norman style, Harold's men bungled their grizzly task. Alfred was found by monks of the abbey with terrible wounds from which he subsequently died. He was buried in the south chapel at the west end of the pre-Conquest church. This truly dreadful tale shocked even contemporaries and was never forgotten by Edward the Confessor, remaining a cause célèbre with him until Godwin's death in 1057.

Half a mile south of the cathedral William the Conqueror established a motte and bailey castle after expelling Hereward the Wake from the Isle of Ely. Only a low **motte**, known as **Cherry Hill**, survives in a park and even this may have been raised during the later Anarchy of the mid-twelfth century. Nevertheless this site is all we have to celebrate the semi-legendary figure of Hereward as the last real threat to the Norman occupation of England.

Hereward certainly existed however, and was of aristocratic but modest family probably in southern Lincolnshire. In the spring of 1070 he and his English rebels were joined in the Isle of Ely by none other than King Sweyn of Denmark and members of his fleet, which had wintered in the Humber. With the Danes, Hereward led a successful raid on Peterborough Abbey, but in the summer the Danes made peace with King William and departed. Hereward took on the defence of Ely and was joined by a fugitive, Earl Morcar of Northumbria, in the spring of 1071. William besieged the island by land and water and the garrison surrendered without terms: Morcar was imprisoned and died soon afterwards, but Hereward and a few companions managed to elude the Normans, were lost to history but graduated to legend.

GREAT CANFIELD, Castle and St Mary the Virgin Church **
Hamlet is 1 mile north-east of B184 Leaden Roding–Great Dunmow road. Turn off just north of High Roding on minor road. Turn left at T-junction and left again on sharp right-hand bend.

Great Canfield is a little gem. It is also a great example of the juxtaposition of Norman castle and church (plus later manor house) in the subjugation of Old England. The remains of the large **motte** and **bailey** lie south-east of the church in trees on private land. However a good view can be obtained from the High Roding road or the footpath south of the church – but be sure not to go in winter.

Before the Conquest, Great Canfield was held by Robert Fitz Wymark, one of Edward the Confessor's Norman imports (he was probably Norman-Breton). He most likely built an early motte and bailey here and so this is a candidate for being 'Robert's castle' whither a number of these Normans fled in 1052 when the Godwins forcibly returned to power under King Edward.

In Domesday the estate belonged to Aubrey de Vere (dc. 1110), the progenitor of the powerful Earls of Oxford, who played an important role in English politics for nearly 500 years. Pettifer is clear that the earthworks visible today date from this later post-Conquest period. De Vere became one of Henry I's most trusted household administrators. Along with Robert Basset he became joint sheriff of eleven shires, part of a drive by Henry to centralise government of the counties (little is new in English politics). His son, Aubrey II, rose to be Henry's master chamberlain in 1133 and was given extra lands. This Aubrey was killed in London 'in a tumult' in 1141 during the Anarchy. St Mary's is a virtually unchanged early **Norman church** (the bell tower is later) with unusually fine doorways, tympanum and chancel arch. The church is dated to the first half of the twelfth century so it is likely that all three of the first Aubrey de Veres had a hand in its building.

GREAT DUNHAM, St Andrew's Church **
2½ miles south-west of Litcham on Litcham–Little Dunham minor road. Next to school.

You are in deepest Norfolk country here. Pevsner tells us that this delightful Anglo-Saxon church is of the 'overlap' period at the end of the eleventh century. Look out for the triangle-headed west entrance, long and short work, and the bell openings of the tower. Internally there is Anglo-Saxon blank arcading, an Anglo-Saxon east arch of the tower but a Norman west arch. At Domesday, land in the parish was held by the king directly and by Ralph de Tosny amongst others. Castle Acre and Newton are nearby.

GREAT PAXTON, Holy Trinity Church *

North end of village, just west of B1043 St Neots–Huntingdon road. Turn north-west off B1043 towards railway.

Before the Conquest Great Paxton was a royal manor of some size. This resulted during the eleventh century in the construction of one of most sophisticated Anglo-Saxon churches in England. As you approach however, little clue is given to the splendours inside! In a rare moment of emotion Pevsner describes both the aisled nave and crossing tower as 'amazing'. Built in around 1020, it is thought that the church served as a minster. Interestingly, at Domesday this manor was held by Countess Judith, half-sister of the Conqueror and widow of Waltheof, the only prominent Englishman to be executed by William (see Crowland).

HADSTOCK, St Botolph's Church **

South end of village on B1052 Saffron Walden–Linton road.

This church contains a number of Saxon elements: the arches to the two transepts, the high nave, the nave windows and most especially the **north doorway** and **arch**. Here, it is claimed, is the oldest surviving wooden door in England; it is of oak and dated to around 1020, but is quite different from a Norman door. Tradition has it that a Dane committed sacrilege and was punished by being flayed alive and his skin nailed to this door. Centuries later, repair work on the door revealed a piece of human skin (or so it was claimed). The skin can be seen in the **Saffron Walden Museum** nearby. Unfortunately modern analysis has shown that the skin comes from a cow. The west door of the church may also be Saxon.

Detailed investigation has revealed that the church on this site received its third major rebuild early in the eleventh century, raising the prospect, given its large crossing tower, that it might have been the minster known to have been erected by Cnut in celebration of his great victory at Assandun (believed to have been sited at either Ashingdon or Ashdon, both in Essex) over King Edmund Ironside in October 1016. It is not clear which is the true location of the battle. Neither village church offers any suggestion of sufficient antiquity or of minster proportions, but Hadstock is less than 3 miles from Ashdon on the same raised plateau (and could have been built to commemorate the battle). So could this be the minster whose first priest was Stigand, later to become Archbishop of Canterbury? Perhaps, but most modern historians prefer Ashingdon as the battle's location (see Ashingdon).

HALES, HECKINGHAM AND HADDISCOE Parish Churches *

1 mile south of village. Take left fork on minor road to Ravingham off A146 Beccles road. Church is ½ mile on right on its own.

East Anglia specialises in delightful round-tower churches identified as Saxon, Norman or of the Saxo-Norman overlap. There are 168 in all, of which 119 are in Norfolk. My personal favourite is **St Margaret's, Hales**.

Pevsner describes it as 'a perfect Norman village church'. It has a round tower, apse, lovely north and south doors and thatched roofs – as charming a church as you will find anywhere in England. Unfortunately St Margaret's has lost its village, which migrated 2 miles north over the centuries.

The round-tower church at Hales complete with apse and thatched roof.

The church is now under the care of the churches Conservation Trust.

The area of Norfolk south of the river Yare abounds in round-tower churches.

1½ miles north of Hales (and 1½ miles east of Loddon). On minor road to Thurlton is **St Gregory's, Heckingham**.

Once again the Norman round-tower church is thatched and has a marvellous south doorway.

3 miles east close to village centre on A143 Yarmouth–Beccles road is **St Mary, Haddiscoe**.

This tower is identified from the bell openings of the Saxo-Norman overlap. There is a fine Norman south doorway with an unusual Norman sculpture above it.

ISLEHAM, Priory ** KAL
On the north side of the village, on the B1104 Ely road and just north of the parish church.

At Domesday **Alan the Red of Brittany** held estates in both Isleham and nearby Linton. Either Alan or one of his successors built this delightful structure as the church for a Benedictine priory. Alan fought at Hastings and was rewarded with huge estates largely in the north of England (see Richmond, North Yorkshire). Sometime in the twelfth century the priory was given to the Abbey of St Jacut-de-la-Mer in Brittany. As the Hundred Years War progressed in the fourteenth century, Isleham became an alien priory and was finally confiscated by Henry V in 1414. It was later granted to Pembroke College, Cambridge and became a barn.

Now happily renovated, the building is believed to date from around 1100 and provides a splendid example of early Norman architecture, never having been extended or extensively altered.

THE BATTLE OF MALDON (10 August 991) +++

Strategic Background and Campaign
Strictly speaking, this battle was of only regional significance and occurred twenty-five years before the eventual demise of the Anglo-Saxon monarchy. However it does hold significance nationally for two reasons: it is a rare example from the reign of Aethelred II of an organised military response to Viking raids and, because of the unusual survival of an epic poem written soon after the battle, its location is known with curious accuracy for the period.

After Edgar's 'golden age' in the mid-tenth century when all England was united and at peace, the scourge of the Viking attacks on the country restarted, when at least two fleets operating in the Irish Sea and the Channel attacked Southampton, Thanet and Cheshire in 980. The English defences of naval squadrons backed up with fortified burghs – as set up by Alfred the Great – had fallen into disuse and were in need of repair. Over the next ten years further raids occurred along the northern coasts of Devon and Cornwall (981), Dorset and London (982), and Watchet in Somerset (987), where local resistance was led unsuccessfully by the thegn, Goda.

For the 991 raiding season a fleet of ninety-three Viking ships arrived in the English Channel. It is unclear whether it was led by Olaf Tryggvason (later King of Norway) or Sweyn Forkbeard, King of Denmark, or by both. They attacked Folkestone, Sandwich and Ipswich before landing on Northey Island near Maldon and threatening the town. For once a substantial English land army was on hand to resist the raid led by Byrhtnoth, Ealdorman of East Anglia.

The Battle

The English force drew up on the banks of the river Blackwater opposite the causeway access to Northey Island, which still exists today. It was apparently high tide so battle was impossible, but the Vikings gathered their troops opposite the English and a chaotic mixture of shouted insults and negotiations ensued. The Vikings first asked for tribute money but Byrhtnoth refused. As the tide dropped the Vikings prepared to cross the causeway but their path was blocked, according to the poem, by three brave souls. Eventually the Vikings asked to be allowed to cross to the mainland unmolested and then to line up opposite the English ready to do battle. Heroically, but perhaps surprisingly, Byrhtnoth agreed.

The battle itself was conventional. It started with a hail of arrows and javelins before the Vikings attacked Byrhtnoth's shield wall. The wall held firm until, fighting in the midst of his troops, Byrhtnoth was struck twice by spears and then cut down by axes – his head may have been cut off as a trophy. The death of their leader quickly led to the rout of the English army possibly started by one Godric. The poem does recount however how Byrhtnoth's household troops staged a chivalrous fight to the death, ensuring that Viking battle casualties were also high on that day.

Participants and Casualties

Julian Humphries has estimated Viking numbers at 3,000–6,000 based on a fleet of ninety-three ships, led by Sweyn Forkbeard and Olaf Trggvason. We can assume that the Essex fyrd and Byrhtnoth's housecarls together amounted to a somewhat higher number, say 5,000–8,000, but these were less well trained.

The causeway from Maldon to Northey Island, across which the Danes were allowed to march in 991.

Aftermath and Commentary

Although the English army was heavily defeated in the field, the high toll extracted from the Vikings by Byrhtnoth's household troops ensured that, in the short term at least, this was something of a Pyrrhic victory for the Vikings. Maldon town was saved, and the raiders called an end to the 991 'season' in England and returned home to lick their wounds. So Byrhtnoth's decision to allow the Vikings to engage in battle may have been right – after all, he surely had no fleet available for the alternative strategy of blockading Northey Island. The Vikings could simply have sailed away unmolested and returned another day. Byrhtnoth wanted to teach them a lesson through battle.

However the long-term consequences for the English nation were much more severe. This battle is a prime example of the dangers of the medieval battle for the military-political leader. Byrhtnoth, at over 6ft 8in tall and with a lifetime's military experience behind him (he was over 60 in 991), was the supreme English military leader of the time. His decision to engage the Vikings, not appease them, led to his immediate death (the Vikings may have employed a hit man, a renowned warrior who targeted Byrhtnoth in the battle). Aethelred II was not a fighting man but perhaps he should not be criticised too strongly at this time for he was the only fully mature member of the ruling House of Cerdic – his death would have been a disaster for England. However the death of Byrhtnoth at Maldon can only have re-inforced Aelthred's 'leading from the rear' approach to confronting the Viking raids, which was to eventually lead to the kingdom being overrun by Sweyn Forkbeard in 1013.

The net result was that after Maldon, England made the first payment of the infamous 'Danegeld' to the Vikings to stay away. This amounted to £10,000, a high proportion of contemporary English GNP. A slippery slope had been engaged. The Vikings returned in the very next season (992) to raid London.

Location and What to See

There is no battlefield monument but it is reasonably certain that the causeway to Northey Island has not changed its position since 991.

The battle is believed to have been fought in the fields immediately north-west of the causeway near South House Farm. For battles of this period this is very exact. A fine round walk from Paradise Park can be undertaken.

On the south side of **All Saints church** in Maldon's High Street is a nineteenth-century statue of <u>Byrhtnoth</u> (he is also commemorated in Ely Cathedral). Enjoy a pint in the next-door Blue Boar Inn, once home to the de Vere Earls of Oxford.

MOUNT BURES, Castle and St John's Church **

1 mile south of Bures village on minor road to Wakes Colne off B1508.

Situated on the high ground above the Stour Valley, this is not a location where you will be bothered by the crowds. The surviving motte and ditch were built soon after the Conquest by **Roger de Montgomery II, Earl of Shrewsbury**, one of the Conqueror's principal lieutenants, whose role in 1066 was to remain behind in Normandy to advise William's regent, Duchess Matilda. A **plaque** at the entrance records that in 1079 Roger's wife, **Mabel Talvas**, was murdered at Bures by one Hugh Bunel, son of Robert de Jalgeio, in a property dispute.

However it is much more likely that this occured at Bures-sur-Dives in Normandy

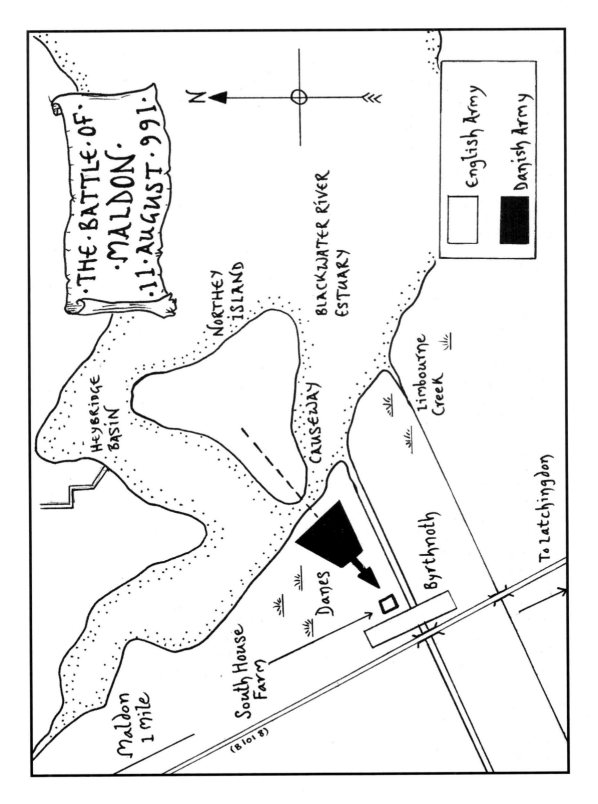

THE·BATTLE·OF·MALDON· ·11·AUGUST·991·

English Army

Danish Army

N

BLACKWATER RIVER ESTUARY

NORTHEY ISLAND

Limbourne Creek

HEYBRIDGE BASIN

CAUSEWAY

Byrthnoth

To Latchingdon

Danes

South House Farm

Maldon 1 mile

(B 1018)

where Mabel had a castle; she is not recorded as having visited England. Nothing survives at Bures in Normandy, so let's commemorate her passing here anyway! The normally discreet *Dictionary of National Biography* describes her as 'a forceful and worldly woman, cunning, garrulous and extremely cruel'. She was an heiress in her own right. The dictionary continues: 'four vassals cut off her head as she lay in bed after a bath.' No one was ever charged with her murder and her husband Roger re-married. His and Mabel's eldest son Robert immediately inherited her Bellême estates in Normandy, but unfortunately also inherited her character. He fell foul of Henry I in the early 1100s and ended his life in prison.

The **church** next door provides another example of the juxtaposition of castle and church in the subjugation of Old England by the Normans. The church's patronage by the wealthy and powerful Montgomery family explains the size and relative sophistication of the structure with a crossing tower and transepts.

NEWTON (West Norfolk), All Saints Church *

1 mile east of Castle Acre on A1065 Swaffam–Fakenham road, opposite George and Dragon public house.

Sensitively restored in the nineteenth and twentieth centuries, this church is almost completely Anglo-Saxon. The tower and the chancel arch are particularly noteworthy. The remains of an older, higher nave roof are visible on the outside of the tower. At Domesday land in this parish was held by the king and by Ivo Tailebois. The survival of the Anglo-Saxon church through the Norman period is surprising given its proximity to the Norman plantation town of Castle Acre only 1 mile across the river Nar.

NORWICH **

Castle £
City centre, south side.

At the Conquest Norwich was the third-largest conurbation in England behind London and York. In early 1067 the Conqueror moved against East Anglia, soon after his coronation at Westminster. During this campaign it is thought that a wooden motte and bailey castle was erected on the current site, probably by Ralph Guader, Earl of East Anglia, on William's orders. A natural hill was heightened and deep ditches dug. From the start this castle was as much a royal palace as a defensive structure. During its construction almost 100 Saxon houses were destroyed to create room for the bailey. This original castle was besieged by royal forces during the rebellion of Ralph Guader, Roger of Breteuil and Waltheof of Northumbria in 1075.

From about 1094 work began on the present stone **keep**, the motte being extended in order to support this very large Norman structure. The new building was certainly finished by 1121 when Henry I is known to have spent Christmas here, newly re-married. Although the exterior of the keep looks modern because the outside was refaced in 1834–9, inside it reveals itself as a thoroughly genuine and indeed lavish Norman building. Many Norman features are on view. The **Bigod arch**, the original entrance to the royal hall, celebrates the Bigod Earls of Norfolk and Suffolk and hereditary constables of the royal castle.

Cathedral
City centre north-east side.

In 1066 the principal see in Norfolk was located at North Elmham. In 1070 this was moved to the much bigger town of Thetford.

However, in accordance with the Norman policy in England of locating cathedrals in the biggest towns, in 1094 the see was moved again, this time to Norwich. The Norman bishop Losinga had been given the task of managing this transition when he was appointed to Thetford in 1091. Losinga laid the foundation stone in 1096 and the building was completed in 1145.

From a distance the cathedral is dominated by its magnificent spire and so does not advertise its Norman origins. However, once inside, the building reveals itself as an unusually complete survival from the twelfth century. Nave, chancel transepts, ambulatory and bishop's throne are largely original – only the east end has been rebuilt. An additional bonus here is the memorial **floorslab** to founder Bishop Losinga (d. 1119) in the **presbytery**, whose life is well documented and whose appointment is typical of the approach taken by the Norman kings to the management of the English church.

ST ALBANS, Cathedral **
City centre.

The cathedral has its origins in the shrine and early Anglo-Saxon church built on the site of the execution of St Alban by the Romans in around 250 – the earliest martyr in Britain. King Offa refounded the monastic church in 793 under Benedictine rule. In 1077 Paul of Caen, a kinsman of Archbishop Lanfranc, began the total rebuilding of the Anglo-Saxon church in the early Norman style, incorporating many Roman bricks from nearby Verulanium. This was achieved in only eleven years; when dedicated in 1115 it was the largest church in England. It was extended and partially rebuilt in the early English style, but the cossing tower, transepts and eastern end of the nave remain in the plain (but not grim) early Norman style.

Overall St Albans is a strange shape for a cathedral: extremely long but with an unusually squat tower. Internally however,

Lovely Norman nave arches at St Albans Cathedral.

this is a lovely example of early Norman architecture. At the Dissolution the once mighty abbey came to an end but the abbey church survives as a cathedral.

SOUTH LOPHAM, St Andrew's Church **

On B1113 South. Lopham–Kenninghall road ½ mile north of A1066 Thetford–Diss road.

The glory of this church is its fabulous Norman tower. Pevsner describes it as 'the most powerful in Norfolk' and dates it to no later than 1120. The tower displays Norman arching, arcading, windows and bell openings. It was probably built by William Bigod, second Earl of Norfolk, one of the most powerful men in the county. He gave the church living to Thetford Priory. Internally the church contains a surprise. High up on the north wall of the nave can be seen a round Anglo-Saxon window indicating that the tower was added to an existing Anglo-Saxon church.

STANSTED MONTEFICHET, Castle ** £

By the station on the east side of the town.

This motte and bailey castle was established after the Conquest by William Gernon, a significant landowner in Essex. His sons changed their names to Montefichet. Although the surviving earthworks are not spectacular, Stansted offers something completely different – a reconstruction of the wooden defences of the castle carried out in the 1980s. A great place for children and convenient for the airport.

THETFORD ***

Castle

East of town centre. Signposted, best approached from A1065 Diss–Thetford road from Diss. Castle is in park on left.

At the time of the Norman Conquest, Thetford was the sixth-largest town in England, commanding the crossing of the Little Ouse on the Icknield Way. The Conqueror moved against East Anglia early in 1067 soon after his coronation. Thetford's splendidly tall motte and bailey was probably raised on William's orders soon afterwards, either by Ralph Guader, Earl of East Anglia, or by Roger Bigot. It was constructed within an existing Iron Age fort. The motte rises to almost 70ft and is England's tallest. There is no evidence of any stone masonry ever having been used here and the site fell out of use in the thirteenth century as Thetford's importance declined.

Priory of St Mary
North of the Little Ouse, ½ mile north-west of town centre by bridge over the river.

Founded by Roger Bigod, Earl of Norfolk and Suffolk, as a Cluniac house in 1104–5. Roger had vowed to go on pilgrimage to the Holy Land but decided against it. The price of the Pope's agreement was the foundation of this priory. Originally sited on the other side of the river on the location of the ill-fated cathedral (the Norfolk see was centred here between 1075–91 before moving to Norwich, which had become the biggest town in the county), the priory moved to the current site a short while later. Roger attended the foundation ceremony in 1107 but died only eight days later, where he was buried after an unseemly dispute between the prior and Bishop Losinga of Norwich. The church was in use by 1114 and was probably completed 1130–40. Roger was a very wealthy official of the royal household who was a trusted advisor to both William Rufus and Henry I.

One for the children at Stansted. Montefichet.

The massive motte at Thetford.

The crossing and transepts and parts of the monastic buildings survive from the original but in ruin. A delightfully tranquil spot with a fine fifteenth-century gatehouse.

WALTHAM, Abbey ****
East side of town, south of B194 Nazeing road. Signposted.

It is likely that a church has existed on this site since the seventh century. Early in the eleventh century Tovi the Proud, 'staller' to Cnut, had a hunting lodge here. Tovi discovered a miracle-working crucifix (the Holy Cross) on his lands at Montacute, Somerset, which he transferred to Waltham and endowed a new church and two priests. On Tovi's death in the 1050s Edward the Confessor gave Waltham to Harold Godwinson who re-founded the church and built a new minster by 1060. It is said Harold was cured of paralysis through praying before the cross.

The fate of Harold's body after the Battle of Hastings is unclear. Some sources have him buried by William on the Sussex coast near Hastings, or possibly Bosham looking perpetually out to sea. Others have that his body was given by William to William Malet, who had befriended Harold during the latter's stay in Normandy. A famous version is that, because the corpses on Senlac ridge were so mutilated, Harold's first wife, Edith Swan-Neck, was brought along to identify his body which was then transported to Waltham for burial in his minster church.

Nothing now remains of that church and further uncertainty surrounds the exact location of burial. Nevertheless, in 1960 a **memorial slab** was constructed in the graveyard to the east of the present church. It is very understated but is all we have to commemorate one of Anglo-Saxon England's heroes, **King Harold II**. A modern

statue also stands on the southern corner of the **west front** of the present abbey, together with a portrait in **stained glass** at the east end of the north aisle.

After the Conquest the church was given to the bishops of Durham. From around 1110 the **nave** was rebuilt very much in the style of Durham Cathedral, with deeply grooved, circular piers, and this survives in its splendour today. After Thomas Becket's murder Henry II re-founded Waltham as an Augustinian abbey as one of his penances. It almost tripled in size and became a rival to Canterbury but at the Dissolution it was denied cathedral status and only the parish church is now left. This important site needs more visitors.

WISSINGTON (WISTON), St Mary's Church *
Close to the river Stour between Bures and Nayland, 1½ miles west of Nayland. From Nayland take minor road west to Bures, off A134 Colchester–Sudbury road. After 1 mile turn left and continue straight to Wissington (cul-de-sac). After ½ mile park and walk rest of way to church.

Although not mentioned in Domesday Book, this manor is known to have been owned by Robert Godbold in 1135 because he gave the living to the Cluniac priory of Little Horkeley in Essex, an increasingly popular act in Norman times. The church is delightfully situated next to the Victorian hall and within an ancient moated enclosure. Though heavily restored by the Victorians the church survives in its original structure as a fine example of Norman nave, chancel and apse (the last has been rebuilt). Good thirteenth-century wall paintings.

WYMONDHAM, Abbey **
West side of town centre.

Like a medieval galleon, the two towers of the abbey dominate much of the surrounding countryside. Founded as a Benedictine priory in 1107 by <u>William d'Aubigny (d. 1139)</u> the building originally had twin west towers. These were demolished later in the Middle Ages when the central octagonal tower and the present west tower were built, and stand as monuments to centuries of quarrelling between the priory and the population of the town to whom d'Aubigny had granted access to the nave. Originally a daughter House of St Albans Abbey where d'Aubigny's brother was abbot, the priory gained abbey status only in 1448. The interior of the nave is particularly impressive. However the highlight of the abbey lies to the east of the present church. D'Aubigny's original church was twice the length of the existing one. In front of the scant remains of the old altar is a modern **memorial slab** to the founder William d'Aubigny, whose career provides a perfect example of how William the Conqueror and his sons relied heavily on talented men from modest backgrounds who were promoted into senior positions.

The d'Albinis (or d'Aubignys) were one of several families from the Cotentin in Normandy to be favoured by Henry I. They formed part of his first powerbase in the 1090s after he had purchased lands there from his elder brother, Duke Robert. William is described as a '*curialis*' or courtier, and witnessed many royal charters. From a modest background he had risen within the royal household under William Rufus and, by 1101 at the latest, was royal pincera (butler). He married Maud, daughter of Roger Bigot, another courtier and wealthy landowner in East Anglia. Their son, William II, was even more upwardly mobile: he married Henry I's widow, Adeliza, in 1138–9, and became Earl of Arundel. William's

younger brother Nigel also prospered under Henry I. William Senior lived at Old Buckenham Castle.

EAST MIDLANDS

BARTON-ON-HUMBER, St Peter's Church * £
Town centre east side, north of the A1077 Grimsby road. There are two fine medieval churches in this small town within 150yds of each other. St Peter's is the further east. (EH)

St Peter's was made redundant in 1972 but is now well managed by English Heritage. The church is justly celebrated for its fine Anglo-Saxon Danish **tower** and unusual adjoining baptistery, built at the beginning of the eleventh century. The top of the tower is of the Saxo-Norman overlap, added after the Conquest. The remainder of the church was rebuilt later in the twelfth century and now houses an interesting exhibition based on the archaeological work undertaken in recent years by English Heritage in the nearby Anglo-Saxon cemeteries.

BLYTH, Priory Church of St Mary and St Martin **
North side of village centre. Tel. 01909 591229. Open daily in February.
This church was founded as a Benedictine priory in 1088 by <u>Roger de Buscli (or Bully) (d. 1089)</u>, who was based at nearby Tickhill Castle and whose massive landed wealth stemmed from the Honour of Tickhill. Roger may have been present at the Battle of Hastings. The **nave** and **north aisle** of the church are excellent examples of the early Norman style. To quote Pevsner: 'There is nothing like Blyth … to get a feeling of Early Norman grimness'. The priory was subordinated to Holy Trinity Priory, Rouen. It became a kind of motorway

service station for travellers on the main route northwards in medieval times. Contrast this plain styling with the exuberance of late Norman at Kilpeck, Herefordshire.

The church was originally much larger but the chancel and other parts have been lost because they were walled off during a dispute between the lay vicar and the monks in the late fourteenth century, and were subsequently demolished after the Dissolution.

BRIXWORTH, All Saints Church **
North end of village just west of A508 Northampton–Market Harborough road.

The most impressive Anglo-Saxon church in this book. A large building, comprising nave, chancel, apse, stair turret, ambulatory and tower, originally seventh century but with much alteration in the eleventh. The many internal arches incorporate Roman bricks. Originally the building was even larger. The south door is Norman. The church was well restored in the nineteenth century. At Domesday Brixworth was held by the king.

EARLS BARTON, All Saints Church *
Village centre. Turn off A45 Wellingborough– Northampton road 3 miles west of Wellingborough.

The main point of interest in this church is the mighty late Anglo-Saxon **tower**, at its very best when viewed from the west side. The tower has good bell openings and doorway. The Normans extended/rebuilt the church in two phases in the early and late twelfth century. Evidence for this can be seen inside the church (chancel and tower arches) and in the late Norman south door. The early phase is probably attributable to Simon de St Liz, first Earl of Northampton.

It is thought the Saxon tower was built as early as the mid-tenth century during the relatively peaceful reign of King Edgar. In the time of Edward the Confessor the manor was held by Bondi, one of Edward's stallers, or courtiers. By Domesday the manor was held by Countess Judith, sister of the Conqueror and widow of Earl Waltheof, the only prominent Englishman to be executed by William. Judith was also to become widow of Simon de St Liz, above.

LAXTON, Castle *
½ mile north of church and village centre. Accessible by public footpath.

This hilltop site has an unusual **motte** and **bailey**, which was first established soon after the Conquest by Robert de Caux, later to become hereditary forester of Sherwood. It consists of one motte on top of another, broader one (total height 71ft) and two baileys. At Domesday Geoffrey A'selin also held land in this parish. Laxton still possesses some open strip fields.

LINCOLN, Castle * £
'Old' city centre on hilltop next to cathedral.

As a result of Danish settlement from the late ninth century, Lincoln became one of the Five Boroughs in the Danelaw and one of the largest towns on England, with a population of around 10,000 by 1066. The Conqueror established a castle here when returning from his first campaign in Yorkshire in autumn 1068. In the process, 166 Anglo-Saxon houses were destroyed. Four years later the vast bishopric of Dorchester-on-Thames was relocated here, ensuring the city's importance in the early medieval period. The newly constructed castle housed the English hostages taken by William after his northern campaign of 1068, Waltheof and Gospatric.

The surviving structure of the castle is much cluttered by the later defences and the

old gaol. However the really special feature of this site is the existence of **two early mottes** (as at Lewes), presumably for even greater security. **The Observatory Tower** (the lower part of which is Norman), and **the Lucy Tower** stand on these mottes. The latter was built after a fire in 1110 and named after <u>Lucy Taillebois</u>, wife of Ivo, Sheriff of Lincolnshire (she had previously been married to the Earl of Chester). Lucy was the niece of Thorold, who had also been Sheriff in 1086 – by then a rarity for a non-Norman.

MELBOURNE, St Michael and St Mary Church **

South-eastern edge of village on road to Wilson and Isley Walton.

The Domesday Book tells us that in the time of Edward the Confessor and in 1086 Melbourne was a royal manor with a church and priest. This royal connection undoubtedly explains why we have such a splendid and exotic church here in a relatively small village. It is one of the most complete and best preserved larger parish churches of the mid-Norman period in the country – especially inside. The nave with aisles, the chancel walls and arch, and the transepts and crossing tower are especially fine. The top of the tower was added later. Originally the church had a two-tower façade at the west end and an apse at the eastern end. Altogether rather like a mini-cathedral and unique in England. In fact the overall design owes much to the Romanesque style of tenth- and eleventh-century Germany. Be very careful not to miss the fabulous stone **carvings** on the chancel arch, especially the **Melbourne Cat**.

Dating the building has proved difficult. Broadly the span of 1120–50 looks sensible, with building progressing as usual from east to west. **King Henry I** was a great builder.

In 1114 he had married his daughter Matilda (or Maud) to Henry V, Emperor of Germany (d. 1125), which was as prestigious a match as it was possible to achieve in that era. Henry took great pride in his achievement and uncharacteristically parted with a massive 10,000 marks as dowry. So does Melbourne represent a celebration of this new connection by Henry, or perhaps a wedding present to Matilda? What is known is that the living of Melbourne was given by Henry to <u>Aethelwold (or Adelulf)</u> when he was appointed bishop of the newly created see of Carlisle in 1133. Aethelwold was Henry I's confessor (in what must have been a colourful and challenging job) and completed the building of the church.

It has been conjectured that Melbourne provided Aethelwold with a 'bolt hole', as Carlisle was still being disputed with the Scots and was indeed overrun in 1136. However there could be another reason. Melbourne lies just 2 miles or so south of **Swarkestone** bridge over the river Trent. In the twelfth century this was part of the main route to the north-west and probably commanded lucrative tolls to the royal manor. This would explain the sumptuousness of the church.

Head north from the church on the main A514 Derby road. After 1 mile the road runs over an ancient causeway across the Trent floodplain to Swarkestone bridge.

NEWARK, Castle * £
Riverside on north-western edge of town centre by bridge for A616 Ollerton road.

The latest thinking is that William the Conqueror may have established a castle at this strategic point during his notorious campaign in the north in 1068–9. Newark lies at the junction of the Great North Road and

The Melbourne Cat – the charming side of the Normans.

the Fosse Way, as well as being an important north-south crossing of the river Trent. It would almost certainly have been a motte and bailey located on the site of the present castle ruins. William granted the manor to the bishops of Lincoln. From around 1130 Bishop Alexander (bishop 1129–48) began his programme to rebuild and upgrade the castle. Alexander, the natural son of Bishop Roger of Salisbury (they did things a little differently in those days), was, like his father, a prodigious builder (see Salisbury).

The ruins of the castle make a fine sight from across the Trent. Alexander's **gatehouse**, the **lower curtain** on the **riverside** and the **south-west tower** survive from this period. King John is said to have died of dysentery in this tower in 1216, but that's another story.

SOUTHWELL, Minster **
Town centre.

The minster was founded before the Conquest, probably in the tenth century. Building on the current structure began in 1108, led by Archbishop Thomas II of York (archbishop 1108–14). To begin with, Southwell was, like Beverley and Ripon, a major church within the see of York. It was recognised early on as the mother church of Nottinghamshire but did not achieve independent cathedral status until 1884. The archbishops of York maintained a palace here until the seventeenth century, the remains of which can be viewed.

Work on the new building proceeded quickly, starting, as was normal, from the east end. The original Norman chancel was rebuilt in the thirteenth century but **nave, crossing, transepts and splendid western towers** survive from the first Norman work and are dated to 1120–60. The west end elevation dominated by the towers gives Southwell a very special feel. In the **north** transept is a **tympanum** of Anglo-Saxon date, which survives from an earlier church.

STAMFORD, St Leonard's Priory *

Eastern edge of town on by-road just south of its junction with the A16 Stamford–Spalding road.

Founded in the seventh century by Wilfrid, tutor to King Oswy's son, and rebuilt by William of Carilef, the Norman architect of Durham Cathedral, for the monks of that cathedral. The priory served as a base for the management of Durham's considerable southern estates – a good example of the widespread landed power possessed by the church after the Conquest. The delightful remains comprise the north arcade of the priory church, built in about 1100 and the west front, rebuilt around 1150.

STOW-IN-LINDSEY ***

Village centre, 1 mile north of A1500 Marton–Lincoln road.

St Mary's church is a wonderful example of a large Saxo-Norman church with little embellishment after 1200 except for the tower. Perhaps the biggest question is why such a fabulous and large church is located in this small and very rural village? Before the Conquest, Stow lay at the centre of a large block of estates that belonged to the bishops of Dorchester-on-Thames. In around 975 Bishop Aelfnoth built or rebuilt a church here as a head minster for the Lincolnshire part of his diocese. This work can be found in the **lower parts of the transepts** and of the **crossing**. In 1073 the diocese was translated from Dorchester all the way to Lincoln, then the third-largest town in England, as part of the Norman policy of re-centring dioceses in major conurbations. At the time the diocese covered a massive

area of the Midlands. Stow's head minster role was thus superseded by nearby Lincoln, though the bishops of Lincoln continued to use nearby Stow Park as a country residence (possibly to combat plague), probably funding St Mary's at the same time.

Aelfnoth's church was destroyed by fire and rebuilt by Bishop Eadnoth II (bishop 1034–50). This church was re-endowed in 1054 by none other than **Earl Leofric of Mercia and his wife Lady Godiva** (see Coventry). The **upper parts of the transepts** and the **crossing** survive from this rebuild. Remegius was appointed bishop in 1067 and was translated to Lincoln before his see, where he built the present **nave**. The **chancel** was rebuilt in its current form in the second half of the twelfth century – a fine example of late Norman display. At this time efforts were made to turn Stow into a bigger market town but, as with so many other Norman plantations, these failed and the markets moved to nearby Marton.

WEST MIDLANDS

BARROW, St Giles Church *

In centre of hamlet just south of B4376 Broseley (south end)–Much Wenlock road.

This quiet location has a most interesting church. Anglo-Saxon churches are rare in Shropshire, and Norman churches incorporating Saxon remains are rare anywhere. The chancel and chancel arch are Anglo-Saxon dated to the tenth or eleventh centuries but with later Norman windows and doors. The nave, tower arch and tower are Norman, perhaps late eleventh-century. The latter is massive in size (its roof and battlements are later additions). Of note are the south doorway, the font and the tympanum under the tower. Barrow was not mentioned in

Domesday Book and remains a hamlet today. The living belonged to Much Wenlock Priory.

BEAUDESERT *

At the north end of the village just across the river Alne from Henley-in-Arden. The earthwork castle extends eastwards from the church.

Beaudesert may seem today like just a suburb of the more prosperous Henley, but in the late eleventh century it was much the more important of the two. It had both a castle and a church; Henley had neither.

Castle

In the late eleventh century Thurstan de Montefort built an earthwork castle on the long, low hill, known locally as the Mount, probably ring work with two bailies. In the thirteenth century this family gained fame and notoriety through their descendant Simon de Montfort. Peter de Montfort was lord of the manor here at that time and was killed alongside his kinsman at the Battle of Evesham. The Mount provides a pleasant walk and affords fine views over the locality. The castle was later rebuilt in stone but little survives.

St Nicholas Church

This church is only 700yds from Henley parish church across the river Alne. It is thought to have been built in the twelfth century but is difficult to date accurately. The south doorway, chancel east window, chancel and arch all survive as fine and sturdy examples of late Norman work.

BRINKLOW, Castle *

¼ mile east of village centre on high ground behind church. Access via minor road east to Easenhall.

The fabulous Anglo-Saxon church at Stow.

A splendid example of a motte and bailey with a high (40ft) motte, two bailies to the west and well-preserved ramparts and ditches. Pettifer suggests the castle was first owned by the de Mowbrays around 1100 but that ownership was disputed by the Stutevilles. The castle probably dominated the Fosse Way that passes through Brinklow village.

CAUS, Castle **

1½ miles south-west of Westbury. Turn off B4386 Montgomery–Worthen road 1 mile south of Westbury on minor road heading west to Rowley, Lower Wallop and Broomhill. The castle is high up on the left in trees after 1½ miles. Take public footpath

south up steep slope by house to tree-lined ridge. Map ref: 337078.

As you arrive in the Lower Wallop area it is hard to believe that this spectacular site once represented one of the most formidable fortresses in medieval England, surrounded by its own town, now entirely lost. The castle was built on the summit of the ridge with very steep slopes falling away to streams on both sides. It must have appeared virtually impregnable.

Actually, Caus was probably first established about 1070 by William Corbet on another site close to nearby Hawcocks Farm to the south-east. His son Roger Corbet transferred the castle to this new site. The family hailed from Pays de Caux in Normandy and were followers of Roger de Montomery, Earl of Shrewsbury. Caus was established as a major springboard base to support Earl Roger's incursions into Wales from Shrewsbury as he advanced across Offa's Dyke. Caus commanded the important Shrewsbury–Montgomery supply route. In 1102 Roger Corbet was deprived of his estates by Henry I because of his part in Roger de Belleme's revolt (this Roger was Roger de Montgomery's son), but was restored to them in 1105.

In the late twelfth century the castle was rebuilt in **stone** and a fragment survives as the base of Wallop Gate at the south-west corner of the site. Once you have ascended the ridge in trees, head along it to the south-west towards Lower Wallop. Extensive earthworks survive as multiple bank and ditches plus a fine motte. Go in winter, but you are unlikely to meet crowds here at any time.

CLUN, Castle *
North-west edge of village, right by bowling green off A488 Bishop's Castle road.

This fine castle occupies a commanding position above the river Clun utilising a bend in the river for protection. It comprises a motte and bailey structure with two bailies and later, thirteenth-century stonework. It is believed to have originally been constructed in wood by the Norman Picot de Say (d. 1098), a follower of Roger de Montomery, Earl of Shrewsbury, soon after the Conquest. Say established a marcher lordship here, the Honour of Clun. In the mid-twelfth century the castle passed by marriage to the powerful Fitz Alan Earls of Arundel. It was sacked by the Welsh in 1195. While in Clun, also visit the impressive late Norman church of St George at the south end of the village.

COVENTRY ***

The Priory £
City centre: west of the cathedral complex.

In 1043 **Earl Leofric of Mercia** and his wife **Countess Godifu or Godiva** founded a Benedictine priory of St Mary on what is now the crowded hilltop of Coventry's centre. Dissolved in 1539 only scant remains survive. However the city has done a great job to preserve and display these. Following excavations in 1955 it is clear that the priory church eventually reached 425ft in length and extended eastwards almost as far as the new, post-war cathedral. In fact from 1102–88 St Mary's became a cathedral, when Bishop Robert de Lindsey transferred his see from Chester because of incursions by the Welsh across the border (see Chester).

So Lady Godiva was a real person, married to one of the most powerful men in the England of Edward the Confessor. She is known to have been a substantial patron of the church – for an example see Stowe-in-Lindsey. Whether she actually rode naked though the streets of Coventry it is impossible to say, but it would certainly fit in with the ironic, black humour often shown by the Anglo-Saxon warrior elite at that time. Godifu outlasted her husband and is recorded in Domesday Book as holding lands in Coventry, Atherstone and other Warwickshire villages, probably as dowry.

Statue of Lady Godiva
Broadgate in city centre.

Here is a city that knows how to exploit its historical connections. Larger than life-size and 'dressed' as in the legend, there is no missing this one! What would the countess make of this memorial? Why not stay and have lunch at the nearby **Leofric Hotel** in Broadgate while you are in Coventry. It's not quite in period though.

EWYAS HAROLD, Castle **
⅓ mile north-west of village on minor road to Dulas and Maerdy hamlets. Climb footpath from road to view the remains.

A fine motte and bailey standing on a spur above the river Dore. The tree-lined motte rises to 42ft. A small Benedictine priory, founded in around 1100, stood to the south-east. The Domesday Book refers to this castle and indicates that **Earl William Fitz Osbern**, one of the Conqueror's closest confidantes, re-fortified it after the Conquest as one of the first chain of castles built by the Normans, both to protect their western flank against incursions by the Welsh and then to provide bases from which to invade Wales. Most historians have interpreted the Domesday Book entry as indicating that this is also the site of Pentecost's castle built by Osbern Pentecost in 1051–2. Osbern was a retainer of the Norman Earl Ralph of Hereford, Edward the Confessor's nephew who had been appointed by Edward to the great opposition

of the Godwins and other Englishmen in the 1040s. Ralph developed Herefordshire into a 'mini' Normandy, introducing castles for the first time in England and persuading the locals to fight as cavalry.

Traditionally, therefore, historians have accepted that this is most probably the site of the first castle built in England (though a recent book by Terry Wardle claims the location is Burghill, west of Hereford). Regardless, this was one of the first of many castles in Herefordshire, quintessentially a county full of them.

Osbern Pentecost was compelled to leave England in 1052, along with many other Normans, when the Godwins forced their way back into power. The castle was named after Osbern's son, Harold. It is unlikely that any of the remaining **earthworks** date back to the pre-Conquest castle which was suppressed when Harold Godwinson took control of the region in 1057. William Fitz Osbern was killed in 1071 and by 1086 the castle belonged to Alfred of Marlborough, a nephew of Osbern's.

HEATH, Chapel *** KAL
Set deep in the countryside 3 miles east of Diddlebury and north of Ludlow – not easy to find. From Diddlebury on B4368 Ludlow–Bridgnorth road take minor road east through Peaton and Bouldon. At the end of Bouldon village take minor right to Abdon and Clee St Margaret. Ascend hill towards Heath. After 1 mile reach chapel which is behind hedge on the left and diagonally opposite Heath House. Map ref: 557856.

Be assured it really is worth the effort of getting here. Originally built alongside Heath manor house (now long since disappeared, along with its attendant medieval village), the chapel survives today as the most complete Norman parish church in this

Coventry is proud of Earl Leofric and his wife, Lady Godiva.

book – the only alteration to the original twelfth-century structure (dated to *c.* 1140) was the enlargement of the window in the north wall around 1700. Services are still held here as a chapelry of Stoke Milbrough. The surroundings are totally rural. If this building were within reach of London it would be nationally famous, but it would no doubt have been altered over the centuries and spoiled. A must-visit site.

KILPECK, St Mary and St David's Church and Castle ***

Village centre on minor road 1 mile south of A465 Hereford–Abergavenny road. Signposted but ignore more recent church en route. 3 miles north-east of Pontrilas.

Pevsner describes this small church as 'one of the most perfect Norman churches in England' and there is absolutely no need to disagree. I would only add 'and spectacular', for the combination of red sandstone and the sumptuous decoration throughout generates a truly unique church. The structure comprises nave, chancel and apse

and is almost totally Norman – only later windows and the bellcote intrude. Do not miss the ornate south door, indeed it would be difficult to do so. The external corbel table with bizarre carvings of wild animals, wrestlers and a 'sheila-na-gig' (a fertility symbol) is the icing on the cake. The church leaflet gives a full list of all carvings; spend a fun twenty minutes identifying them.

The whole church represents the triumph of the so-called Herefordshire School of Norman Sculpture (see also Shobdon and Moccas) and is the most spectacular example of late Norman architecture in a small church in England. It was probably built by Hugh de Kilpeck from 1130–45. He also built the adjoining motte and bailey **castle** immediately to the west. Although somewhat overgrown, this is freely accessible. Earthworks survive as well as two pieces of masonry from a shell keep on the motte. If you find yourself betwixt Hereford and Abergavenny do not miss this marvellous site.

Not to be missed! The most complete Norman church in this book at Heath, Shropshire.

LEOMINSTER, Priory Church of St Peter and St Paul **
North-east corner of town near river Lugg.

A church has existed on this site since 598. In the first half of the eleventh century an Abbey of Benedictine nuns was re-founded by Earl Leofric of Mercia and his wife, Godiva (yes, she of riding fame – see Coventry), but was most likely dissolved in 1046. In 1123 **King Henry I** founded a new Benedictine priory of monks who rebuilt the church in the late Norman style. Much remains of this building, particularly the north side of the **nave** with its arcades and piers.

While viewing the nave, ponder on why a nunnery should close so peremptorily in 1046. It is a bizarre story, and one we are able to commemorate in this book. In 1046 Sweyn (d. 1052), eldest son of Godwin and elder brother of Harold, was returning from an expedition to South Wales with Gruffydd

ap Llywelyn. They had been attacking the lands and interests there of Earl Leofric of Mercia when Sweyn 'ordered her [Eadgifu, the Abbess of Leominster and possibly a blood relation] to be brought to him and kept her as long as it suited him and then let her go home'. It is unclear whether the episode represents seduction or rape – one source claims Sweyn kept her for a whole year until the threats of the Archbishop of Canterbury were successful in securing her release. Whatever the case, Sweyn had to flee the country within a year and escaped to Flanders.

Sweyn comes across as a most unstable and unpleasant character. He once claimed to be the son of Cnut (his father was actually Godwin – see Bosham) and later murdered his cousin, Beorn, after which he was declared 'nithing' (i.e. without honour) by King Edward and fled once again to Flanders. To atone for these sins and no doubt many more, Sweyn decided

The exotic Kilpeck.

to go on pilgrimage to Jerusalem in 1052, walking barefoot. He died of cold near Constantinople in September 1052. Such a wasted life for a man who could have been King of England (though surely not a good one). The wronged Eadgifu retired to her nearby manor of Fencote after this 'excitement', and was still in occupation at Domesday thirty years later.

LUDLOW, Castle ** £
Town centre, signposted.

This marvellous castle was most probably originally built by <u>Walter de Lacy</u> or <u>his son, Roger</u>, not long before Walter's death in 1085. Walter was a member of the military household of William Fitz Osbern, a close confidant of William the Conqueror who held 'palatinate' powers over the border counties of Hereford, Gloucester, Worcester and southern Shropshire after the defeat of the local English in 1069. Fitz Osbern secured his border by building a string of castles from Wigmore in the north to Chepstow in the south. Walter sited his castle at Dinham in his manor of Stanton Lacy. Only later did it become known as Ludlow. The site commands the strategic crossroads of a north–south border route and the east–west, Knighton–Worcester route together with a crossing of the river Teme.

This castle is remarkable for the early date of its stonework in the **inner bailey**. This walled enclosure, large gatehouse tower and corner towers all date from around 1080. Within the inner bailey (ward), do not miss the round Norman **chapel** (rare in England) dating from the mid-twelfth century.

A town grew up around this important castle and resulted in the development of a planned settlement during the twelfth century, from which Ludlow derives its grid street system. Ludlow was one of the more successful Norman plantation towns so a walk around its pleasant surroundings is a must. Although no Norman buildings survive, the street plan remains with the juxtaposition of castle, market place and parish church at its centre. By the late Middle Ages Ludlow had become nationally important because of its links to the Yorkist dynasty, and played a crucial part in the politics of the turbulent fifteenth and early sixteenth centuries.

MOCCAS, St Michael and All Angels Church **
In the grounds of Moccas Court, ¾ mile north of B4352 Hay-on-Wye–Hereford road and 2 miles south of Bredwardine.

A fine and almost complete small Norman parish church built around 1130. Only the windows and bellcote are later intrusions. The nave, chancel and apse are on a downward progression and internally comprise a most attractive sequence of Romanesque arches. The two doorways are also Norman with tympana, which have unfortunately decayed over the centuries. The stonework is of the Herefordshire School (see Kilpeck). At Domesday the manor belonged to Nigel the Physician and comprised of just one hide and one plough.

RICHARD'S CASTLE **
1 mile north-west of village centre and pub, which lie on B4361 Leominster–Ludlow road. Turn west off B4361 at pub onto minor road.

Not so easy to find but very rewarding, this castle is one of those rarities – a pre-Conquest castle, just one of three or four in Herefordshire (see Ewyas Harold). In all probability this is the castle of Avretone/ Auretone, mentioned in Domesday Book as being held by <u>Osbern Fitz Richard</u>, who was the son of <u>Richard Fitz Scrob</u> – a Norman knight who came over to England with Ralph of Nantes in the 1040s at the request of Edward the Confessor, his uncle. Richard avoided expulsion from England when the Godwins returned to power in 1052 and Osbern became Sheriff of Hereford in 1060, during Harold Godwinson's earldom, and retained his lands after the Conquest. Osbern married Nest, the daughter of the Welsh prince Gruffydd ap Llywelyn and his wife Eadlgyth, daughter of Aelfgar, Earl of Mercia.

Substantial **earthworks** from the motte and bailey remain on this site west of the church on a spur above the valley of the Teme. The splendid motte rises 60ft above the ditch (access steps have recently been cut but the site is somewhat precipitous). Fragments of a bailey wall survive. You will not be disturbed here.

The adjacent St Bartholomew's **church** is largely from a later era but offers an interesting guidebook that gives details of recent excavations. Unfortunately but not surprisingly, these have shed little new light on whether the castle earthworks date from pre- or post-Conquest. They are probably a mixture of both, with even later modifications.

There is yet more interest in this village. It represents a classic example of a failed Norman plantation town as the road patterns around the castle/church complex indicate. Prospering for over 200 years from the early twelfth century the town is recorded as having 103 burgesses in 1304. However decline set in in the later Middle Ages perhaps overshadowed by the growth of nearby Ludlow, owned by the dukes of York. Failure of such towns was quite common, e.g. Huntington and Caus in Shropshire.

SHOBDON, Arches *
½ mile north of village in grounds of Shobdon Court. 200yds north of church at top of avenue of trees.

At the top of the tree-lined avenue stands what is called an 'eyecatcher' by Pevsner. What remained of the Norman priory church was re-erected in this splendid position by the Bateman family in 1756. The original church was built around 1130 by <u>Oliver de Merlimond</u>, chief steward to the Mortimer family of Wigmore. It comprises chancel arch, two doorways and their tympana with sculptures all in the so-called Hereford School of Norman Sculpture. The existing church, which was rebuilt in an amazing Rococco style, is nearby and well worth a visit.

SHREWSBURY, Abbey Church ****
Just across English Bridge east of river Severn beside 'old A5' London Road, now A458 to Much Wenlock.

This monastery was founded in 1083 by **Roger de Montgomery II, Earl of Shrewsbury**, as a Benedictine house on the site of a wooden Anglo-Saxon church. Roger was one of William the Conqueror's inner circle, his importance being demonstrated by the fact that William chose him to remain behind in Normandy in 1066 to assist his wife Matilda in governing the duchy during William's absence in England. The original early Norman centre bays in the nave, the transepts, chancel arch plus others; the west door and the north porch all remain from Roger's church. Towards the east of the **north aisle** lies a splendid **effigy** of Roger, who died a few days after being admitted to the monastery as a monk in 1094. The effigy probably dates from the late twelfth century. Full marks to the abbey for their recognition of Roger's historical importance in their excellent guidebook and in the signage in the church. Roger's son, Hugh, was also buried here after his death at the hands of Danes in 1098.

Shrewsbury, with its motte and bailey castle, served as Roger's principal residence in the north – he also owned large areas of West Sussex around Arundel and Chichester, as well as other lands. Roger held palatine status in Shrewsbury and was charged by William with defence against Welsh incursions across the Severn. The Normans judged that attack was the best means of defence against the Welsh and Roger was no exception. He was soon establishing a castle near the newly named Montgomery in modern day Powys (see Hen Domen). As early as 1069 Shrewsbury withstood an attack by the Welsh.

STAFFORD, Castle *

Just north of A518 Stafford–Telford road, 1½ miles west of town centre just before bridge under M6.

The castle overlooks the M6 but no longer commands this main route to the north-west! In 1069–70 Stafford was heavily involved in the Mercian uprising against the Conqueror led by Edric the Wild of Herefordshire. In suppressing the revolt, William personally led armies to the town and achieved easy victories on both occasions. The second involved his famous lightning march across the Pennines from York in the middle of winter, during which even his disciplined Norman troops came close to mutiny. In the aftermath, castles were built at Chester and Stafford, the latter on a site nearer to the town and defended by the river Sow.

Before the end of the eleventh century the castle was moved to the present site for reasons unknown. Either Roger de Tosny or his son Robert built the new structure as a motte and bailey. Roger had been granted

substantial lands in Staffordshire in 1071. His son adopted the name de Stafford, whose descendants moved up to greater things, becoming the dukes of Buckingham. The substantial earthworks of the motte and bailey survive and are well maintained by the local authority. A woodland trail within the 26-acre site has been developed, together with a visitor centre. The keep is clearly of a later vintage.

STOCKTON-ON-TEME, St Andrew's Church *

At the T-junction of A443 Tenbury Wells–Worcester road and minor road from Stockton to Stanford Bridge.

This church and surroundings just ooze rural charm. The nave is Norman of 1130–40 with a splendid south doorway and chancel arch. Note the carved stones of Norman vintage either side of the chancel arch. At Domesday the manor was held by Roger de Lacy; before the Conquest it had been held by Godric.

STOULTON, St Edmund the Martyr Church *

Village centre just north of A44 Worcester–Evesham road.

Delightful early Norman nave and chancel (with three original windows), which are shown to best effect inside the church. The memorable north and south doors feature Norman 'blind' arcading and the chancel arch is simple early Norman. The admirable guidebook dates the church to 1120, while Pevsner dates it to 1130–40. At Domesday the church was held by Worcester Cathedral. St Edmund the Martyr was killed by the Danes in East Anglia in 879.

Effigy of Roger Montgomery, founder of Shrewsbury Abbey.

YORKSHIRE

ALNE, St Mary's Church *
South-west end of village, 2 miles west of A19 York–Thirsk road on minor road. Turn off A19 west, 2 miles south of Easingwold.

This church may not look Norman from the outside but nave, chancel and west tower date from the 1120–30s. The south doorway is particularly fine and ornate and the tower arch and lintel of the priest's doorway are also noteworthy. Note also the corbel table and delightful small Norman window in the vestry north-side. The parish belonged to the archbishops of York but at Domesday was described as 'waste', no doubt a victim of the harrying of the north by the Conqueror in 1069–70.

KIRKBURN, St Mary's Church **
Village is 3 miles south-west of Driffield. The A614 Driffield–Howden road now the village. Church is signposted off A614.

This church was founded by <u>Robert le Brus</u> and the living given to Guisborough Priory which he also founded in 1119. Robert was the ancestor of the Robert the Bruce and an example of Anglo-Norman nobility who were induced to live in Scotland by grants of land by the Scottish monarchs and then who became involved in Scottish politics. The nave survives as a fine example of late Norman work, built 1130–40, including windows, south and north doorways, plain tympanum, corbel table and the splendid chancel arch. Note also the delightful Norman font. The chancel was originally

179

apsed but rebuilt in the early nineteenth century. Excellent church literature. Pre-conquest this was Earl Morcar territory.

KIRKDALE, St Gregory's Minster ***
1½ miles south-west of Kirbymoorside, ¾ mile north of A170 Thirsk–Pickering road. Signposted off A170.

Delightfully situated by a stream, this unusual church is dedicated to Pope Gregory (590–604). The sundial in the south porch has an old inscription referring to 'the days of King Edward and … of Earl Tostig' – approximately 1060 when **Tostig Godwinson** was Earl of Northumbria. The narrow west arch is also Anglo-Saxon, as are the quoins and the chancel arch.

The powerful Norman interior at Kirkburn.

The church was rebuilt around this time by <u>Orm (son of Gamel)</u>, of a major Northumbrian family and married to Aethelthryth, daughter of Ealdred, an earlier Earl of Northumbria. One of Orm's brothers-in-law was the powerful Siward, earl from 1041–55. Orm owned a large estate based on Kirbymoorside, which passed to the Mowbrays during the twelfth century. It is believed the church was linked to the abbey at nearby Lastingham, serving as a minster, i.e. a community of non-monasterial clergy proselytising over a wide area in an era before most villages had parish churches.

KIRKSTALL, Abbey ** £
3 miles west of Leeds city centre on A65 Skipton road. Signposted.

A stone's throw from the city centre but set in glorious surroundings on the banks of the river Aire. First founded at Barnoldswick near Skipton in 1147, the monks moved to this site in 1152 as the area finally recovered from the Conqueror's harrying of the north (many other monasteries were founded at this time in the north). These dates are considerably later than those normally encountered in this guide. I have included Kirkstall because its architecture remains predominantly late Norman, having been little altered in later centuries. The impressive size of the abbey church is cathedral-like and the remains include a fair proportion of the associated outbuildings. Quite simply, Kirkstall has the best abbey remains I have visited.

The initial construction of the abbey was completed by 1182. Some early gothic pointed arches were used, but overall the buildings have a real Norman feel to them. This Cistercian monastery held lands throughout West and South Yorkshire. The

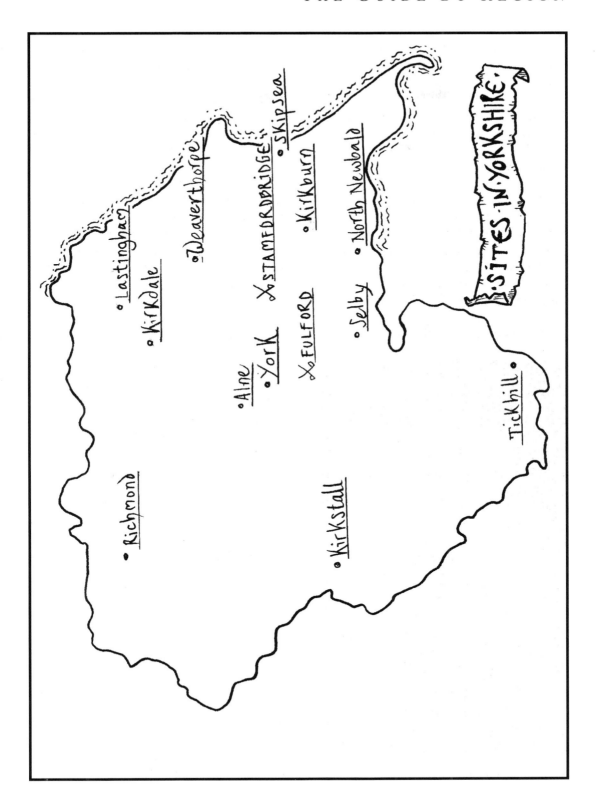

Sites in Yorkshire

Lastingham
Kirkdale
Weaverthorpe
Skipsea
Stamfordbridge
Kirkburn
North Newbald
Fulford
Alne
York
Selby
Richmond
Kirkstall
Tickhill

Kirkstall Abbey, Leeds.

whole site exudes the affluence enjoyed by most of these early medieval abbeys. The founder was <u>Henry de Lacy</u>, Lord of Pontefract. There is a fine guidebook to the site which is run by Leeds City Council and entry is free – a must see. This is of course the Kirkstall as in 'Gough from the Kirkstall Lane End' beloved of cricket commentators, so why not combine your visit with a couple of sessions of decent cricket at nearby Headingley.

LASTINGHAM, St Mary's Church *
West side of village, 4 miles north of A170 Thirsk–Pickering road on minor road via Hutton-le-Hole.

St Cedd founded a monastery here in 654, which was destroyed by the Danes. Refounded in 1078 by Stephen of Whitby, first Abbot of St Mary York but then abandoned by 1086. The highlight of this church is the 'unforgettable' **crypt** (Pevsner), virtually all of which is dated to the early Norman period and intended as a shrine to St Cedd. It is unique in England having within it an apse, plus chancel, nave and aisles. The main body of the church retains the original early Norman **columns**, plus added work of the thirteenth century, and produces a lovely atmospheric effect helped by the existence of another apse.

NORTH NEWBALD, St Nicholas's Church ** KAL

Village centre, off A1034 South Cave–Market Weighton road. Tel. 01430 801068.

Pevsner tells us this is 'the most complete Norman church in the East Riding'. It is also the finest – particularly outside. Dated to around 1140, this large building is a good example of late Norman decoration. Windows and doorways abound and there is a corbel table. Inside, the crossing provides the climax with all four original Norman arches in place. As is often the case, the chancel was originally apsed but is now a perpendicular rebuild. The unexpectedly wonderful architecture is probably explained by the fact that the manor was held by the archbishops of York. A church and priest are mentioned in Domesday Book, presumably using an earlier wooden structure.

RICHMOND Castle *** £

Town centre south side. Overlooks the river Swale.

After Durham this is the finest Norman monument in the north. At the Conquest King William granted vast lands to **Alan the Red, Count of Brittany**, who led the Breton contingent at Hastings. Most of these were in the north so Alan constructed a castle on this magnificent site after 1071 as his principal residence. The castle was built of stone in the first instance and much of this original work survives – both curtain walls, the great gateway embedded in the ground floor of the later keep, **Scolland's Hall** and **St Nicholas' Chapel**. Scolland's Hall is justly claimed as the oldest hall in England (Chepstow now being in Wales) while the design of the main gatehouse keep is rare.

Alan's grant included the lands of Earl Edwin of Mercia from the Conqueror in 1071. These formed the basis of the Honour or Earldom of Richmond, the lands of which were so vast that recent research concluded

that the epithet 'wealthiest Briton ever' belonged to Alan the Red. Alan's great nephew Conan, who became Duke of Brittany, was probably responsible for adding the upper two storeys to form the great keep. Despite these illustrious beginnings, history has largely passed this castle by, perhaps because of its 'off the beaten track' location. Henry Tudor inherited the Earldom of Richmond well before he fought his way to the throne of England at Bosworth in 1485. After a fire at his palace at Sheen in 1497, he built a new one on the Thames – Richmond, after his northern Honour. A fine place to visit, but summer will usually be much warmer.

SELBY, Abbey ****

Town centre signposted.

An enigma wrapped up in a paradox? This abbey is the finest Norman church in the north after Durham. Selby is also by tradition the birthplace of **King Henry I** in September 1068. Yet this event is little celebrated here and the abbey is little known outside Yorkshire.

The abbey was founded in 1069 by Benedict, a French monk from Auxerre who was introduced to the Conqueror while the latter was spending Christmas at York in 1069 after suppressing the first wave of Northumbrian risings. The next year William presented Benedict with a charter, perhaps suggesting that Selby should commemorate his victory over Northumbria in 1070 in the same way that Battle Abbey celebrates Hastings. This first abbey was built of timber. The exciting aspect here is the involvement of Queen Matilda in the foundation. If Henry was born here in 1068 then Matilda must have accompanied her husband on his first ever visit to Yorkshire at a time when Norman control was only just being exerted there. Surely it was

Richmond Castle from across the river Swale.

The magnificent late Norman west door at Selby Abbey; hints at the royal connection here.

more sensible for her to remain safely in Winchester during pregnancy? Selby was the only occasion **Queen Matilda** and **King William** co-operated in the founding of a Benedictine monastery. It clearly commemorates something important: if not Henry's birth, then what?

Selby is actually only 3 miles south of Riccall, where Harold Hardrada and Tostig had based their fleet in September 1066. In the aftermath of the Battle of Stamford Bridge there was fighting around the ships at Riccall (excavations have unearthed weapons and other items). Does Selby Abbey in some way commemorate Tostig? After all, he was Matilda's brother-in-law; he was married to her half-sister Judith, daughter of Count Baldin of Flanders. There would be a macabre symmetry, with Battle Abbey in Sussex commemorating Harold Godwinson and Selby Abbey his brother Tostig Godwinson.

It does however seem strange that King William should risk bringing his pregnant wife up to York during his first ever visit to Northumbria, a potentially hostile territory. In 1068 the northern earls, Edwin and Morcar, were still loyal to William and, during this particular visit, no significant violence ensued. But nevertheless, bringing the newly crowned and pregnant queen of England 'along for the ride' seems a huge gamble.

Unfortunately in the course of his duties, Abbot Benedict overreached himself when disciplining two thieving monks, whom he had castrated and blinded in the Norman style. He was forced to resign and the monks talked of leaving Selby. Henry I, by now king, refused to allow this and thus saved the abbey. New abbot Hugh de Lacy (abbot 1097–1122) moved the abbey to its current site a little further from the river Ouse and began the construction of the current church around 1100. By implication

Henry was motivated by Selby having been his birthplace. He actually made quite a lot of the fact that he was the only son of the Conqueror born when the latter had become King of England.

The revamped abbey went from strength to strength. It was granted vast lands throughout Yorkshire, Lincolnshire and other parts of the north. When Abbot Hugh retired, the abbey went into a long period of decline. As a result the building of the early Norman church was interrupted, resulting in a particularly long gestation period for its construction. The **nave** provides an excellent comparison of the differing styles of architecture from 1100–1225. To quote Pevsner: 'It is warmly recommended to students (of architecture)'. The piers are particularly fine and are in the style of Durham Cathedral. The transepts are also noteworthy examples of mid-Norman work, but the chancel has been often rebuilt. Windows in the north and south transepts illustrate the lives of abbots Benedict and Hugh (not original of course). The late Norman west door is quite sensational, while the 'deformed' nave arches furthest east demonstrate the almost uniquely difficult location of this abbey for a builder, as it is only 3ft above the water table.

Over the centuries this fine church has suffered many vicissitudes: initially the tower began to sink, then after the Reformation it fell into disuse for eighty years before becoming a parish church in 1618. It suffered military action in the Civil War and a major fire in 1906, but still it has survived. It needs and deserves more visitors.

**SKIPSEA, Castle **

¾ mile west of village. Access from Skipsea Brough on footpath, north (ten minute walk).

A fine, accessible example of an early motte and bailey castle, built before 1086 by Drogo de la Beauvriere, Lord of Holderness. The information board suggests that Drogo was present at Hastings but he is not included in the lists of most commentators. His descendants became Counts of Aumale with substantial lands in Upper Normandy. Stephen, Count of Aumale was restored to the lordship of Holderness by Henry I after the fall of the Montgomeries in 1102, but by 1116 he had sided with William Clito, Duke Robert of Normandy's son, against Henry. However by 1120 he had been reconciled to Henry.

The motte was originally an island in the now drained Skipsea Mere. A failed Norman plantation town stood on the higher ground to the west of the motte. The castle remained the principal residence of the Lords of Holderness until the late twelfth century when it moved to Burstwick.

TICKHILL, Castle **
South end of village on bend in A60 Worksop road near the Millstone public house. Has open days in high summer.

Roger de Buscli (Bully) moved his castle here from nearby Laughton-en-le-Morthen sometime before his death in 1098. Tickhill (referred to as Dadsley in Domesday Book) lay on one of the main routes north via Newark, Worksop and Doncaster. This important castle acted as principal residence to the vast estates of de Buscli's Honour of Tickhill and was the gateway to Yorkshire, being just 2 miles north of the Nottinghamshire border. Beware you are in Fred Trueman country – he was born in the nearby village of Stainton.

The physical remains of the castle are impressive but privately owned, and rarely open to the public. Do not be put off; the massive **motte** (still standing to 70ft and one of

Henry I's gatehouse at Tickhill Castle.

the tallest in England) is easily visible and close to a public footpath to the south. Park behind the public house by the duck pond in charming surroundings beside a helpful information board. The delightful **gatehouse** built by __King Henry I__ in 1129–30 is immediately visible.

De Buscli's wealth ensured that he was amongst the top flight of nobles in the late eleventh century and he is known to have witnessed many king's charters. On his death in 1098 the castle passed to the infamous __Robert de Belleme__, who had just inherited the Earldom of Shrewsbury from his elder brother Hugh de Montgomery. Robert had become one of the very wealthiest Anglo-Norman lords with vast estates in England (including the palatinate of Shrewsbury) and lands in Normandy inherited from both his brother and mother. In 1102 he chose to back Duke Robert of Normandy rather than Henry I in the succession crisis that followed the death of William Rufus. Belleme fortified his castles at Shrewsbury, Bridgnorth, Arundel and Tickhill. Tickhill was besieged by Henry but within a month all the castles had been reduced and Belleme had been banished to Normandy, where he was eventually captured and imprisoned by Henry after the Battle of Tinchebrai in 1106 (along with Duke Robert). Tickhill was confiscated by Henry I and remained in royal hands.

*De Buscli had built his first motte and bailey castle at nearby **Laughton-en-le-Morthen** just after the Conquest. This charming village is 5 miles south-west of Tickhill, 2 miles south of Maltby. The remains of the motte and bailey site adjoin the church at the west end of the village. It is on private land but can be observed from both the churchyard and from a public footpath accessible 200yds west on the Thurcroft road.*

An unusual entry in Domesday Book indicates that this was also the site of an aula (hall), built pre-Conquest by Edwin, Earl of Mercia. All the major players in late Anglo-Saxon England held lands in South Yorkshire presumably because of its traditional border status. Edwin as stated, King Harold at nearby Conisborough with its hunting park, Tostig held Doncaster, while Morcar, Earl of Northumbria, also held some manors in the area.

The exterior of the adjoining **All Saints church** includes a splendid Anglo-Saxon north doorway in the tower with a later Norman door inside it, plus pilaster strips.

WEAVERTHORPE, St Andrew's Church *** KAL
Delightful village set in the heart of the Wolds. 10 miles east of Filey, 2½ miles north of B1253 Sledmere–Bridlington road. Set high above village on north side. Tel. 01944 738315.

This is it: the Holy Grail. Of all the parish churches I have visited this comes closest in my view to giving the true 'feel' of a Norman church. Its structure, west tower, nave and chancel are all Norman and, most importantly, its windows are chiefly original – a good few remain. Externally the church is austere and simple in the early Norman style. The interior is similar but the scarcity of windows leaves it dark, just as it would have been in medieval times. Note also the Norman font (you may need a torch to get the full effect of the inside).

This manor was held in the eleventh century by the archbishops of York. At Domesday it was waste – presumably as a result of the harrying of the north. In 1108 it was sold by Archbishop Thomas to <u>Herbert the Chamberlain (d. 1130)</u>, a court official of Henry I based in Winchester. The wonderful sundial above the south door commemorates

The 'Holy Grail' of Norman parish churches: Weaverthorpe.

Herbert's building of this church around 1110. However Herbert seems to have had a darker side. Henry I biographer C. Warren Hollister has suggested that Herbert was the organiser of an assassination plot against Henry in around 1120. This was the third such plot on his life in as many years and quite unnerved Henry. Herbert was blinded and castrated in the Norman tradition. Charter evidence suggests that Herbert's eldest son, also Herbert, acquired his father's lands by 1121 and married one of Henry's mistresses, Sybil Corbert. Herbert's second son William by contrast acquired Weaverthorpe and went on to be Archbishop of York (1143–54) during the Anarchy. William was later canonised as St William. Do not miss this wonderful church. If it lay within 50 miles of London it would be much celebrated.

YORK ***

York was the capital of Northumbria, the only region of England to offer substantial and sustained resistance to the all-conquering Normans. This resistance is symbolised by the fact that the Normans constructed not one but two motte and bailey castles in York, on either side of the river Ouse.

Clifford's Tower
In the east bank of the Ouse between that river and its tributary, the Foss. Signposted for Castle Museum.

Baille Hill
On west bank of Ouse by Skeldergate Bridge. By the corner of Bishopgate Street and Cromwell Road.

The Conqueror ordered the construction of a motte and bailey castle here during his first visit in the autumn of 1068, when he entered the city without a fight and obtained the submission of many local magnates. It later became known as Clifford's Tower. Command of the castle was entrusted to <u>William Malet</u> from Le Havre, the man who may have been entrusted with the burial of King Harold after Hastings (he was probably a member of the Norman hit squad dispatched by William to kill the king late in the battle). In February 1069 the castle was attacked by rebels. Malet was killed but the castle held out and was relieved by William with all speed. William immediately ordered a second castle to be built on the west bank of the Ouse opposite the first one, known as Baille Hill. William entrusted this to his right-hand man, **William Fitz Osbern**.

Despite this action, when the autumn 1069 rebellion (led by King Sweyn, Estrithson of Denmark, Edgar Aetheling, Earls Gospatric and Waltheof) attacked York, both castles capitulated and the city fell to the rebels on 20 September. Stenton sees this as 'the heaviest defeat which the Normans ever suffered in England'. However, at the rumour that King William was speeding towards the city, the rebels withdrew.

Jorvik Museum
City centre, Coppergate.

Displays a reconstruction of Viking York – a great family outing.

THE YORKSHIRE CAMPAIGN
(September 1066)
Strategic Background and the Campaign
On the death of Edward the Confessor in early January 1066, the throne of England was technically vacant by historical precedent (see chapter two). On his deathbed Edward was said to have nominated Harold Godwinson, the head of the most powerful family in England, as his successor. The next day the Witan hastily ratified the choice,

Edward was buried and Harold was crowned in Westminster Abbey. Harold had no links at all with the House of Cerdic however, which had ruled Wessex and England for over 400 years and of which Edward had been the last. This unfortunate position encouraged two powerful overseas claimants to the English throne: on one hand Duke William of Normandy who possessed a bogus claim through his aunt, Emma, twice Queen of England and Edward's mother; on the other hand and even more obscurely, Harald Hardrada the Ruthless, King of Norway. Hardrada had succeeded to the throne on the death of his nephew, Magnus the Good. A Scandinavian tradition held that in around 1040 Magnus had reached an accord with Harthacnut, King of England and Denmark, by which both would be recognised as each other's heirs if one was to die childless, which is exactly what happened to Harthacnut in 1042. Obscure maybe, but a good enough excuse for a renowned Viking warrior to invade England. Before becoming king Hardrada had spent seventeen years as a mercenary in the Mediterranean, rising to be head of the Varangian guard in Byzantium. By 1066 he had a reputation as a military commander bar none.

Hardrada spent the summer of 1066 preparing for an invasion of England and amassed a fleet as large as 300 vessels, probably setting sail from Norway in mid-August. He achieved some surprise by sailing directly across the North Sea to the Shetlands and Orkneys. Taking advantage of favourable northerly winds, the fleet then sailed down the coast of Scotland to rendezvous in early-mid September with his ally, Tostig, King Harold II's exiled brother and formerly Earl of Northumbria under King Edward. A Northumbrian rebellion late in the summer of 1065 had swept away Tostig's regime in York and replaced him

Clifford's Tower, York.

with Morcar, the younger brother of Edwin, Earl of Mercia. Tostig had been forced into exile when his brother Harold subsequently refused to back him. He fled to Flanders under the protection of his wife's half-brother, Count Baldwin. Tostig's subsequent actions appear to indicate that he was keen to exact revenge on his brother and the northern earls. Tostig is reported as having visited both Hardrada in Norway and King Sweyn Erithson, presenting himself as a potential ally for the conquest of England. He may also have visited Duke William in Normandy – keeping his options open perhaps? Whatever the truth of it, Tostig was quickly off his moorings in the spring of 1066 and sailing to the Isle of Wight, whence he harried the south coast of England with a force of sixty ships. By May he had moved up to Norfolk where he raided the country around the mouth of the Burn River. He

tried his luck in Lincolnshire but was beaten back by Earls Edwin and Morcar. Crucially Tostig's raids resulted in the militia (fyrd) being brought out by King Harold all over England early in the campaigning season.

The combined fleets of Hardrada and Tostig sailed down the Yorkshire coast, raiding Scarborough and Holderness en route. They rounded Spurn Point and, no doubt using the strong tidal flow in the Humber and Ouse to their advantage, made landfall at Riccall, 9 miles south of York, between 16–19 September. Meanwhile Earl Morcar would have received early warning of Hardrada's progress down the Yorkshire coast and begun to muster his troops in York. At some stage he was joined by his brother Earl Edwin, who most probably mustered at Chester, the capital of West Mercia, and marched the 125 miles across the country.

THE BATTLE OF GATE FULFORD (20 September 1066) ++

Location and Battle

At first light on Wednesday 20 September and 8 miles north of Riccall, King Hardrada ordered his troops to move from Riccall towards York. They used two parallel routes, represented today by the A19 Selby–York road and the B1222 Cawood–York road. These roads meet at Water Fulford just south of Fulford village. As the armies recombined they would have seen English troops to their north guarding the ford that crossed **Germany Beck**, a tributary of the nearby river Ouse. The exact location of this battle is the subject of much debate, but recent work by Charles Jones of the Fulford Battlefield Trust suggests this very ordinary beck as the focal point of a large engagement. Edwin and Morcar had advanced their armies the 1½ miles from the walls of York that morning and had spread their troops along the northern bank of Germany Beck, between the east bank of the Ouse on their right and marshy ground some distance to the east towards Heslington on their left. River levels in 1066 were higher than today (it was the medieval warm period) so, in my view, ignore the marshes right next to the Ouse at this point. The battle would have been fought on the higher ground slightly further east where the A19 crosses Germany Beck and on which most of Fulford village is now built. In 1066 Edwin and Morcar were in their late teens or early twenties – mere callow youths in comparison with Hardrada – so their decision to engage with his army was certainly brave, if not foolhardy. There seems no suggestion of their agreeing with King Harold II to dig in behind the walls of York until the king could come to their rescue from London.

The English had lined up with Germany Beck in front and with Morcar and his Northumbrians on the left flank, opposing Tostig and his Flemish mercenaries. The elder brother, Edwin, opposed Hardrada on the Norwegian left, right up against the east bank of the Ouse. Just a little is known of the battle tactics; the English were unsurprisingly targeting Tostig, so the battle started with Morcar's flank charging and pushing back the latter's force (clearly a grudge match). However Hardrada's preferred tactic was to let the melee develop and then strike with his best troops at a developing weakness. Edwin's Mercian troops were no match for the battle-hardened Norwegians and were pushed back towards York, some drowning in the Ouse as they tried to escape. Hardrada was able to wheel his force to the right and envelop Morcar's Northumbrians, pushing them eastwards towards marshy ground in the direction of Heslington. A large body of them were surrounded (perhaps 500 or so) and slaughtered. Miraculously however, both Edwin and Morcar escaped from this debacle. Edwin managed a fighting retreat back to the safety of York, while Morcar disappeared north-east beyond Heslington. His eventual destination is not known, but if he had any sense he would have kept well away from York given the history with Tostig. Casualties on both sides are seen as heavy, but no doubt much heavier on the English side during the rout.

Aftermath

We can assume Hardrada took his army back to Riccall after the battle. Negotiations secured the surrender of York and a victory parade on Sunday 24 September, with the handing over of hostages and provisioning of the invasion force fixed for Monday 25th. The whereabouts of the defeated Edwin and Morcar are vague; Edwin may have been in

York overseeing the negotiations.

THE BATTLE OF STAMFORD BRIDGE (25 September 1066) +++

Strategic Background and Campaign (continued)

We are now shaping up for one of the most prodigious military feats of the Middle Ages. It is likely, but not recorded, that King Harold II was by now based in London and learnt of Hardrada's arrival at Tynemouth on the 18–19 September (it had probably occurred on the 14th) – unless it came a day or two earlier by sea? The king already would have known that Duke William's fleet had moved up to Valery-sur-Somme on the 12 September. And yet by the 21th at the latest he was saddled up and leading an army northwards to confront Hardrada. A true moment of decision in the history

Harald Hardrada's force combined at this crossroads called Water Fulford, prior to the battle in September 1066.

of England. He was clearly on horseback because his army arrived in Tadcaster, which is south-west of York but 180 miles from London, on the evening of Sunday 24th after a journey of only four or five days. No army marching on foot could have achieved that: it would have taken more like eight or nine days.

Hardrada, meanwhile, had led his army back from Fulford to his ships in Riccall to spend Sunday night there. The next morning he made his way to Stamford Bridge with perhaps 3,000 men, 8 miles north-east of York on the river Derwent, where the Northumbrian hostages and provisions were to be assembled. By late morning Hardrada's force had arrived and was relaxing on the banks of the river. What's more, it was a warm, late summer's day and many of the warriors had left their body armour behind in the ships. The army was obviously not expecting to fight that day. Then, over the rise at Gate Hemsley, 1 mile on the road towards York, a great army of soldiers came into view, some probably mounted. Initially Hardrada thought these may be the hostages but it soon became obvious that there were too many for that. It was a hostile Anglo-Saxon force which had covered the 17 miles from Tadcaster through York to Stamford Bridge that morning, having picked up further recruits in both towns. It was probably bigger than Hardrada's army, perhaps 4,000–5,000 strong.

The Battle

Hardrada's army was taken completely by surprise, i.e. he had posted no scouts at York or Tadcaster. The majority of his men were on the east bank of the Derwent, with the river between themselves and the enemy, so they were immediately able to begin the process of achieving battle formation on the conveniently located level and open

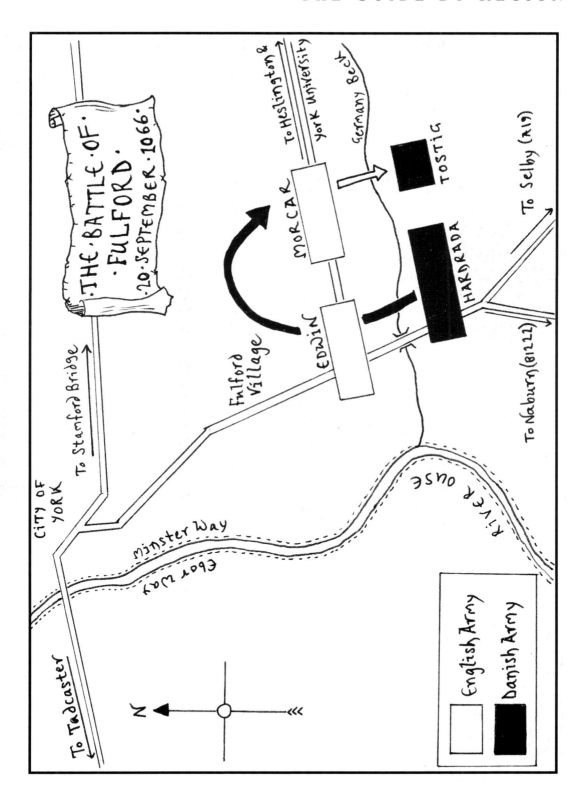

THE·BATTLE·OF·FULFORD·
-20·SEPTEMBER·1066·

To Stamford Bridge
City of York
To Tadcaster
Ebor Way
Minster Way
RIVER OUSE
Fulford Village
To Heslington & York University
Germany Beck
MORCAR
EDWIN
TOSTIG
HARDRADA
To Selby (A19)
To Naburn (B1222)
N

English Army
Danish Army

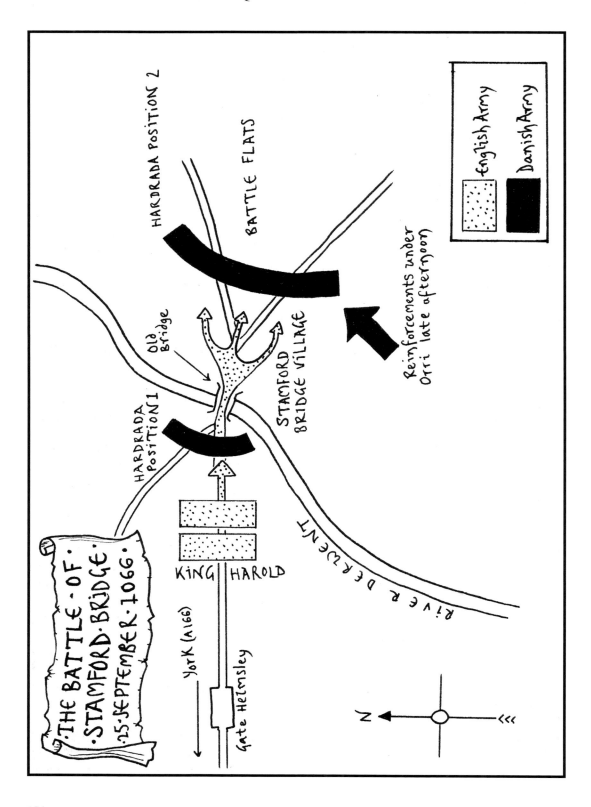

THE · BATTLE · OF ·
· STAMFORD · BRIDGE ·
· 25 · SEPTEMBER · 1066 ·

HARDRADA POSITION 2

BATTLE FLATS

Old Bridge

HARDRADA POSITION 1

STAMFORD BRIDGE VILLAGE

Reinforcements under Orri late afternoon

KING HAROLD

York (A166)

Gate Helmsley

River Derwent

N

English Army

Danish Army

fields nearby, now called **Battle Flats**. A contingent remained on the west bank to hold the bridge and delay the English (clearly the Derwent was not fordable despite its being late September and despite the name of the bridge). In 1066 the bridge was located several hundred yards upstream of the present bridge, more directly in line with the Roman road. Tradition has it that the bridge was held by a solitary Viking who could only be dislodged by the English rowing under the bridge in a swill tub and spearing him from below! The English poured across the bridge towards Battle Flats. At some stage attempts were unsuccessfully made to parley by both sides, during which it would have become apparent that the English were led by no other than King Harold II who had ridden up from London with his housecarls in less than five days. Hardrada did manage to despatch fast horsemen back to Riccall to bring reinforcements.

Few details of the battle tactics have survived. Sources talk of English cavalry movement and English archers. Hardrada appears early on to have led a charge of his housecarls in berserker fashion, but to have been struck in the throat by an arrow and killed. Tostig took over command but he was eventually cut down alongside the Norwegians and his Flemish mercenaries – lack of body armour no doubt proving a great handicap. In mid-afternoon the Norwegian reinforcements arrived hotfoot from Riccall, but their effectiveness was much reduced by the physical exertion expended in the long march from the ships while wearing their body armour. They immediately engaged with the English in what became known as Orri's Storm, but were also put to the sword. The slaughter was immense but would also have taken its toll on the English housecarls.

There is evidence that the Viking ships at Riccall were attacked too. In any event, the sources tell us that out of the 300-ship fleet that Hardrada brought on campaign, only twenty-four were needed to transport those survivors that King Harold was allowing to return home to Norway. These might actually have been different ships brought in for the purpose. At no stage is there any mention of prisoners.

Aftermath

With the deaths of Hardrada and Tostig, the Norwegian claim to the English throne collapsed. King Harold's awesome ride to York and stunning victory greatly enhanced his military reputation. For the Vikings the defeat was so calamitous that they were never the same threat to England again. Further raids did follow in the 1070s but these were quite easily dealt with by William the Conqueror.

The most important result of Stamford Bridge occurred just four days later however, when Duke William's invasion fleet landed at Pevensey in East Sussex completely unopposed. Harold was still at York, 250 miles away, sorting out the damage caused by Hardrada's invasion. He is likely to have heard this dreadful news around 2 October. Oh, to have been a fly on the wall when he did!

No figures survive but the fearsome slaughter of the Norwegians will have also taken its toll on Harold's housecarls, highly skilled and experienced warriors who could not be replaced in the short term. The next day, 3 October, the king left for London to deal with Duke William's threat, accompanied by his remaining housecarls and any other troops who had access to horses.

King Harold may have been the victor in the short term but the real beneficiary of Stamford Bridge was Duke William, who was handed not only an unopposed landing in Sussex but also the initiative in the subsequent Hastings campaign. Harold's disappearance to the north was crucial to his final defeat at Senlac. William couldn't have planned it better if he had tried.

Discussion

This battle is something of a puzzle. At midday on 25 September one of the greatest European warrior-kings of the age found himself in the following strategic position:

- His invasion army was split in two: 3,000 men with the king at Stamford Bridge, the remainder back with the invasion fleet at Riccall, 15 miles away across the river Derwent. His immediately available force was probably outnumbered – reinforcements would take some hours to arrive from Riccall.
- Many of the men at Stamford Bridge had left their body armour behind and perhaps other specialised weaponry, e.g. that of the archers.
- Scouts do not seem to have been posted in York or Gate Hemsley, so the arrival of the Anglo-Saxon force under King Harold at the bridge over the Derwent came as a complete surprise to the Norwegians.
- Stamford Bridge does not appear in the Domesday Book. Presumably at that time it was just a bridge (and ford?) on the York–Bridlington Roman road. The nearest manor however is Catton, just 1¼ miles to the south. Before the Norman Conquest this manor was owned by none other than the Godwins, and was certainly well known to Tostig after his time in Northumbria – possibly to Harold also.

There are four ways of explaining this disastrous situation:

- It was strategic incompetence of the highest order; difficult to believe given Hardrada's massive military experience.

- The facts are wrong, always possible after 1,000 years.
- Logic points to Hardrada and Tostig having completely discounted the possibility of King Harold arriving so quickly from London. Yet Tostig had fought alongside his brother not two years before and obviously knew his character. To march on foot from London so quickly was impossible, but to ride with an elite band of men was an entirely different prospect.
- When Hardrada recognised that King Harold was upon him, he must have been furious. Had he been deceived by Anglo-Saxons unknown? Had he been told Harold was definitely still in London? I worry about Tostig: he was known in England as a tricky and secretive operator, he was something of a Francophile in being married to Judith of Flanders, and he had been Edward the Confessor's favourite. Trustworthy? Definitely not! Was he playing a double game? Interestingly there is no suggestion of any attempt at reconciliation between the brothers after Harold secured the throne in early 1066.

Other worrying features of this battle are the complete absence to date of archaeological finds at Stamford Bridge (although some remains have been found at Riccall). There is also no mention in the sources of Edwin or Morcar, who escaped from the battlefield at Gate Fulford. You would perhaps have expected Edwin, who negotiated the surrender of York to Hardrada, to have been in the Norwegian party as a hostage.

Location and What to See

Unsurprisingly this village makes quite a lot of the battle. In the centre near the river are two modern **monuments** and a mural **display** for young people. A pub by the river celebrates the legend of the Danish hero on the bridge.

Stamford Bridge makes much of the battle connection with two monuments.

For the children.

Even the pub is in on it!

Battle Flats can be viewed from a minor road south-east to Fangfoss and Full Sutton.

THE NORTH

CARLISLE, Cathedral **
City centre, south-east of castle north of railway station.

In the tenth and eleventh centuries Carlisle was part of the Scottish kingdom of Strathclyde, captured by William Rufus in 1092. Consolidation of the Scottish border in the 1090s represents one of the major achievements of Rufus. Marcher lordships along the lines of those on the Welsh border were established for border defence and English settlers were brought in from the south, even bringing with them their own livestock. By the early twelfth century marcher lords like Robert de Boivill of Kirklington had begun moving north of Hadrian's Wall.

King Henry I granted lands for a religious establishment in 1102 and founded a priory here in 1122. Construction may not have commenced straightaway because of border problems, but a Norman church was being built in 1130. In 1133 Henry declared Carlisle a bishopric under Aethelwold of Nostell in South Yorkshire (he was Henry's Augustinian confessor, surely a most fascinating job), who also had been given Melbourne in Derbyshire. This first cathedral in Carlisle has similarities to the superb Norman church in Melbourne (see East Midlands) and survives today at the **west end** of the later cathedral as the **transepts** and part of the **nave** of the original building. They make a fine sight. Henry I visited the city in 1122 to found his priory and ordered the construction of the castle in stone.

CHESTER, St John the Baptist Church **
City centre (not the cathedral).

Chester has been an important town in this border region since Roman times at the latest. This was recognised by the Conqueror in 1070 by the building of a castle after the collapse of the Mercian revolt of 1069–70. In 1071 Hugh d'Avranches was made Earl of Chester, providing one of the key links in the chain of marcher defences. In 1075, in accordance with the Norman policy of moving cathedrals to major centres of urban population (perhaps for defensive reasons?), this church was granted cathedral status by Bishop Peter of Lichfield (d. 1085) who moved his see here. A church had stood here since the seventh century and had been re-founded in 1057 by Leofric,

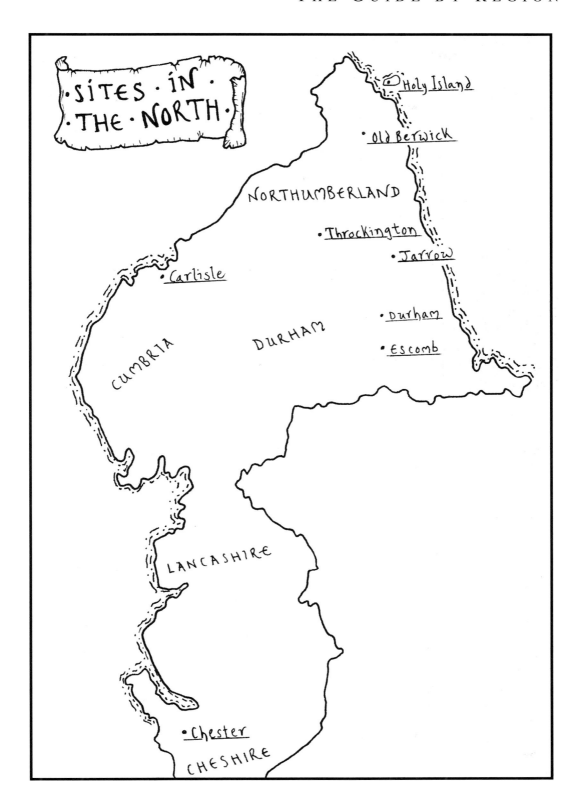

Earl of Mercia. Peter quickly started to build a new Romanesque church, but the structure had not even been completed when his successor, Robert de Lumesay, in turn moved the see to Coventry in 1095 – perhaps because of frequent incursions by the Welsh. A turbulent border town indeed. The unfinished building was left roofless until the sixteenth century when St John's became a collegiate church, only to be dissolved by Edward VI later in the century and the renovated/extended building partly demolished. What a chequered history. Meanwhile, a Benedictine abbey had existed in Chester since 1092 and had been granted cathedral status by Henry VIII in 1541 as the current cathedral.

Much of the early Norman work survives in St John's as the **nave**, the first bay of the **chancel** and the splendid **crossing**, together with the ruins outside of the former choir, partly demolished in 1541. A most interesting survival. Much less of Norman interest survives in the current cathedral.

DURHAM, Cathedral and Castle *****

City centre. You would have to work hard to miss this tremendous location, on a hilltop in a bend of the river Wear. Park in a multistorey and walk up.

Externally, the cathedral looks interesting, with the long nave displaying its Norman windows, but nothing prepares the visitor for the splendour of the interior. To all intents and purposes, inside, Durham remains a Norman **cathedral** except for the east end. Quite simply this is the most glorious survival in this guide and one of the marvels of European architecture. Enjoy! In addition to its beauty, the cathedral is also important from the viewpoint of its architecture. It was the first building in Europe to incorporate tunnel vaulting in its nave. This was constructed in 1128–33 and thus points the way to the change to Gothic architecture with its pointed arches towards the end of the twelfth century.

Durham does not have as long a religious history as one might think. The site only gained importance in 995 when the relics of St Cuthbert (d. 687) were brought to this naturally defendable hilltop for safe keeping from the Danes. A stone church was quickly built by the Anglo-Saxons to house them. The Normans chose this defendable location as their forward base within the Northern March to counter any threat from Scotland. A new cathedral was founded in 1093 by Bishop William of St Carileph (bishop 1080–96) and largely completed by his successor **Bishop Ranulph Flambard (bishop 1099–1128)**. By 1133 it was completed. In addition to that of St Cuthbert, look out for the tomb of the Venerable Bede (d. 735). His remains were stolen by a Durham cleric from Jarrow in around 1020 and brought here to be kept safe.

The first building constructed by the Normans in Durham was the **castle** across Palace Green. It was ordered by the Conqueror in 1072 on his return from Scotland. Before 1100 the castle had been fortified in stone. Little of this early work survives (under croft, chapel and some walling) but the motte survives and the modern fortifications occupy the original site. It was first commanded by Bishop Walcher, in effect the first of the prince-bishops of Durham. In the early years after the Conquest, Durham had experienced much violence, not only from the local inhabitants whose resistance formed around displaced Anglo-Saxon Earls Morcar and Gospatric, but also from raids by the Scots taking advantage of the chaos in northern England. Robert de Commines, newly appointed Earl of Northumbria, was burnt to death in the bishop's house

Anglo-Saxon charm at Escomb.

in January 1069. In spring 1080 Bishop Walcher was murdered at Gateshead and Durham Castle was then besieged. King Malcolm of Scotland devastated the area in 1070 and besieged the castle in 1088. Much violence has occurred on this lovely hilltop.

ESCOMB, St John the Evangelist's Church ** KAL
1½ miles west of Bishop's Auckland in village centre. Take minor road right off B6282 Bishop's Auckland –Etherley road.

The church guide admits that little is known about the origins of this building: its date, founder or why it is here. This is of absolutely no consequence since it is an unmistakeably Anglo-Saxon church and, what's more, one of only three in Britain which survive complete. Like other Anglo-Saxon churches in Northumbria it has a long, tall and narrow nave. This is a fabulous building both inside and out. Be sure to take in the almost windowless north wall. Enjoy a relaxing pint in the pub opposite.

HOLY ISLAND, Priory Church *
Village centre. Walk from car park. ½ mile south of Haggerston on A1 turn off to Holy Island via Beal. Beware road floods at high tide and take care.

The island is a much more interesting place to visit than it looks from the mainland. A religious centre since St Aidan arrived from Iona in 635, the monastery was destroyed by the Danes in 875. It was re-founded by <u>William of St Carileph, Bishop of Durham (bishop 1080–96)</u> in the late eleventh century as an offshoot of the monastery at Durham. What remains of the original monastery is the atmospheric ruin of the priory church. Architecturally it has much in common with Durham Cathedral, which was built around the same time – in fact the piers in the nave are copied from Durham. A delightful ruin in a delightful setting.

JARROW, St Paul's Church *
¾ mile east of town centre in park surroundings just east of B1297 ring road.

Founded as a monastery in 681 by Benedict Biscop with monks sent from nearby Monkwearmouth, Jarrow became the home of the Venerable Bede who died here in 735. By around 700 a stone church had been constructed, of which the east church gloriously survives as the chancel of the present church. There is no question that the Anglo-Saxons had the technology to build in stone, and 400 years before the Conquest! The monastery was sacked by the Danes in 794 but re-founded in 1074 by Aldwin, Prior of Winchcombe Abbey, in far-off Gloucestershire. The **tower** and **monastic**

buildings survive from this era. Jarrow became a cell of Durham. Bede's body was stolen in 1020 by a Durham cleric, and his remains lie in that cathedral.

OLD BEWICK, Holy Trinity Church ***
Take B6346 Alnwick–Woolverton road. About 4 miles out of Alnwick go straight on minor road to Chillingham/Chatton through Old Bewick hamlet. ½ mile out of hamlet turn right up very minor dead end to church.

You are well off the beaten track here. Tradition has it that this lovely church was built by **Queen Matilda (or Edith) (c. 1080–1118)**, first wife of Henry I and daughter of Malcolm Canmore, King of Scotland (king 1058–93), and St Margaret – herself daughter of Edward the Aetheling who fled to Hungary in 1016 upon Cnut's accession to the English throne. Matilda was therefore a member of the House of Cerdic.

This delightful Norman church

Yes, the Normans got this far north. Holy Island Priory, which had connections to Durham.

incorporates earlier work in the north and west walls. Although restored on a number of occasions over the centuries, the essentials of the church remain Norman: apse, chancel, chancel arch and nave. A great spot, apparently once a thriving market town.

Matilda gave the church and manor of Bewick to Tynmouth Priory in 1107 in memory of her father, who was slain alongside her brother at Alnwick in 1093 by retainers of Robert Mowbray, and initially buried at Tynmouth. Malcolm is known to history as the man who killed Macbeth in 1057. In the uncertain times ruling immediately after the Conquest, Malcolm raided Northumberland on a number of occasions. William Rufus took a dim view of this behaviour and Malcolm and his forces were ambushed north of the Lion Gate at **Alnwick**. A **monument** called Malcolm's Cross, restored in 1774 stands on the east side of the B6341 Alnwick–South Charlton road in trees by a roundabout.

WALES

CARDIFF, Castle *** £

City centre near National Rugby Stadium and south of Cathays Park. Signposted.

In 1081 the Conqueror undertook an expedition to St David's, his one and only visit to Wales. He received tribute and homage from the princes of South Wales and he ordered a motte and bailey castle to be built on this site en route – within the remains of the Roman fort that commanded the lowest fording point of the river Taff. The structure is massive, and at 35ft high the **motte** is the highest in Wales. Originally it also had a ditch that was filled in during the eighteenth century. From 1093 the castle became the administration centre of Robert

Fitz Haimon's lordship of Glamorgan. Fitz Haimon, a close confidante of William Rufus, strengthened the castle's defences.

The shell **keep** in stone was probably added by **Robert, Earl of Gloucester**. Robert, the eldest illegitimate son of Henry I, had married Fitz Haimon's daughter and heiress, Mabel, and succeeded to the latter's estates, including Glamorgan on his death in 1107. The exact date of the keep is not known but one possibility is around 1126, when it could have become necessary to strengthen the castle's security and comfort in order to house **Duke Robert of Normandy**, Henry I's elder brother and prisoner. On the Conqueror's death in 1087 Robert inherited only the Duchy of Normandy, while his middle son William Rufus inherited the kingdom of England. Robert was, in contrast to his brothers, an easy-going but ineffective duke, whose rule led to constant breakdown of law and order. This provided the perfect excuse for Henry I to invade Normandy from 1104. Robert was defeated by Henry at the Battle of Tinchebrai in southern Normandy in 1106 and taken prisoner. Henry kept his brother imprisoned in a variety of castles in England and Wales for twenty-eight years until his death. Cardiff was the last. Despite being a crusader of note and a man of great charm, Robert appears to have made no attempt to escape. It is thought that the prisoner was transferred here in 1126 because Henry had begun to doubt the loyalty of Bishop Roger of Salisbury, his gaoler at Devizes.

CHEPSTOW, Castle and Priory Church *** £

Town centre north-side by river Wye. Signposted.

One of the great castles of Britain, Chepstow is sited on a near impregnable cliff on the west bank of the Wye, commanding the main route into South Wales from England. Although the site contains much later fortification, its centrepiece remains the great tower, one of the earliest stone structures in Britain. The Domesday Book records that a castle was built here by **William Fitz Osbern, Earl of Hereford**, soon after the Conquest. It was built on the west (i.e. Welsh) side of the Wye as a base for expeditions into Wales. It was probably a wooden motte and bailey construction.

Originally it was thought that the marvellous **great tower** was built at the same time but recent research suggests a somewhat later date. Turner has suggested that the tower may have been ordered by William the Conqueror during his one and only visit to Wales in 1081. After Earl William's death in 1071 his son Roger de Breteuil rebelled against the Conqueror in 1075 and forfeited all his estates to the Crown. The suggested date also fits the tower well, putting it alongside London's White Tower and Colchester Castle, two other early stone keeps. Progress with subduing the Welsh in South Wales was at first slow. By Domesday the Normans had only just crossed the Usk at Caerleon, but from 1093 progress was more rapid.

300yds to the south-east of the castle.

William Fitz Osbern founded a Benedictine priory. Much of the **priory church** survives from the early twelfth century. Built on a lavish scale, the nave and west end survive as the parish church in the early Norman style.

DEGANNWY, Castle *
½ mile east of railway station, which is on A546 Llandudno Junction–Llandudno road. Close to village church where footpath access is possible up to castle remains on twin peaked, low hill (or from adjacent housing development).

This prominent site had long been used for defensive purposes when Robert of Rhuddlan (d. by 1093) established a royal castle here, probably sometime after 1081 when Gruffydd ap Cynan, Prince of North Wales, was captured by the Normans. This enabled them to penetrate westwards along the coastal plain towards Anglesey. But, as was so often the case, the Welsh did not give up that easily. Robert of Rhuddlan, who was a cousin of Earl Hugh of Chester, was killed here in around 1088, probably by the same Gruffydd. On 3 July of that year Gruffydd beached three ships under the Great Orme close to Degannwy. Caught unawares, Robert impetuously sallied forth with only one companion to confront the raiders who were busy loading their booty aboard their ships. He was surrounded, slain and decapitated.

The twin peaks here were made into a double motte castle linked by ramparts and ditches. Little remains but the impressive natural features. There is a modern **plaque** and the coastal views are extensive. In the thirteenth century Edward I built Conway castle on the opposite bank of the eponymous river in order to at last secure the conquest of Wales.

EWENNY, Priory ***
1 mile north-east of village on dead end minor road. Signposted off B4524 Cowbridge–Ewenny road.

When Robert Fitz Haimon, one of William Rufus' closest confidantes, was granted the lordship of Glamorgan in 1093 he sub-divided the county amongst his followers in order to settle the fertile Vale of Glamorgan. One of them, William de Londres (d. 1126), built a castle at nearby Ogmore and, between

SITES·IN·WALES

- Degannwy
- Rhuddlan
- Hen Domen
- New Radnor
- Nevern
- Llandovery
- Abergavenny
- Chepstow
- Newport
- Ewenny
- Cardiff
- Ogmore

Chepstow Castle looms over the west bank of the river Wye.

1116 and his death, founded this Benedictine priory, building the church as a daughter House of St Peter's Abbey, Gloucester.

This church is the finest Norman building in Wales and amongst the very finest in this book. The whole interior is preserved. The vaulted presbytery (which the monks used) is stunning, and the nave is not far behind, along with the south transept. Original wall paintings from the 1140s survive in the presbytery. In the south transept lies the splendid **tomb slab** of William's son, the notorious <u>Maurice de Londres (d. before 1171)</u>. In 1141 Maurice is recorded as having confirmed the grant of the priory to Gloucester and as founder (perhaps he re-founded it after destruction by the Welsh). At any rate, he had many crimes to atone for: he murdered Gwenllian, wife of the Welsh Prince of Deheubarth, in Kidwelly Castle and was denounced by the Pope in 1128 for robbing and defrauding Llandaff Cathedral.

Unusually, the priory is fortified: the original twelfth-century work was extended 100 years later. A fine guide book is available.

ABERGAVENNY (Grwynne Fawr), The Revenge Stone ****

You could say this is tucked away. Located on a spur of the Black Mountains in the Grwynne Fawr Valley, north of Abergavenny. Turn north off A40 Abergavenny–Brecon road at Glangrwyney onto minor road signposted to Llangenny/Llanbedr. Proceed north then east for 6 miles to crossroads by Grwynne Fawr River. Turn left on minor road north to Grwynne Fawr reservoir. After 1 mile turn down sharp right across river to Non-conformist chapel. Park here by river and walk up the road past Ty-mawr and Upper House farms. From the latter continue on public footpath to the top of the ridge. Just before the top bear right to cairn-like stone. A 1 mile climb. Map ref: 284 240.

Degannwy Castle has magnificent views on a fine day.

This is the most unusual entry in this guide: no plaque, no road, no toilets. Just two stones on a ridge, one with a hierogly and one with history! The stones commemorate the ambush and killing of **Richard Fitz Gilbert, Lord of Clare, Chepstow, Cardigan and Tonbridge**, on 15 April 1136 by the disgruntled Welsh princes Morgan and Iorwerth ap Owain, who held the nearby province, Ystradyw. The de Clare family was one of the wealthiest in England, taking its name from the Honour of Clare in Suffolk. Family members had been present in the New Forest when William Rufus was killed in 1100. Although not close to Henry I they were always treated well by him. One of the 'perks' they received was the lordship of Ceredigion in 1110, an invitation by Henry to re-conquer this territory in West Wales, which had been devastated in the 1094 Welsh uprisings.

At Easter 1136, only a few months after the death of Henry I, Richard Fitz Gilbert had a big argument with the new ruler, King Stephen, and then returned to his estates. Travelling from Usk to Ceredigion, accompanied by Brian Fitz Count, Lord of Abergavenny, and his escort, Richard, he followed the medieval route into Mid-Wales via Abergavenny, the Grwynne Fawr Valley in the Black Mountains and Talgarth. The Grwynne Fawr forms the boundary between Monmouthshire and Powys and at the time the lordships of Abergavenny and Ystradyw. As Richard's party approached the forest of Grwynne Fawr and the county boundary, they dismissed Fitz Count and his men. The reduced party of Normans (with the escort now amounting only to a '… fidler and a singer') was soon afterwards set upon by Welsh troops, led by one or both of the ap Owain brothers. Richard and his son Gilbert were killed. The **Revenge Stone (Dial**

Garreg) high up on the ridge may mark the spot where Richard was killed. However the OS map shows a Coed Dial ('wood of revenge') ½ mile north down in the valley so that may be the spot to which the Welsh charged downhill from the ridge.

Presumably they were righting earlier wrongs wrought against their family or 'clan' by Richard. By the end of spring 1136 all of South Wales was aflame. Henry I's firm but careful handling of Wales had led to a generation of inexorable expansion of Norman colonisation in South Wales. Within weeks of his death in December 1135, the Welsh had defeated the Normans at Llwchwr near modern-day Swansea and later that year defeated them again at Crug Mawr near Ceredigion. The assassination of such a powerful Norman lord only fanned these flames of widespread revolt. With the subsequent confusion and lack of purpose which characterised the Norman presence in Wales during the Anarchy in England 1138–53 the Norman Conquest of Wales was set back generations. This memorial symbolises that defining year for the Welsh. Morgan and Iorwerth themselves regained many of their family lands in Gwent during 1136 and continued to rule there for many years, with Iorwerth succeeding his elder brother and lasting into the 1170s.

Do visit on a fine day. The views of the Sugar Loaf, the Black Mountains and the Vale of Ewyas are superb. A personal favourite.

HEN DOMEN (near Montgomery), Castle **

1½ miles north of Montgomery on west side of village on minor road between B4385 Montgomery–Welshpool and B4388 Montgomery–Kingswood road.

In 1071 Roger de Montgomery was granted widespread lands by the Conqueror and, in 1074, was created palatinate Earl of Shrewsbury, charged with defending his section of the border with Wales. Between these dates Roger had crossed nearby Offa's Dyke from Shrewsbury and established a motte and bailey castle here as a forward base for expeditions into Wales. One of the few castles mentioned in the Domesday Book, it was probably constructed by a younger son of Roger's, **Hugh de Montgomery**, who inherited the earldom on his father's death in 1094.

Hen Domen has a fine motte (although tree-lined) and extensive bailey earthworks, commanding the Severn Valley between Welshpool and Newtown as well as the road from Shrewsbury into Mid-Wales. Excavations have revealed the presence of numerous wooden buildings in the bailey together with the existence of no fewer than five generations of wooden bridges linking the bailey with the motte. In 1073–4 Hugh led expeditions deep into Wales from here, which resulted in the annexing of Cardigan and Pembrokeshire where Arnulf, Roger's youngest son, was established. Hen Domen was captured during the Welsh revolt of 1094 but re-taken by Earl Hugh in 1095 with much bloodshed. There is some suggestion that the intervention of William Rufus was required in 1097 to again recapture the castle. On the fall of the House of Montgomery in 1106, Henry I granted the site to Baldwin de Bollvers, but in the thirteenth century this important castle was moved 2 miles down the road to the virtually impregnable site above Montgomery.

LLANDOVERY, Castle *

South side of town near cattle market.

A well-preserved motte and bailey constructed beside the river Bran in 1116 by <u>Richard Fitz Pons</u>, Lord of Clifford in western Herefordshire and Cantref Bychan in Mid-Wales as he thrust westward into Wales from his English base. Later that year the bailey was attacked by locals and torched (no doubt the first structure was of wood). Like so many castles in Wales over the next century it was besieged and fought over many times by Norman and Welsh opponents. The unusual 'D'-shaped tower was added in the late thirteenth century.

NEVERN, Castle *

The village is just north of B4582 Newport–Cardigan road (off the A487). Remains are north-west of church up a steep hill on minor road north to Gethsemane. Motte is on east side of road.

An ancient defensive site encompassing an Iron Age hill fort and a Norman motte and bailey. This castle was first established by <u>Robert Fitz Martin</u> (Lord of the Honour of Blagdon in Somerset and Devon, Cemais in Pembrokeshire and Llangybi in Gwent) in around 1105. Fitz Martin was one of Henry I's favoured young courtiers. The bailey is triangular in shape, bounded to the east by the narrow-gorged river Gamman. There are in fact two mottes here, both tree-lined. The original (and largest) is to the north-west of the site by the road, with a later (but stronger) one to the south-west corner by the river, built in the late twelfth century.

At that time the Welsh Lord Rhys captured the castle from William Fitz Martin, Robert's grandson, despite or because of William being married to Rhys' daughter. Subsequently Rhys himself was imprisoned here by his unruly sons. The castle fell into disuse soon after as the Fitz Martins developed their site at nearby Newport. This delightful spot lies 1 mile north-west of and above the **parish church**. By the south chapel in the churchyard

stands the Nevern **Cross**. The Buildings of Wales tell us this is 'one of the outstanding Celtic crosses of Wales' dated 1033–5.

NEWPORT, Cathedral *

On hill west of river Usk, ¾ mile due south of railway station in residential area. Map ref: 309 876.

The Gloucestershire Domesday Book tells us that by 1086 the Normans had just begun to infiltrate across the Usk around Caerleon. In 1093 Robert Fitz Haimon was granted lands

The Nevern Cross.

in Glamorgan and its lordship by his friend William Rufus. At the same time Rufus granted this church (as St Gwynllyw's) to Gloucester Abbey. So a Norman church existed on this ancient Christian site before 1100. The present structure hides its Norman origins very well externally, but inside the visitor immediately encounters a splendid internal **west door** of Norman origin, leading onto an equally splendid five-bay Norman **nave** of round piers and clerestory. The styling of this work is Gloucester's, said to date to the 1140s after a dispute over the church's ownership had been resolved.

NEW RADNOR, Castle *

North-east edge of town that the castle hill overlooks. Access is up lane north just before exit from town centre towards Kinnerton. It is a very small town.

A lovely setting high above the town, this motte and bailey site is both extensive and dramatic. The earthworks are particularly impressive. The steep drop down from the motte to the town is spectacular, but take care. The site was probably developed around 1095 by Philip de Broase, Lord of the Rape of Bramber in West Sussex, although William Fitz Osbern, close confidant of the Conqueror, may have first fortified it around 1070.

The town still conforms to the grid pattern of its Norman plantation. Surely this was the smallest county town in England and Wales, whose status was achieved in 1536 only because the castle was being used as a prison. This site provides a typical example of how the Norman kings gave opportunities to their successful aristocrats to conquer and hold lands in Wales but rarely engaged directly in the Conquest themselves.

OGMORE, Castle **

Lies just north of B4524 Ewenny–Ogmore-by-Sea road at Ogmore village, 1½ miles west of Ewenny.

The Norman Conquest of Glamorgan began in earnest in 1093, when Robert Fitz Haimon, a close confidante of William Rufus, was granted the lordship of Glamorgan. Robert sub-divided the county between his followers. William de Londres (d .1126) was granted lands in this area on what was for a while the western boundary of the Conquest. Before 1107 he erected a ring work castle at the confluence of the Ogmore and Ewenny rivers. During the 1120s, his son, Maurice de Londres (dc. 1171) built the first masonry structure on the site: the stone keep, the dominant ruin today. In 1116 Maurice had apparently abandoned the castle when an assault by the Welsh Prince Gruffydd ap Rhys ap Tewder threatened. This did not materialise so Maurice re-occupied the site and resumed his wicked ways (see Ewenny).

RHUDDLAN, Twthill Castle *

1 mile south of a later stone castle at south-west edge of village, on the banks of the river Clwydd. Accessible by road from the later stone castle.

Long a region of North Wales disputed by the Welsh and English, Rhuddlan was the site of the palace of Gruffydd ap Llywelyn, Prince of Gwynedd, which was burned by Harold Godwinson during his lightning strike on North Wales in early 1063. After the Conquest the Normans quickly pushed on from Chester along the coastal plain into Wales. At the lowest fording place of the river Clywd, Robert of Rhuddlan, a cousin of Hugh d'Avranches, Earl of Chester, established a motte and bailey castle in 1073. In co-operation with cousin Hugh a small Norman plantation borough was also developed. The castle became the base for

Ogmore Castle near Bridgend.

Norman expansion westwards towards Anglesey. Robert held his castle and lands directly of the king and was recognised by the Conqueror as Lord of North Wales.

However in 1075 the castle was sacked by Gruffydd ap Cynan, one of the Welsh leaders vying for control of Gwynedd, but recovered by Robert. The Welsh would not give up – Robert was killed near Degannwy (modern-day Llandudno) in 1088 (see Degannwy), with Earl Hugh taking over the lordship. In succeeding decades Rhuddlan was sacked in 1094 (probably), during the Anarchy in the 1140s and in 1167.

A fine, tall **motte** survives beside the Clywd plus limited earthworks. In the thirteenth century Edward I moved the castle downstream and canalised the river 2 miles to the sea so that the new castle could be readily supplied by water.

NORMANDY

BARFLEUR ***

Harbour
You can't miss it. Park at north-east end.

Close to the lifeboat station are two **plaques** that commemorate the fact that Duke William's flagship in the 1066 invasion fleet was built here that same year. It was given to William by his wife, Matilda, and named the *Mora*. Its captain was a Barfleur man called Stephen, son of Alrard. However there is something much more interesting to be seen at Barfleur.

Walk through the alleyway northwards for a few metres and you will reach the other side of the harbour wall with a view of the beach and the largest lighthouse in France. That lighthouse is there for good reason, for on 25 November 1120 the *White Ship* is said to have struck submerged rocks, capsized and sunk somewhere between the harbour mouth and the lighthouse – a view little changed today. A **plaque** commemorates the disaster. At low tide these rocks become visible (many other ships have been lost here over the centuries). This was one of the greatest disasters of medieval England. Over 300 passengers and crew were drowned, only a butcher from Rouen survived. Amongst the dead were Henry I's son and heir, <u>**William Aetheling**</u>, his natural son Richard (although some scholars suggest Richard was a younger legitimate son). Henry now had no direct male heir and he was already over 50 years old. He quickly re-married – Queen Matilda had died in 1118 – but no children resulted. He considered promoting his eldest natural son, Robert of Gloucester, but in the end decided against it, so his daughter, Matilda, became his heir. She was married to Geoffrey of Anjou and so, after the interval of civil war between Matilda and Stephen, England came to be ruled by the Plantagenets from 1154. Without the *White*

Ship disaster English history would have been very different. A number of Henry's key household officials also drowned and his travelling treasury went to the bottom.

The *White Ship* had set sail in the early evening darkness of 25 November, on a moonless night. Henry was returning to England after four years of campaigning in Normandy against rebellious barons and Louis, King of France. Victory at the Battle of Bremule had secured Henry a favourable peace with Louis. On the eve of departure, Henry was approached by one Thomas, son of Stephen, who asked Henry to sail in his newly refitted vessel, the *White Ship*, because Stephen, his father, had in turn piloted William the Conqueror's ship the *Mora* across the Channel during the invasion of England. Henry declined Thomas' offer but agreed to let both William Aetheling and Richard travel in the *White Ship*. William and Richard were then joined by many young companions whose high spirits led to the consumption of much wine by passengers and crew alike. The degree of drunkenness became so bad that Count Stephen of Blois (who usurped the throne of England on Henry's death) and a number of companions disembarked. With captain and crew inebriated, the *White Ship* set sail somewhat behind King Henry's vessel. The unruly passengers urged the crew to overtake the royal fleet with the result that they got too close to the submerged rocks.

For a whole day nobody in England dared tell the newly arrived Henry the awful news. On finally hearing it he is said to have fallen to the ground, overcome with anguish and 'never smiled again'. His own decision had sent two sons to their deaths, but what was his rationale behind it?

Plaque to the White Ship *disaster at Barfleur Harbour.*

Pointe de Barfleur Lighthouse
Take D911/D10, 4km from village to the point.

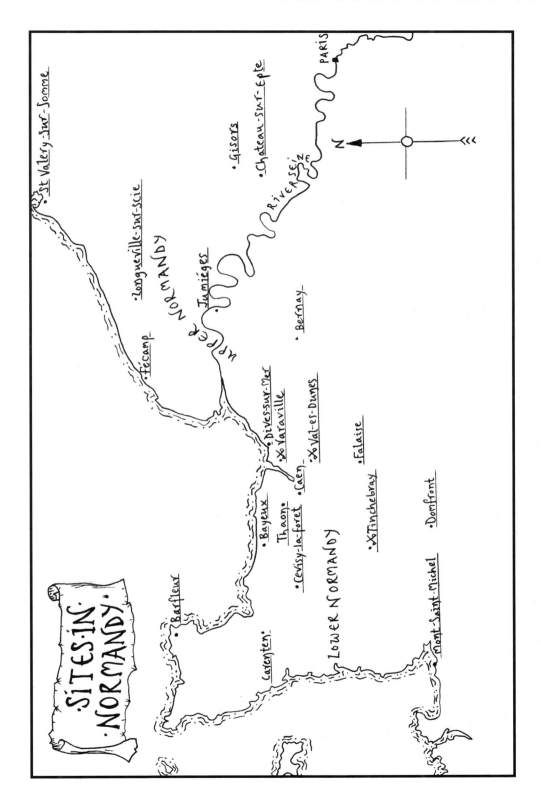

SITES·IN· NORMANDY·

St Valéry-sur-Somme

Longueville-sur-Scie

Gisors

Château-sur-Epte

PARIS

N

River Seine

UPPER NORMANDY

Jumièges

Fécamp

Bernay

Dives-sur-Mer

Varaville

Caen

Val-ès-Dunes

Falaise

Bayeux

Thaon

Cerisy-la-forêt

Tinchebray

Domfront

LOWER NORMANDY

Barfleur

Carentan

Mont-Saint-Michel

A short drive gets you nearer to the offending rocks and a view back to the harbour. Go at low tide if possible. Ascend the lighthouse for yet another angle and a commanding view of the Saire region.

BAYEUX *****

Tapestry (Tapeserie) €
Museum 0.5km east of cathedral. Signposted.

An absolute must for any student of the Conquest who is visiting Normandy. The display is exemplary: exhibition, cinema, followed by the tapestry with audio commentary. It will not disappoint! However choose your time because it does get busy. No need to tell you the story in the tapestry since it is all in the rest of this guide.

Cathedral
City centre.

An early centre for Christianity in Normandy, Bayeux sprang to prominence in the eleventh century with the construction of the mighty Romanesque cathedral. This was started by Bishop Hugues d'Ivry and completed by **Bishop Odo of Conteville**, the Conqueror's half-brother and comrade in arms at Hastings. This church was consecrated on 14 July 1077 with much splendour and in the presence of William and his queen, Matilda.

Unfortunately this structure did not last long. In 1105 Henry I invaded Normandy via Barfleur and made for Bayeux. Accompanied by Helias, Count of Maine and Geoffrey of Anjou, he invested the city. Very soon, however, Henry's men managed to set light to the city, driving out both the population and the garrison. High winds whipped up the flames and destroyed many houses, as well as the new cathedral. Henry captured Gunter

d'Aunay, the garrison commander, and many of his soldiers. The brutality continued, with Henry allowing his Manceaux and Angevins troops to plunder the remains of the city. A massive blot on Henry's career. Only the **crypt** and **parts** of the **western towers** survive from this building. Later in his reign **King Henry I** did arrange for the building to be rebuilt, but the replacement structure itself suffered another fire in 1160. The **nave arches** survive.

BERNAY, Abbey ** €
Town centre.

This splendid building was founded by Judith of Brittany, wife of Duke Richard II of Normandy (and grandmother of the Conqueror), before her death in 1017. The wealthy Judith bequeathed lands for the abbey from her extensive dower. In 1025, after some considerable deliberation, her husband issued a charter supporting the project but declaring Bernay to be a daughter house of the ducal abbey in Fécamp. Nevertheless, with this support Bernay played a part in the religious revival that swept Normandy in the middle decades of the eleventh century. Designed by William of Vulpiano from Fécamp, the church survives almost unaltered from its eleventh-century origins (the apse at the eastern end has been restored). The abbey was sold off during the French Revolution.

CAEN *****

Château
North side of city centre. Signposted.

In the years immediately after the Battle of Val-ès-Dunes in 1047, at which he regained control of Lower Normandy, Duke William the Bastard took steps to build up the fledgling

Bernay Abbey with Norman arches galore.

urban area of what is now Caen as a military stronghold. He built a ducal palace and a castle, and Caen became a favourite location and second city in the duchy at the expense of Fécamp. The surviving stone fortifications are of a later date but the **excavated** remains of the **ducal palace** can be viewed in the north-west corner of the château. Next to the ruins is a fine survival of a secular Norman building. Built by **King Henry I** in the early 1100s, it is known as the **Treasury**, but is more likely to have been intended as a banqueting hall. Not open on Tuesdays.

Abbaye aux Hommes (St Etienne) and Abbaye aux Dames (Holy Trinity)
West and north-east side of city centre respectively. Signposted.

These two abbeys on opposite sides of the city centre constitute arguably the finest medieval memorials in Western Europe. They were built in the 1060s by Duke William on the express instructions of the Pope as part of the 1059 settlement, which enabled the Pope to at last recognise William's marriage to Matilda of Flanders. In 1049 William had announced his intention of marrying Matilda but this was opposed by Pope Leo IX. The reasons were obscure at the time and have remained so. Consanguinity is often quoted, but William and Matilda were not that closely related. Political objections from the Holy Roman Emperor are more likely. William was not impressed and went ahead with the wedding despite the Pope's objections. The date of the wedding is again not certain but is likely to have been in the early 1050s. So it took a long time and a new pope for papal approval to be obtained. The settlement was negotiated by Abbot Lanfranc on behalf of William (note that the date of birth of Matilda's first child Robert is also shrouded in mystery: 1051–3).

In other words the anomaly was significant and required a significant penance to ensure expiation. These two splendid Romanesque abbeys were the price Duke William had to pay. Aux Hommes was finished in 1063, while aux Dames was consecrated on June 18 1066. **King William I (d. 1087)** is buried in **Abbaye aux Hommes**. A modern **floor slab** in front of the altar commemorates him but only his femur survives beneath it. The rest of his remains were lost during the French Revolution. **Queen Matilda (d. 1083)** is buried in **Abbaye aux Dames** in front of the altar. Time has been kinder to her. An older **slab** marks her grave, which contains much fuller remains. Not to be missed!

CARENTAN, Notre Dame Church **
Town centre, east side.

The current building is largely of the fifteenth century but inside remain parts of the original Norman structure, particularly the **nave** and **arcades**. These unusual survivals commemorate a well-documented piece of history from 1105: **King Henry I** returned to Normandy at Easter, determined to wrest control of the Duchy of Normandy from his elder brother, Robert. He landed at Barfleur and made his way to Carentan accompanied by a large force and much money. Here Henry met Bishop Serlo of Sees (in southern Normandy), a refugee from the excesses of Robert of Belleme, Duke Robert's ally.

Henry took his place at the back of the old church amongst the chests and belongings of the peasants (put there for safety against the ravages of the civil war raging in Normandy), ready to hear the Easter Mass. Perhaps having done a 'deal' with Henry, Serlo proceeded to deliver a memorable sermon, which has come down to us care of Orderic. To quote Warren Hollister p. 186–7:

Above: Henry I's treasury within Caen Castle. His dream home?

Right: Grave slab of William the Conqueror in Abbey aux Hommes, Caen.

… and the general breakdown of civil order because of the lethargy and boundless extravagance of the duke [Henry's elder brother Robert Curthose]: 'Often he dares not rise from his bed … because he has no breeches, socks, or shoes. Indeed, the jesters and harlots who constantly accompany him steal his clothes while he lies snoring in drunken sleep.'

It recalls that Curthose's predecessors among the Norman dukes had been active and capable, 'not for lust of earthly power but for the defense of your homeland [*pro defensione patriae*]'. With the avid support of Robert, Count of Meulan, and other nobles present in the church, Henry responded, 'I will rise up and work for peace in the name of the Lord and will devote my utmost endeavours to procure, with your help, the tranquillity of the church of God'. Having just crossed the Channel with a large army and war chest, and having already arranged to be joined by allied forces from Maine, Anjou, and Brittany, Henry was only too easily induced to proceed. But although Serlo's sermon – and propaganda similar to it – obviously served the royal ambition, it also represented a genuine and widespread yearning for the return of peace and order.

Serlo now turned to his second subject, that of cutting one's hair and trimming or shaving one's beard. These were vitally important, divisive issues in the church of the early twelfth century. Long hair and beards were widely censured at ecclesiastical synods and in the writings of church reformers, often along with the wearing of flowing, extravagant clothes and shoes with pointed toes that curled up like scorpion tails. Most recently and immediately, such practices had been condemned at Anselm's primatial council of 1102 at Westminster as well as in the archbishop's correspondence. At

Carentan Serlo quoted St Paul's admonition: 'If a man have long hair it is a shame unto him'; he went on to complain that long beards give men 'the look of billy goats, whose filthy viciousness is shamefully imitated by the degradations of fornicators and sodomites … and by growing their hair long they make themselves seem like imitators of women'.

The Easter Mass at Carentan reached its emotional crescendo when Serlo, having observed that Henry and all his court 'wear [their] hair in woman's fashion, received the king's consent to correct the situation. The bishop pulled out a pair of shears that he had conveniently brought along in his bag and proceeded personally to cut King Henry's hair. He then cropped the count of Meulan and most of the magnates.'

The Normans certainly were different … For Henry this was not so much a deal with Serlo, more some excellent propaganda against Curthose plus a cheap haircut! Bishop Serlo had begun by commenting on the piles of goods and equipment stored in the church and how they testified to the breakdown of order in the Cotentin for lack of a just protector. He went on to observe that such conditions had become common to all Normandy under (Duke) Robert Curthose. He spoke of the burning of churches and their congregations within them.

CERISY-LA-FORÊT, Abbey Church **
Between St Lô and Bayeux, 2km north of D572. From D572 take D8 or D34 minor roads north to village.

This celebrated abbey was founded in 1032 by Duke Robert the Magnificent of Normandy (d. 1035) as a Benedictine house. Robert, William the Conqueror's father, was lending support to the ecclesiastical revival then sweeping Normandy. This led to the duchy becoming famous throughout Europe for the number of its monasteries. This church dates from the second half of the eleventh century and inside it is a particularly magnificent celebration of Romanesque.

CHÂTEAU-SUR-EPTE, Castle **

The village lies on the D146 Gisors–Vernon road. The castle lies above and west of the village up a minor road which links to the D9.

This spectacular ruin was built in 1087 by **William Rufus** as the first in a chain of forts to protect the Norman border with the French Vexin along the river Epte. Originally the castle may have been fortified only in wood and its main feature was, and still is, the enormous **motte**. Also surviving from the early twelfth century are a curtain wall and two fine gate towers. The keep is later. This castle was besieged in the summer of 1119 by King Louis VI of France but successfully held out during the manoeuvring ahead of the nearby Battle of Bremule between Louis and Henry I in which Henry triumphed over the French king thus emulating his illustrious father.

DIVES-SUR-MER *

River and Harbour Mouth
From A13 auto route take D400 for Cabourg and Dives. After 6km turn right on D513 to Dives and Houlgate. After 2km river mouth and marina will be seen on left.

This small town briefly entered the history books in 1066. Although there is some dispute between the sources, most historians accept Dives as the port of concentration for Duke William's invasion fleet in early August of that year. The whole of the estuary and surrounding sea would have been covered with hundreds of ships from all over Normandy and elsewhere. In addition, new ships had been built here in Dives in the preceding months.

It is said that the fleet was delayed by contrary winds for a month. However on the 12 September, just four days after King Harold had stood down the fyrd in southern England, William's fleet set sail with his flagship, the *Mora*, leading. What happened next is unclear but the fleet ended up not in England but at Valery-sur-Somme, 60km north-east up the Channel. William finally set sail from there for Pevensey on the evening of 28 September.

Town Centre and Parish Church
Retrace footsteps along D513 1km to town centre. Signposted.

Here is a town which is very proud of its association with '**Guillame le Conquerant**'. There is a Conqueror's shopping village and restaurant, a Hotel Hastings, and a list of all the participants in the invasion placed on the inside of the west wall in the nineteenth century in the church (open summer weekends).

DOMFRONT, Castle ***
Ruins situated in north-west corner of this small hilltop town.

Duke William besieged the castle in 1052. On its surrender he annexed the surrounding Passais region. However the splendid **keep** was built in the late eleventh century by the Conqueror's youngest son, who was to become **King Henry I**. Its splendid ruin is situated in a superb naturally defensive position and celebrates the special place that Domfront occupied in Henry's career. By 1092 the three sons of the Conqueror were at loggerheads. After the siege of Mont St Michel, Henry was banished from Normandy. At Christmas in 1091 William Rufus and Robert Curthose fell out and the Treaty of Rouen was repudiated.

Henry gained possession of this strategically important hill town in mid-1092 in a bloodless coup. The townspeople, fed up with the heavy-handed and abusive rule of their lord, Robert of Belleme, invited Henry to take his place and opened their doors to him. It is thought that the castellan, Archard, probably engineered the coup. Formerly a landless exile with few companions, Henry now had a power base. Living like a robber baron, he avenged his banishment by making war on Robert of Belleme and his own brother, Robert Curthose, Duke of Normandy. From the moment he assumed the lordship of Domfront Henry's cause prospered. By 1106 he was not only King of England but had deposed Curthose in Normandy too – an awesome man (see Tinchebrai).

FALAISE, Statue and Castle
Town centre.

The marvelous statue of William the Conqueror (see frontispiece) commemorates his birthplace. The castle's donjon was built by Henry I and allegedly stands upon the rock from which William's father, Duke Robert the Magnificent, first set eyes on his beautiful mother, Herleve.

FÉCAMP, Abbey Church and Ducal Palace ****
Town centre on opposite sides of major road.

Abbey Church
A convent was founded here in the seventh century but destroyed by the Vikings in the ninth. On the same site Duke Richard I of Normandy founded a collegiate church in 990, together with a ducal palace close by that became one of his favourite residences. In 1001 his son, Duke Richard II, asked the celebrated William of Volpiano, from Piedmont, to establish a Benedictine abbey on the site. Fécamp became renowned as a

centre of Christian learning and teaching in the eleventh century.

A Romanesque stone church was consecrated in 1106 but destroyed by fire in 1168. Little of the original survives today, yet in the south transept can be found the grave slabs of the first two dukes of Normandy: Richard I (d. 996, duke 955–6), and his son, Richard II (d. 1026, duke 996–1026). Richard I in particular is important to our story for two reasons: in 991 he was the first duke to make a peace agreement with Aethelred the Unready, brokered by the Pope to counter the growing threat of Viking raids so that neither party would shelter the enemies of the other. Richard I was also the father of the inimitable Queen Emma, wife to both Aethelred and Cnut. Duke Richard II initially ignored his father's obligations but then negotiated with Aethelred the agreement that saw Emma established as Queen of England in return for Richard's closing of his ports to Viking ships. We know who got the better deal in the long run.

Note also the **wall plaque** to William of Volpiano in the north transept. The outside wall of the west front of the church contains statues of the two dukes.

Ducal Palace
Originally built in wood by Duke Richard I during his long reign. He loved the place and in fact died here. The structure was rebuilt in stone by Duke Richard II (d. 1026) in the early years of the eleventh century. The remains are scant but well cared for. Fécamp's finest hour came at Easter 1067 when the Conqueror returned here in triumph from England, complete with hoards of booty and treasure, a great gathering of Norman nobility and even prominent English hostages like Edgar Aetheling, Edwin and Morcar. This palace

witnessed great splendour, which has probably never been repeated in the town.

GISORS, Castle *** €
North-west edge of town centre, north of D14 Gisors–Rouen road.

In medieval times the river Epte formed the border between Normandy and the French Vexin. Over the centuries it saw much fighting between the King of France and the dukes of Normandy and thus attracted much castle building on both sides of the river. In 1097–8 acting as Duke of Normandy during his brother Robert's absence on crusade, **King William Rufus** laid the foundations of a castle here, designed to oppose the King of France's great fortress across the river at Chaumont-en-Vexin. William was prosecuting the Vexin War against the French king, which saw him advance towards Paris but fail to capture the king's fortresses. There was later fighting here in 1123–4 involving rebels against Henry I: Amary de Montfort, William Crispin and Waleran de Meulan.

A fine **motte** and **curtain wall** survive from the original structure. The castle is noteworthy for being sited and designed by **Robert de Belleme**, the notorious eldest son of Roger of Montgomery. During Rufus' time in Normandy Robert had gained favour for his military and engineering talents. **King Henry I** later added the marvellously irregular and polygonal keep, which was subsequently heightened by Henry II.

JUMIÈGES, Abbey *** €
From D982 Pont de Brotonne–Rouen road turn south at sharp bend near river Seine close to Le Trait on D143 to Jumièges. Abbey is signposted 3km along.

Here in a great bend of the Seine you get two ruined churches for the price of one. The left-hand church of Notre-Dame provides a wonderful example of mid-eleventh-century Romanesque architecture. The abbey was originally founded in the seventh century but suffered sack by the Vikings. In 1040 a rebuilding of the church was set in motion by Abbot Robert Champart (d. 1052), friend and advisor to Edward the Confessor. Edward may have spent time here during his long exile in Normandy during 1016–42. By July 1067 the church was ready for dedication, which was carried out by the Archbishop of Rouen in the presence of Duke William (now King of England) and a large gathering of the Norman aristocracy, as William travelled in triumph after his return to the duchy earlier that year. For good measure William granted Hayling Island to this great monastery – England was under the cosh!

LONGUEVILLE-SUR-SCIE, Castle *
East of and above village, just south of D149 Longueville to St Foy road on hillside after hairpin. Heading east turn right off D149 past school/college.

These ruinous remains celebrate the Giffards, an important and talented military family who were major landowners in both Normandy and England. Walter I (d. before 1090) fought with Duke William at the siege of Arques in 1053 and was present at Hastings – he may even have been one of the hand-picked knights detailed by the Conqueror to seek out and destroy King Harold. Walter was rewarded with 107 lordships in England, with over half in Buckinghamshire. Walter II (d. 1102) supported William Rufus and led his army in 1097–8 during the Vexin War with the King of France. He initially supported Duke Robert in 1101 but later (and very sensibly) became a firm supporter of Henry I. He was rewarded with the

Jumièges Abbey, which had strong links to Edward the Confessor.

Earldom of Buckinghamshire. Walter III fought for Henry at the Battle of Bremule in 1119. Sometime after 1106 the family founded a Cluniac priory at nearby St Foy.

A fine **plaque** at the castle entrance commemorates Walters I and II. In actual fact, this is not the site of the first castle built at Longueville (*c.* 1050) from which the Walters departed for Hastings. That was down in the valley. Early in the twelfth century the castle moved to the current site, perhaps to provide better protection to the newly established priory. The charming oval enceinte with walls survives, together with a fine example of a gatetower.

MONT ST MICHEL, Abbey *** €
Impossible to miss, but note causeway floods at high tide.

This dramatic location has a long religious history. The church dates back to the abbey buildings constructed in the 1050–60s and is a fine Romanesque survival – especially the nave, transepts, crossing tower, crypt and some of the convent buildings.

The previous church had been the setting for the marriage of Duke Richard II of Normandy to Judith of Brittany in around 998, from which survive the first details of a ducal marriage in Normandy, but it is the sons of the Conqueror who provide the colour here. In 1088 the youngest brother, Henry, used some of the quantity of silver inherited from his father to buy Mont St Michel and other lands in the Cotentin from his elder brother, Duke Robert, who was already short of money within a year of the Conqueror's death. This purchase provided Henry with a secure base from which he made his successful bid for the Duchy in the early 1100s once he had become King of England. Then, in a move that typified the dysfunctional behaviour

of the three brothers, in 1091 Duke Robert made peace with his middle brother, King William Rufus, and the two turned on young Henry. Henry took refuge in this natural fortress and both his elder brothers arrived mob-handed to lay siege. Tournaments for the besiegers were organised at low tide. Henry ran out of fresh water but Duke Robert typically allowed water to be sent in (Rufus was furious). After a fifteen-day siege Henry was allowed to ride away and lost his lands (but not for long).

Duke Robert came back here on a solemn pilgrimage soon after his return from the First Crusade in September 1100 – St Michel is the greatest of the warrior saints. The abbey became Cluniac under Henry I and owned vast lands through Western Normandy. It also owned St Michael's Mount in Cornwall and other lands in England given to it by King Edward the Confessor; another demonstration of his partiality towards Normandy.

THAON, St Peter's Church **
5km north-west of Caen, 1km north of village on D170. Park on bend and take footpath down through wood 1km to church in clearing. Open in July and August on Sundays only: 3–6 p.m.

There is nowhere else quite like this in this guide. A truly rural idyll where one is confronted by delightful Romanesque arches on the exterior of the church. Built in two stages 1050–70 and 1080–90, the church was controlled by the powerful lords of nearby Creuilly, but was also under the patronage of both Bayeux Cathedral and the Abbey of Savigny. An uneasy governance for certain, but the reason for the beautiful architectural decoration that adorns the building. In the 1090s Robert Fitz Haimon was Lord of Creuilly. A lovely picnic spot.

The church at Thaon, a rural idyll.

THE BATTLE OF TINCHEBRAI
(28 September 1106) ++

Background

In 1105 Henry, the Conqueror's youngest son and by now King of England, launched a full-scale invasion of Normandy against his brother Robert Curthose, Duke of Normandy. Robert's rule in the dukedom was seen as weak and had led to constant fighting amongst the barons, thus placing the brothers' inheritance from the Conqueror in jeopardy. The 1105 expedition stalled in front of the walls of Falaise but Henry returned the next year with his usual determination. After setting fire to the fortified Abbey of Saint-Pierre-sur-Dives Henry moved south-west against William of Mortain's castle at Tinchebrai. Henry's initial siege force proved too small so he assembled a 'very large army' in front of the castle and sealed it off. The army was commanded by Robert, Count of Meulan; William, Count of Evreux; Helias, Count of Maine; and

William Warenne, Earl of Surrey. Also with Henry were Alan, Duke of Brittany, Ranulf of Bayeux, Ralph of Tosny and most of the great magnates in Normandy.

William of Mortain was reinforced by only his uncle Robert of Belleme and cousin Duke Robert Curthose; they positioned their forces against Henry's besieging troops.

The Battle

On 28 September – forty years to the day the Conqueror set sail for England – two of his sons met in battle. Henry is said to have had much the larger army, especially in terms of cavalry. His army was arrayed in three columns led by Ranulf, Robert of Meulan and Warenne, while Henry dismounted and led a force of Englishmen and Normans on foot. He also positioned a force of mounted Bretons led by Helias at a distance and out of sight.

Battle commenced with a mounted charge by Curthose's knights. Initially they made some inroads but soon the two forces became locked in a close and deadly melee as both sides dismounted. Crucially Helias' reserve force, backed up by Duke Alan of Brittany, then charged against the flank of Curthose's infantry. Ducal casualties were high and a rout ensued. Robert of Belleme, commanding the rear of Curthose's army, then fled with his troops. The ducal army collapsed and Curthose and William of Mortain were captured. The fighting is said to have lasted only an hour.

Aftermath

This battle was the supreme military victory of Henry's career. He displayed much the superior diplomacy skills in assembling a larger force than his brother before the battle and superior tactics during it. But then Curthose was never much of a general, even if he was a brave and chivalrous soldier. As a result of the battle Henry became Duke of

Normandy and thus was able to reconstruct his father's Anglo-Norman realm. Not bad for a youngest son who inherited 5,000 sovereigns but no land from his father in 1087.

Curthose by contrast did not fair well. He was dispossessed by Henry, dispatched to England and incarcerated there in various castles for the rest of his long life. He died just months before Henry in 1134 aged 80 years.

Location

Nothing survives of the castle, but a modern **monument** to **Robert Curthose** and a **plaque** of the battle are situated at the roadside by a small park on the D911 Tinchebrai–Sourdeval road just at the western exit from the town. This is said to be the location of the battlefield 'in front of the castle'.

VALERY-SUR-SOMME, Monument **
Quayside at harbour.

A very pleasant little town with a marina and views across the reclaimed salt marshes. A modern **plinth** commemorates the fact that **William the Conqueror** used this harbour as a stopover prior to sailing on the evening tide for England on 27 September 1066. The Normans are rightly proud of their Conqueror. St Valery was actually in Ponthieu, not Normandy, but relations were good (it was also here that Harold Godwinson was shipwrecked in 1064). The narrower Channel crossing from here offered the attractive prospect of a twelve-hour overnight crossing for William's invasion fleet. In the medieval period once out of sight of land it was much easier to navigate at night by the stars than during the day.

St Valery at that time provided the largest haven on this part of the coast. The current river estuary is of modest width, but the extensive coastal marshes surrounding it

Modern monument commemorating the Battle of Tinchebrai.

give a clear picture of how the anchorage would have looked with the higher sea levels existing in that globally warm medieval period. The Conqueror's fleet of nearly 700 vessels would have been comfortably accommodated – afloat at high tide but many aground around low water. The fleet arrived here on 12–13 September from Dives-sur-Mer, 50km west along the Norman coast, where it had assembled during late summer of 1066. Along the way it is clear that a number of its ships were damaged or sunk. The sources suggest that the fleet ran into a westerly gale – some ships being driven onto the Normandy lee shore. In other words Duke William may have intended to sail direct from Dives to England, but was literally blown off course to Valery. Such a plan would have involved a full twenty-four-hour crossing,

which could have presented navigational difficulties during daylight hours. Certainly something untoward happened – there is talk of shipwrecks, damaged ships and even casualties being secretly buried to avoid demoralising the invasion fleet.

Some modern commentators investigate an alternative theory. William's fleet left Dives only four days after King Harold had stood down both the fyrd (militia), guarding the south coast and the Anglo-Saxon navy, which had been based at the Isle of Wight. Most likely he had in fact received intelligence in Normandy that this had occurred. Manuscript E of the Anglo-Saxon Chronicle tantalisingly mentions Harold going out against the Normans 'with a ship-army' but gives no date. Could it have been that William's fleet in fact ran into the Anglo-Saxon navy, which had not yet retired to London? Such a fleet engagement would explain not only William's casualties and his need for secrecy but could also have duped Harold into thinking that William's invasion fleet was crippled for the next few weeks – hence his willingness to depart for the north on 19 September, leaving southern England unguarded.

THE BATTLE OF VAL-ES-DUNES (early 1047) ++

Background

This was the battle that saved Duke William from a potentially disastrous rebellion and marks the turning point in his reign. From 1035, when William acceded to the dukedom at the age of 8 years, his hold on power was tenuous. In late 1046 Norman rebels, largely from Western Normandy, began to support a bid by Guy de Brionne (or Burgundy) to seize the dukedom – he had been a possible candidate in 1035. A plot was hatched to assassinate William while he stayed at

Valognes in the Cotentin. Forewarned, William escaped at night in disguise and made his way back to Falaise in what has now become a famous ride. In desperation the duke appealed directly to King Henry of France, his feudal overlord, for help in defeating the rebels. William travelled to Poissy and prostrated himself at Henry's feet. This did the trick and Henry led an army into Normandy in support of William.

Henry met up with William's meagre forces from Upper Normandy near Mezidon where they encamped for the night. Meanwhile the rebels, led by Guy de Brionne, Nigel of the Cotentin, Rannulf of Avranches, Ralph Tesson of Thury, Grimmoald of Plessis and Haimo of Creuilly, had crossed the river Orne south of Caen.

The Battle

Very early the next morning Henry's force pushed on through the hamlet of Valmeraye to the plain of Val-es-Dunes, a featureless, low plateau bounded by the hamlets of Serqueville, Begrenville, Billy and Airan, where they encountered the rebel army. The ensuing battle seems to have been a purely cavalry affair with no use of men at arms or archers. Detached groups of cavalry engaged in isolated conflicts over the extended plain. Henry and William were helped by the last-minute defection of Ralph Tesson from the rebels. King Henry was unhorsed early in the battle by Haimo but was saved when the latter was killed. The 19-year-old Duke William was meanwhile making a reputation for himself by killing a notable rebel warrior.

The rebels eventually broke – Rannulf first, Nigel of the Cotentin later. Fleeing in small bands they were hunted down as they tried to cross the Orne. Many perished through drowning or were killed at the ford at Arthit between Fontenay and Fleury-sur-Orne (just south of Caen).

Valery-sur-Somme. Duke William's invasion fleet sheltered here prior to departure for England.

Aftermath

The importance of this battle may not have been apparent immediately afterwards. William had certainly been rescued from a difficult position by Henry but Val-es-Dunes was to prove the beginning of William's rise to greatness. Further civil strife and battles lay ahead before he was master in his own country but from now on 'the bandwagon was rolling'. In October 1047 William held an ecclesiastical council at a site close to the battlefield where the Truce of God was formally proclaimed. Private war in Normandy was prohibited from Wednesday evening until Monday morning and during the major religious seasons. Tuesdays must have been murderous!

Location

227

Monument to the Battle of Val-es-Dunes, south of Caen.

*The battle is marked by a **battlefield cross** on the west side of the N13 Caen–Lisieux road, 10km south-east of Caen, just east of the hamlet of Vimont.*

THE BATTLE OF VARAVILLE, 22 March 1057, Modern Plinth ++

3–4km east of village on south side of D27 Varaville–La Bruyere road.

A modern **plinth** and information board commemorates this stunning victory achieved by **Duke William the Bastard** over the French King Henry I. Its importance for our particular story is that it really established William's military reputation throughout northern France and thus made it much easier for him to enlist so many French allies to his project to invade England. In fact the conflict here was purely an internal affair. Despite coming to Duke William's aid in 1047 at the Battle of Val-des-Dunes, by 1052 Henry had turned against Normandy and sided over the next five years with Count Geoffrey Martel of Anjou in a series of largely unsuccessful campaigns against Normandy. In February 1057 these two allies co-operated in another *chevauchée* into Normandy, entering from the south and heading towards Falaise and Caen. They laid waste the countryside and gathered much booty.

Meanwhile Duke William assembled his forces near Falaise, keeping the enemy under observation but not engaging with their much larger army. To continue their progress eastwards the French king had to cross the river Dives. The obvious route was via the Roman road/causeway, running eastwards from Varaville across the marshes and over a wooden bridge. The vanguard of the combined force got safely across the river, including the French king who watched his army cross the river from a nearby hill. Weighed down with the booty the combined force was by now badly strung out along the single-carriageway causeway. And so came the 'tour de force': it happened that the tide in the Dives estuary was up – it was a high spring tide so the sea had covered the marshes right up to the causeway – and the French force could not escape to the north if attacked. Sure enough Duke William, having kept his smaller forces hidden in nearby woods, unleashed a furious attack from the south on the rearguard of Henry's army, still struggling on the left bank of the Dives, and inflicted many casualties. Panic ensued and resulted in the collapse of the wooden bridge. King Henry and Geoffrey Martel could only look on in horror, isolated as they were on the right bank of the Dives, before beating a hasty retreat eastwards back home.

Contemporary sources make little of William's victory – perhaps because the style of the ambush wasn't considered quite 'cricket' when opposing the King of France. It was not until Wace began writing in the thirteenth century that the Norman tradition of a great victory over the French king came into being. Certainly William's careful strategic planning is much in evidence here, something he also demonstrated when invading England. In fact the victory was strategically decisive. Never again in Duke William's reign was the French king to invade Normandy at the head of a hostile army, thus crucially leaving William free to concentrate on his English project.

BIBLIOGRAPHY

Aird, William M., *Robert Curthose, Duke of Normandy*, The Boydell Press, 2008
Barlow, Frank, *Edward the Confessor*, Eyre Methuen, 1970
Barlow, Frank, *The Feudal Kingdom of England 1042–1216*, Longman, 1955
Barlow, Frank, *The Godwins*, Pearson Longman, 2002
Barlow, Frank, *William Rufus*, Yale University Press, 2000
Bartlett, Robert, *The Making of Europe*, Penguin Books, 1994
Bradbury, Jim, *The Battle of Hastings*, Sutton Publishing, 1998
Brooke, Christopher, *The Saxon and Norman Kings*, Book Club Associates, 1963
Carpenter, David, *The Struggle for Mastery*, Penguin Books, 2004
Chibnall, Marjorie, *The Debate on the Norman Conquest*, Manchester University Press, 1999
Chibnall, Marjorie, *Anglo-Norman England 1066–1166*, Basil Blackwell, 1986
Crouch, David, *The Normans*, Hambledon and London, 2002
Delabos, Christian, *Bremule 20 août 1119*, Historic One, 1999
Domesday Book, A complete translation, Penguin Classics, 2003
Douglas, David C., *William the Conqueror*, Yale University Press, 1999
Finberg, H.P.R., *The Formation of England 550–1042*, Paladin, 1976
Fletcher, Richard, *Who's Who in Roman and Anglo-Saxon England*, Shepheard-Walwyn, 1989
Garnett, George, *The Norman Conquest*, Oxford University Press, 2009.
Gondoin, Stephane William, *Châteaux forts de Normandie*, OREP Editions, 2006
Gravett, Christopher and Nicolle, David, *The Normans*, Osprey Publishing, 2006
Green, Judith A., *Henry I*, Cambridge University Press, 2006
Griffiths, Ralph et al., *The Gwent County History Volume 2*, Gwent County History Association, 2008
Harrison, Brian et al., *The Oxford Dictionary of National Biography*, Oxford University Press, 2004
Hardy, Robert, *Longbow: A social and military history*, Sutton Publishing, 2006
Henshall, Kenneth, *Folly and Fortune in Early British History*, Palgrave Macmillan, 2008
Higham, N.J, *The Death of Anglo-Saxon England*, Sutton Publishing, 1997
Hill, Paul, *The Road to Hastings*, Tempus Publishing, 2005
Hollister, C. Warren, *Henry I*, Yale University Press, 2003
Howard, Ian, *Harthacnut: The Last Danish King of England*, The History Press, 2008
Humphrys, Julian, *Clash of Arms*, English Heritage, 2006
Jenkins, Simon, *England's Thousand Best Churches*, The Penguin Press, 1999
Jones, Charles, *The Forgotten Battle of 1066: Fulford*, Tempus Publishing, 2006
Kerr, Nigel and Mary, *A Guide to Anglo-Saxon Sites*, Paladin Granada Publishing, 1982
Kinross, John, *Discovering Battlefields of England and Scotland*, Shire Publications, 2004
Lack, Katherine, *Conqueror's Son: Duke Robert Curthose*, Sutton Publishing, 2007
Lavelle, Ryan, *Aethelred II: King of the English 978–1016*, Tempus Publishing, 2002
Lawson, M.K., *The Battle of Hastings 1066*, Tempus Publishing, 2007
Lawson, M.K., *Cnut: The Danes in England in the Early Eleventh Century*, Longman, 1993

Lloyd, Alan, *The Year of the Conqueror*, Longmans, 1966
McLynn, Frank, *1066: The Year of the Three Battles*, Pimlico, 1999
Magnusson, Magnus, *The Vikings*, Tempus Publishing, 2003
Marren, Peter, *1066: The Battles of York, Stamford Bridge and Hastings*, Pen and Sword, 2002
Mason, Emma, *William II*, Tempus Publishing, 2005
Mee, Arthur, *The King's England Series*, Hodder & Stoughton, 1936
Moore, David, *The Welsh Wars of Independence*, Tempus Publishing, 2007
Mortimer, Richard, *Edward the Confessor: The King who became a Saint*, Dean and Chapter of Westminster
Newman, John et al., *The Buildings of Wales*, Yale University Press, 1994
O'Brien, Harriet, *Queen Emma and the Vikings*, Bloomsbury, 2005
Pettifer, Adrian, *English Castles*, The Boydell Press, 2000
Pevsner, Sir Nicholas, *The Buildings of England* series from 1950s
Pine, L.G., *They came with the Conqueror*, Evans Brothers, 1966
Poole, A.L., *Domesday Book to Magna Carta*, Oxford Univeristy Press, 1985
Rex, Peter, *Hereward: The Last Englishman*, Tempus Publishing, 2007
Richards, Julian D., *Viking Age England*, Tempus Publishing, 2000
Ronay, Gabrial, *The Lost King of England*, The Boydell Press, 2000
Rowley, Antony, *The Normans*, Tempus Publishing, 2004
Rowley, Antony, *The Norman Heritage 1066–1200*, Paladin, 1984
Salter, Mike, *The Castles of Mid-Wales*, Folly Publications, 2001
Salter, Mike, *The Castles of South-West Wales*, Folly Publications, 1994
Sayles, G.O., *The Medieval Foundations of England*, Methuen, 1970
Smurthwaite, Davie, *Battlefields of Britain*, Webb and Bower, 1984
Stafford, Pauline, *Queen Emma and Queen Edith*, Oxford Blackwell, 1997
Stenton, Sir Frank, *Anglo-Saxon England*, Oxford University Press, 1971
Strachan, Isabella, *Emma: The Twice-Crowned Queen*, Peter Owen Publishers, 2004
Swanton, Michael, *The Anglo-Saxon Chronicles*, Phoenix Press, 2000
Tetlow, Edwin, *The Enigma of Hastings*, Westholme Publishing, 2008
Trow, M.J., *Cnut: The Emperor of the North*, Sutton Publishing, 2005
Walker, Ian W., *Harold: The Last Anglo-Saxon King*, Sutton Publishing, 2004
Wardle, Terry, *England's First Castle*, The History Press, 2009
Warren, W.L., *The Governance of England*, Edward Arnold, 1987
Weir, Alison, *Britain's Royal Families*, Pimlico, 1996
Wood, Michael, *In Search of the Dark Ages*, BBC, 1982
Wright, Peter Poyntz, *Hastings*, Phoenix, 2005
Williams, Ann, *The English and the Norman Conquest*, The Boydell Press, 2000
Yorke, Trevor, *English Castles Explained*, Countryside Books, 2003

INDEX OF PEOPLE FEATURED IN THE GUIDE

Bold indicates location in the guide of biographical detail of major participant. <u>Underline</u> means this is the site of a memorial or building associated with this person.

INDEX OF HISTORICAL SITES

SS indicates a secondary site.

Other titles published by The History Press

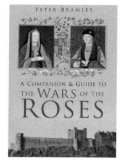

A Companion & Guide to The Wars of the Roses
PETER BRAMLEY £15.29

This updated edition of Peter Bramley's beautifully illustrated book focuses on the rich legacy of physical remains associated with the Wars of the Roses, which have survived for over 500 years in the form of castles, battlefields, houses, church brasses and tombs. A veritable treasure trove of information, this unusual guidebook provides details of the events and people linked with each historical site, together with background on the wars' causes, main events and the personalities involved.

9780752463360

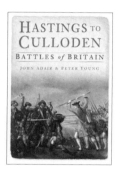

Hastings to Culloden: Battles of Britain
JOHN ADAIR & PETER YOUNG £15.29

This classic army survey by two of Britain's foremost military historians looks in detail at all the major campaigns and battles to have taken place on British soil since the Norman Conquest. Using contemporary documents and eyewitness accounts, and illustrated throughout with battleplans and sketchmaps, the authors offer an insight into the motives of conflict and what it was like to be on the front line at these great battles.

9780752454313

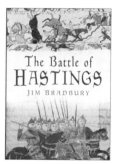

The Battle of Hastings
JIM BRADBURY £8.99

Jim Bradbury here explores the full military background to the battle and investigates both the sources for our knowledge of what actually happened in 1066 and the role that the battle plays in national myth. The core of the book is a move-by-move reconstruction of the battle, including the advance planning, the site, the composition of the two armies and the use of archers, feigned flights and the death of Harold.

9780750937948

The Kingmaker's Sisters
DAVID BALDWIN £18.00

Warwick the Kingmaker, the Earl of Warwick & Salisbury whose wealth and power was so great that he could effectively decide who would rule England during the Wars of the Roses (1455–1487), had six sisters: Joan, Cecily, Alice, Eleanor, Katherine and Margaret. *The Kingmaker's Sisters* examines the role that they played as wives, but also as deputies for their absent husbands, and how the struggle between the Yorkists and the Lancastrians affected them and their families.

9780750950763

Visit our website and discover thousands of other History Press books.

www.thehistorypress.co.uk